Cross–Media Authentication and Verification:

Emerging Research and Opportunities

Anastasia Katsaounidou
Aristotle University of Thessaloniki, Greece

Charalampos Dimoulas
Aristotle University of Thessaloniki, Greece

Andreas Veglis
Aristotle University of Thessaloniki, Greece

A volume in the Advances in
Multimedia and Interactive
Technologies (AMIT) Book Series

Published in the United States of America by
    IGI Global
    Information Science Reference (an imprint of IGI Global)
    701 E. Chocolate Avenue
    Hershey PA, USA 17033
    Tel: 717-533-8845
    Fax: 717-533-8661
    E-mail: cust@igi-global.com
    Web site: http://www.igi-global.com

Library of Congress Cataloging-in-Publication Data

Names: Katsaounidou, Anastasia, 1990- author. | Dimoulas, Charalampos, 1974-
   author. | Veglis, Andreas, author.
Title: Cross-media authentication and verification : emerging research and
   opportunities / by Anastasia Katsaounidou, Charalampos Dimoulas, and
   Andreas Veglis.
Description: Hershey PA : Information Science Reference, [2018]
Identifiers: LCCN 2017049730| ISBN 9781522555926 (hardcover) | ISBN
   9781522555933 (ebook)
Subjects: LCSH: Journalism--Technological innovations. |
   Journalism--Objectivity.
Classification: LCC PN4888.O25 K38 2018 | DDC 070.4--dc23 LC record available at https://lccn.
loc.gov/2017049730

This book is published in the IGI Global book series Advances in Multimedia and Interactive Technologies (AMIT) (ISSN: 2327-929X; eISSN: 2327-9303)

British Cataloguing in Publication Data
A Cataloguing in Publication record for this book is available from the British Library.

All work contributed to this book is new, previously-unpublished material.
The views expressed in this book are those of the authors, but not necessarily of the publisher.

For electronic access to this publication, please contact: eresources@igi-global.com.

Advances in Multimedia and Interactive Technologies (AMIT) Book Series

ISSN:2327-929X
EISSN:2327-9303

Editor-in-Chief: Joel J.P.C. Rodrigues, National Institute of Telecommunications (Inatel), Brazil & Instituto de Telecomunicações, University of Beira Interior, Portugal

MISSION

Traditional forms of media communications are continuously being challenged. The emergence of user-friendly web-based applications such as social media and Web 2.0 has expanded into everyday society, providing an interactive structure to media content such as images, audio, video, and text.

The **Advances in Multimedia and Interactive Technologies (AMIT) Book Series** investigates the relationship between multimedia technology and the usability of web applications. This series aims to highlight evolving research on interactive communication systems, tools, applications, and techniques to provide researchers, practitioners, and students of information technology, communication science, media studies, and many more with a comprehensive examination of these multimedia technology trends.

COVERAGE

- Digital Watermarking
- Multimedia Streaming
- Gaming Media
- Multimedia Technology
- Audio Signals
- Social Networking
- Mobile Learning
- Digital Games
- Digital Technology
- Digital Communications

IGI Global is currently accepting manuscripts for publication within this series. To submit a proposal for a volume in this series, please contact our Acquisition Editors at Acquisitions@igi-global.com or visit: http://www.igi-global.com/publish/.

Titles in this Series

For a list of additional titles in this series, please visit:
https://www.igi-global.com/book-series/advances-multimedia-interactive-technologies/73683

Real-Time Face Detection, Recognition, and Tracking System in LabVIEW™ Emerging...
Manimehala Nadarajan (Universiti Malaysia Sabah, Malaysia) Muralindran Mariappan (Universiti Malaysia Sabah, Malaysia) and Rosalyn R. Porle (Universiti Malaysia Sabah, Maaysia)
Information Science Reference ● ©2018 ● 140pp ● H/C (ISBN: 9781522535034) ● US $155.00

Empirical Research on Semiotics and Visual Rhetoric
Marcel Danesi (University of Toronto, Canada)
Information Science Reference ● ©2018 ● 312pp ● H/C (ISBN: 9781522556220) ● US $195.00

Exploring Transmedia Journalism in the Digital Age
Renira Rampazzo Gambarato (National Research University Higher School of Economics, Russia) and Geane C. Alzamora (Federal University of Minas Gerais, Brazil)
Information Science Reference ● ©2018 ● 348pp ● H/C (ISBN: 9781522537816) ● US $195.00

Image Retrieval and Analysis Using Text and Fuzzy Shape Features Emerging Research...
P. Sumathy (Bharathidasan University, India) P. Shanmugavadivu (Gandhigram Rural Institute, India) and A. Vadivel (SRM University, India)
Information Science Reference ● ©2018 ● 183pp ● H/C (ISBN: 9781522537960) ● US $145.00

Multimedia Retrieval Systems in Distributed Environments Emerging Research and...
S.G. Shaila (National Institute of Technology, India) and A. Vadivel (National Institute of Technology, India)
Information Science Reference ● ©2018 ● 140pp ● H/C (ISBN: 9781522537281) ● US $165.00

Handbook of Research on Advanced Concepts in Real-Time Image and Video Processing
Md. Imtiyaz Anwar (National Institute of Technology, Jalandhar, India) Arun Khosla (National Institute of Technology, Jalandhar, India) and Rajiv Kapoor (Delhi Technological University, India)
Information Science Reference ● ©2018 ● 504pp ● H/C (ISBN: 9781522528487) ● US $265.00

For an entire list of titles in this series, please visit:
https://www.igi-global.com/book-series/advances-multimedia-interactive-technologies/73683

701 East Chocolate Avenue, Hershey, PA 17033, USA
Tel: 717-533-8845 x100 ● Fax: 717-533-8661
E-Mail: cust@igi-global.com ● www.igi-global.com

Table of Contents

Preface

INTRODUCTION

Over the past years, a growing number of people, researchers and analysts have come to realize that information not always has positive social impacts. Among others, the "digital revolution" and the continuous transformation of the mass communications sphere brought forward the liability of accurate data management, obliging individuals to get precaution in a diversity of phenomena, such as misinformation and face news propagation.

Two developments in the media landscape have created quality issues concerning the disseminated news and documents. Firstly, the proliferation of multimedia capturing and processing tools extended the ways of searching and sharing information, allowing people to efficiently and quickly produce, edit and distribute content online. Secondly, the volume and the speed of the exchanged messages /informatory streams have multilaterally influenced individuals' perception of significant aspects of everyday life. For instance, User Generated Content (UGC) has overwhelmed the Internet and Social Networking Sites (SNSs), in which multimodal entities (text, image, audio, video, etc.) can be combined and spread in numerous ways. The arising matter is that large quantities of these digital products may be opinionated, sensationalized, misleading, unverified or manipulated, issue that is further deteriorated by the lack of confidence to the new online services, especially by the average user. The above also impacts negatively on levels of audience trust in news outlets, since the truth holds a significant role in the networked informing ecosystem. Citizen and Participatory Journalism models, while engaging populations /"news consumers" in the newsgathering and publishing works, they also deteriorate the above situation, correlating the offered computing capacities with their unwanted effects on tampering and forgery of informative resources. Within this situation, the public has been confused about the real purpose of media, gets disappointed, therefore stop following the associated journalistic channels, since the provided information is no longer considered useful and necessary.

The current book focuses on the interdisciplinary research and practices, aiming at preventing and/or controlling the misinformation phenomenon. By exploiting contemporary advantages in multi-channel media publishing and storytelling (i.e. cross- and trans-media) and their potentials in correlation analysis and evaluation strategies, the subject of the book is to usher in applicable cross-modal veracity solutions, which are considered tremendously topical, essential and highly demanded.

OBJECTIVE OF THE BOOK

The subject of misinformation forms an exceptionally complicated field, where multiple scientific and applied disciplines are involved. Any attempt to cope with the problem prerequisites an adequate research and understanding of the underlying framing, including all the current journalistic, ethical, operational and technological challenges. The associated perspectives can be classified into the following major categories, constituting the foreseeing prospects to be addressed by the book:

- Estimating the dynamic of massive uncontrolled misinformation, aiming at filling the possible interdisciplinary gaps.
- Comprehending the different views and approaches of the complementary sciences on this multi-perspective matter.
- Cultivating globally informing awareness and digital literacy.
- Establishing friendly practices, methods and tools, policies and procedures, which adequately contribute to ensure the quality of the transmitted information.
- Taking into consideration the recent advantages in multi-channel media storytelling (cross-/trans-media etc.) and their potentials in cross-modal veracity strategies.

Data is the new "lifeblood" of today's ubiquitous society, in which, intense interaction between audience and news outlets is central. It goes without saying that "news influence beliefs, while beliefs affect the way that events are perceived". With the dizzying rhythms of the exchanging communicative streams and the innumerous "user's access to information" scenarios, unreliable content can lead society to a vulnerable position. Hence, related social, political and economic consequences can be triggered, influencing all areas of human activity. For this reason, a new scientific, technological and research industry has been developed, namely the field of Digital Forensics (DF), aiming at facilitating originality evaluation of multimedia resources. In specific, remarkable research effort has been conducted in the field of media veracity, progress that is validated by the development of content forgery tools, online /free document inspection platforms, adoption and elaboration of best factchecking practices. However, while modern computerized systems (software and hardware) made easier the production and distribution of UGC material, they also hardened the detection of manipulation and altering trails. Therefore, multiple /discerned methods and modalities for identifying tampering traces need to be engaged, for which the operating users should have the required marginal know-how with continuous up-to-date awareness. The diversity of the approaches is related to both the multimodal nature of the various formats or entities (text, audio, image, video) and the different algorithmic implementations, thus resulting in a very demanding multi-disciplinary domain.

The innovative aspects of the book are related to the urgent and multidimensional character of the topic and the exploitation of the recent advantages in the digital media world. In specific, considering that multiple publishing and storytelling ways (i.e. cross-/trans-media) form the commonplace in today's journalistic ecosystem, correlation of the various content versions and instances is examined as a promising solution towards cross-modal veracity strategies. No doubt, the maturity of cross-media facilitates easy transformation of informing resources, adapted to the technical specifications of the different communication means. The implied cross-validation mechanisms create a kind of media tampering firewall, since, on purpose processing and falsification have to be applied in all the available instances, i.e. entities and networks. Hence, given that news is now produced once and deployed in various formats for different publication channels, processing inconsistencies that are caused during the tampering actions might be searched for, providing an additional verification approach. Moreover, the multimodal character of the information (and its propagation) allows for the investigation and selection of the most applicable media type, in which originality assessment can be more easily accomplished. In this perspective, both human-operated and machine-driven authentication techniques are presented in this book, forming the necessary grid for fighting and preventing disinformation.

STRUCTURE OF THE BOOK

The book is organized into eight chapters. The most important topics that are covered in this book are listed below, outlining the structure and organization of the chapters:

Chapter 1 provides a smooth "Introduction to Cross-Media Authentication and Verification", helping readers to understand the basics of content tampering and forgery detection processes, as well as their association to multiple media and cross-validation techniques. Based on this, the analysis that is attempted in the following chapters could be more easily comprehended, primarily by the average reader.

Chapter 2, "Media Authenticity and Journalism: An Inseparable Framework", addresses the news authentication principles concerning the cost of misinformation to society, concerning the lost trust in the media agencies and the journalistic profession. In fact, it is the first section where the problem of misinformation is thoroughly addressed in this book. Issues, controversies and problems are discussed with regard to "gatekeeping processes" of the "involved channels", while suggested solutions and recommendations refer to the adoption of essential information verification principles, practices and tools.

Chapter 3 deals with "The Transforming Media Landscape", listing the breakthroughs in communication technologies (and overall ICTs), while illustrating the associated progress in journalism and media services, aligned to the different Web eras. This progress is reflected in the appearance of new (digital) journalism genres, which are associated with various aspects of the misinformation phenomenon, such as the caused discomfort to the non-experts and the lack of trust in the news industry. Solutions and recommendations regarding digital literacy and continuous support for the quick adoption of the advantages, offered through the novel technological trends, are discussed as well.

Chapter 4 addresses issues related to "Misinformation via Tampered Multimedia Content", emphasizing on the use of digital/multimedia documents as proofing evidence while revisiting reliability-based classification of news sites. Solutions and recommendations are provided in terms of informing awareness, cultivation and literacy.

Chapter 5 focuses on "Authentication by Humans", analyzing news fact-checking issues, cross-validation practices and wise verification procedures, assisted by experts or through team-activity collaborations (i.e. crowd computing). Related initiatives on preventing the propagation and dissemination of fake news are listed as recommended solutions to this contemporary problem.

Chapter 6, titled "Assisted Authentication", presents machine-driven algorithmic methods as means of fully or semi-automated forgery detection solutions. The associated research initiatives are carefully inspected concerning their necessary elaboration and adaptation to the needs of the news industry and the everyday journalistic practices.

Chapter 7, "Cross-Media Publishing and Storytelling", provides basic definitions and the historical evolution of these models. The corresponding information is considered essential to illustrate the significant functional attributes, therefore to comprehend the dynamics behind potential cross-modal authentication solutions.

Chapter 8 focuses on the main thrust of the book, namely the presentation of the "Cross-Media Authentication and Verification" framework. Strengths, weaknesses, opportunities and threats of the envisioned media veracity integration are listed, resulting in the recommendation of a prototype modelling solution. Future work on system materialization, maintenance and continuous elaboration is also discussed, implying further multidisciplinary research directions.

TARGET AUDIENCE

The current book is addressed to all individuals, involved (in any way) in the aspects of media veracity. Hence, professional and citizen journalists, who monitor information alerts and disseminate news stories, as well as ordinary news consuming users, will benefit by reading the covered objectives, safeguarding themselves and eventually fighting against the unwanted phenomenon of misinformation. The same applies to the cases of (mediated) communication specialists and ICT experts that could take advantage of the provided information to rapidly acquire knowledge and know-how, best matching their associated urgent needs (in their fields of interest or broader multidisciplinary topics). Furthermore, researchers of all technological, humanoid and social sciences will find a convenient and friendly way of filling the possible interdisciplinary gaps, understanding the different views and approaches of the complementary sciences on this multi-perspective matter. For this reason, extensive /profound analysis on both the involved media communication theories and the associated forensic technologies and algorithms will be avoided throughout the chapters, aiming at serving the balanced presentation of the various topics, while also maintaining a clear purpose on the focused target. Nonetheless, highly profound papers and focused references will be cited where applicable (without any concern of parsimony), so that they could be exploited as further studying sources (and more comprehensive resources) by the demanding readers.

Anastasia Katsaounidou
Aristotle University of Thessaloniki, Greece

Charalampos Dimoulas
Aristotle University of Thessaloniki, Greece

Andreas Veglis
Aristotle University of Thessaloniki, Greece

Acknowledgment

The authors would like to thank Dr. R. Kotsakis, Dr. M. Matsiola, and PhD researchers D. Mantziari and T. Saridou for carefully proofreading and correcting the English language and style of the chapters, as well as for the provided feedback regarding the content and the structure of this book. Moreover, Anastasia Katsaounidou would like to thank the State Scholarships Foundation (IKY) for financially supporting her PhD thesis.

Chapter 1
Introduction to Cross–Media Authentication and Verification

ABSTRACT

The current chapter provides an overview of the objectives being covered in this book, introducing the reader to the values of cross-media authentication in journalism and generally in informing services. Misinformation has social and economic consequences in every aspect of human activity, with critical political implication. The dominance of cross-media publishing and storytelling and the contemporary forms of digital journalism have shaped a new media landscape, raising certain question regarding the applied authentication and verification strategies. While media veracity has received a lot of attention during the last years, content verification practices need to be further supported, adapting to the diverse character of multiple media and sources. The utmost goal of this introductory chapter is to unveil the potentials of an interdisciplinary exploitation of current advantages in multi-channel storytelling and their integration in cross-media veracity strategies, where best practices can be combined with state-of-the-art computational technologies and algorithmic solutions.

DOI: 10.4018/978-1-5225-5592-6.ch001

INTRODUCTION

During the last decades, we have witnessed the digitization of media production that followed the tremendous evolution of Information and Communication Technologies (ICTs) and their widespread adoption in the media business. Undoubtedly, this breakthrough has multi-laterally influenced the roles of journalists, communication professionals and media organizations, as well as their relationships with the end-users and the audience (Kalliris & Dimoulas, 2009). New tools and capabilities have been precipitated, transforming the media landscape with remarkably expeditious research progress, which is still in process. Among others, social media, web and generally ICT services have affected the ways that users are engaged in informing and mass communicating scenarios, where all news /content producing, accessing / browsing and "consuming" services co-exist (Dimoulas & Symeonidis, 2015; Katsaounidou & Dimoulas, 2018; Kotsakis, Kalliris, & Dimoulas, 2012; Spyridou, Matsiola, Veglis, Kalliris, & Dimoulas, 2013, Veglis, Dimoulas, & Kalliris, 2016). The vast expansion in the usage and the capabilities of contemporary mobile devices (i.e. smartphones and tablets) have fueled the materialization of the "information at my finger tip" vision, further advancing flexibility and mobility of both users and services, which can now be launched independently of time and space (Dimoulas, Veglis, & Kalliris, 2014, 2015, 2018; Satyanarayanan, Bahl, Caceres, & Davies, 2009). The proliferation of user-friendly (mobile) multimedia capturing and processing tools have extended the potentials of searching and sharing information, allowing regular users to produce and edit content online, with almost no expense. Hence, the so-called User Generated Content (UGC) has overwhelmed the Internet and social networks, usually having the form of multimodal entities (text, image, audio, video, etc.), which can be combined and propagated in innumerous ways (Dimoulas & Symeonidis, 2015; Dimoulas et al., 2014, 2015, 2018; Katsaounidou & Dimoulas, 2018; Kotsakis et al., 2012; Matsiola, Dimoulas, Kalliris, & Veglis, 2015; Veglis et al., 2016).

Except for the benefits that ICTs and digital revolution have offered to the media industry, there are certain arising issues related to the validity and integrity of the multimodal information that is exchanged through the available media channels. Hence, part of the posted, shared and/or re-published information may be opinionated, sensationalized, misleading, unverified, manipulated or otherwise unreliable. Misinformation has social and economic consequences in all areas of human activity, with serious and, in any case, interesting political implications. This is also one of the reasons explaining why much ongoing research is currently being directed toward the underlying causes and consequences of fake news, where the investigation of preventing measures and practices has major importance. While outstanding progress has been conducted in research terms through the implementation of content tampering detection algorithms and strategies, an integrated methodology is still missing to properly address all the aspects of news and information authentication, taking advantage of all the available modalities (Katsaounidou & Dimoulas, 2018). Considering that publishing in multiple media is nowadays the common place, multimodal authenticity features can be detected and extracted by evaluating the differences between the cross-media publishing versions of a story (Dimoulas et al., 2014, 2015, 2018; Matsiola et al., 2015; Lu, Jin, Su, Shivakumara, & Tan, 2015; Veglis et all., 2016). This also stands as the main objective of the current book, which aims at revealing the potentials of multi-channel media storytelling attributes, thus transforming them into innovative cross-media veracity solutions.

Undeniably, media veracity has received a lot of attention during the last years, where remarkable research progress has been achieved on related methods and algorithms (Katsaounidou & Dimoulas, 2018). However, the deployment of an applicable and user-friendly practical tool remains a question for the users involved in real-world applications (i.e. journalists / citizen-journalists and generally social media users contributing content). At the same time, the daily exposure to a remarkable amount of visualized information (i.e. imaging content and presentation metadata) proves that modern civilization is primarily visual. Thus, images are often used as proofing evidence to convince readers about news truthfulness. In this context, image verification tools were the first approaches that attempted to validate digital content integrity and to reveal potential tampering operations, taking advantage of the inherited visualization means (Farid, 2009; Katsaounidou & Dimoulas, 2018; Schetinger, Oliveira, da Silva, & Carvalho, 2015). This was also dictated by the availability of image processing tools, which could /can be easily handled by non-professional users for basic visual tampering operations (i.e. using common photo editing software, such as the popular Adobe Photoshop, from which the name "photoshopped" was made up for the doctored images). Nowadays, the world has already moved from the age of information to the age of confirmation, where people are becoming the editors, gatekeepers and aggregators of information. Hence, content verification practices need to be further supported, and a potential solution may be found in the exploitation of all the available methods in properly integrated online environments (Katsaounidou & Dimoulas, 2018). The maturity of cross-media publishing technology allows for easy content transformation, adapted to the technical specification of each different channel. The fact that cross-media is a part of everyday life of journalists and media organizations can further be exploited towards the implementation of a kind of media tampering firewall. Specifically, taking into consideration that news production is distributed in various (different) formats through multiple media, on purpose content processing and falsification should be applied to all the involved publishing and storytelling channels. Therefore, processing inconsistencies caused by the tampering operations may be sought, providing additional information validation mechanisms.

MULTIPLE MEDIA AND MULTIMODAL INFORMATION AUTHENTICATION

Background

The processes of news and content validation appeared almost together with the arrival of media publishing services (from the early days of newspapers and print-media) and they co-exist ever since (Dimoulas et al., 2014, 2015, 2018; Reich, 2006; Veglis & Pomportsis, 2014; Veglis et al., 2016). While content tampering and news falsification were even then possible, the technical means and the capabilities to deploy sophisticated media alteration were very limited. However, as evidenced by related propaganda stories, tampering could not be revealed until after some time, where the falsified information was exposed to the public and it was further analyzed by experienced investigators. The slow paces of news production and consumption at that time, as well as the limited number of journalistic and news publishing corporations, could act in favor of directed misinformation. On the other hand, untrue /falsified stories were revealed in time, resulting in a negative impact on the reputation and the credibility of the associated media organizations. Hence, the spread of misinformation could be controlled through the reliability of the limited (at that time) news producers and publishers, so that people could select their own news-informing preferences to avoid hoaxes (Dimoulas et al., 2014, 2018; Ho & Li, 2015; Katsaounidou, 2016; Katsaounidou & Dimoulas, 2018; Siapera & Veglis, 2012; Silverman, 2013; Veglis et al., 2016).

These days, the proliferation of Social Networking Sites (SNSs) and the transition to the era of Web 2.0 (and beyond) have massively extended the ways of mediated communication, resulting in a vast number of news producers (and consumers), in which all professional /citizen journalists and social media users are involved (Kalliris & Dimoulas, 2009; Kotsakis et al., 2012; Spyridou et al., 2013). Consequently, the spread of news has become almost impossible to monitor, exposing infotainment services in many uncontrollable tampering and falsification attacks, thus making users more vulnerable to hoaxes (Katsaounidou & Dimoulas, 2018; Matsiola et al., 2015; Silverman, 2013). Media tampering refers to the processes of intentional altering or falsifying (digital) news reporting content, in an effort to make the story more appealing and/or to purposely misinform the public (i.e. as part of a propaganda campaign). It is well known that photos have been extensively used as proof evident of the associated news stories, also aiming at making the storytelling more attractive, vivid and compelling to the audience. As a result, image processing, aesthetic treatment and/or intentional doctoring are quite common in the effort to stimulate the audience, in order to get high popularity and ratings. Unfortunately, news manipulation can be applied to all the encountered content types or data that accompany a story (i.e. text, image, audio, video, their combination, etc.). In this principle, content authentication refers to the procedures of verifying published content and its multimodal media assets to reveal potential forgery actions, therefore to decide the authenticity of a news story. Considering that the possibility of content alteration is always present, verification actions and policies have become even more important, if not absolutely necessary (Farid, 2009; Gupta, Cho, & Kuo, 2012; Ho & Li, 2015; Katsaounidou, 2016; Katsaounidou & Dimoulas, 2018; Pantti & Sirén, 2015; Pasquini, Brunetta, Vinci, Conotter, & Boato, 2015; Silverman, 2013).

A Theoretical Perspective on Multimedia Evidence and Cross-Media Veracity

As aforementioned, prevention of misinformation is considered extremely critical, due to its subsequent political, social and economic implications. For this reason, fact-checking and confirmation mechanisms were incorporated into the services of journalism and mass informing, from their very early beginning. In particular, along with news-content acquisition, processing, presentation and dissemination, the processes of information validation form a standard procedure that is integral in the end-to-end chain of news reporting (Figure 1) (Dimoulas et al., 2014; Reich, 2006; Veglis & Pomportsis, 2014). The diagram of Figure 1 models a media framework, which established the primary verification rules and practices. The associated theoretical perspectives were also adapted and accommodated to the cases of multiple channels, i.e. with the deployment of cross- and trans-media publishing and storytelling (Siapera & Veglis, 2012; Veglis et al., 2016). However, while this flow model is traditionally followed by most media organizations, the advent of social networks and UGC with the multiple genres of Digital and Online Journalism have complicated the "digital news landscape", thus making media veracity even more demanding. Hence, the domain of Digital Forensics has emerged and is continuously elaborating, constituting an especially interdisciplinary research field, which aims at helping in the authentication of documents, both in scientific and applied level (Ho & Li, 2015). On the one hand, the causes and consequences of misinformation are extensively studied within the research frameworks of humanities and social sciences. On the other hand, experts and scientists on media technologies are trying to cope with the problem through algorithmic /automated solutions, by inspecting digital content for potential context or format inconsistencies that will reveal possible tampering operations. Both approaches are useful, featuring certain advantages and weaknesses when compared to each other, since they provide different evaluation analysis perspectives (Katsaounidou & Dimoulas, 2018).

Extending the above, the integration of all the available media veracity practices and techniques could lead to more reliable outcomes, towards the establishment of universal and easy to apply authentication solutions. However, major unresolved issues and obstacles exist, hindering progress in this direction. As depicted in Figure 1, there is a vast diversity of different sources, channels and paths, where multiple content modalities and plural digital formats are encountered. While this opens a possibility for cross-media authentication strategies (i.e. by correlating all modalities /content versions that refer to the same story), the large-scale heterogeneity and the lack of news propagation controlling and/or monitoring mechanisms are added to the already present difficulties. For instance, the adoption of best practices on fact-checking and the deployment of related crowdsourcing initiatives take some time before they can provide solid authenticity results. The same applies when causes and consequences of misinformation are studied in terms of sociological and humanities research questions, which cannot have the immediate /preventing character of an automated machine-driven method. This is very important when breaking-news come to question, but also because it has been proven

Figure 1. News reporting dataflow model: the role of multiple media and the need for cross-modal validation (Dimoulas et al., 2014; Veglis & Pomportsis, 2014)

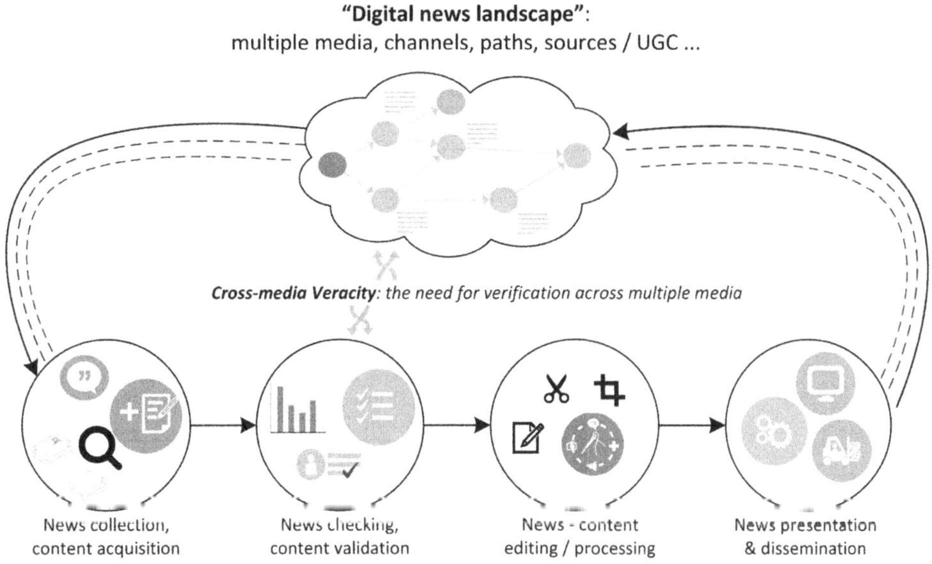

"Digital news landscape":
multiple media, channels, paths, sources / UGC ...

*Cross-media **Veracity**: the need for verification across multiple media*

News collection, content acquisition   News checking, content validation   News - content editing / processing   News presentation & dissemination

very difficult to reveal and diminish the effects of a fake story (i.e. debunk a rumor) after its wide spreading (Silverman, 2015). On the other hand, most algorithmic approaches are regularly associated with some underlying complexity and potential misclassification errors (especially when running in unsupervised modes), so that their outputs require technical know-how and "digital literacy" to be comprehensible and usable by average users. Moreover, in many cases, the above solutions do not exploit the required contextual or sociological framing, which is necessary for being understandable and further elaborated by other scientists.

Table 1 lists typical examples of possible media assets manipulation, providing an overview of the fields in which digital content authenticity can be useful. As it can be seen, multiple disciplines are implicated, where the subject matter experts of the various domains can be valuable in revealing possible forgery attacks and restoring the truth. Thus, gained experience and know-how acquired in one field can also be adapted and propagated to other related situations. Overall, a great number of factors is involved across the media authentication chain, where diverse specializations and different theoretical backgrounds are needed to adequately safeguard against misinformation, aiming at eventually facing this unwanted phenomenon. These complementary skills of the required expertise and competencies can be brought forward

Table 1. Fields in which content authenticity can be useful

Disciplines	Sub Disciplines	Examples of Misused Digital Content
Media	Journalism	• Manipulated Digital Content as evidence at reports
	Social Networking	• Tampered User Generated Content (UGC) • Tampered photos of official documents (Identities - Passports) and misused identity attempts (aiming at succeeding illegal access to profiles /accounts)
	Advertisement	• Doctored (or "photoshopped") images used by Fashion industry • Exaggeratedly aesthetic "sculpting" of media assets presenting products and services associated with financial and commercial activities (e.g. embellished hotel images)
Science		• Inappropriate figures manipulations in scientific publications (results were altered and/ or fabricated) (Farid, 2004)
	History	• Altered audiovisual historical documents, used as misleading evidence
	Art	• Forged works or pieces of Art, falsely attributed to artists for their value to be enhanced, having socioeconomic impact (i.e. financial loss) (Lyu, Rockmore, & Farid, 2004)
	Health	• Exchange of medical images between hospitals and diagnosis centers, with severe consequences on the health of patients (Memon & Gilani, 2008; Periaswamy & Farid, 2006) • Misleads about potential negative effects of important medical procedures (i.e. vaccination-related autism, health-hoaxes) (Poland & Spier, 2010)
Law		• Tampered photographic legal evidences (i.e. fingerprints, shoeprints, DNA images, data of toxicology and ballistic analyses, etc.) • Altered audiovisual legal evidences (e.g. recorded conversations) • Recognition of child pornography footage over digitally-modelled / machine-generated virtual content that have different legal treatment (Farid, 2004) • Altered photos of official documents (Identities/ Passports) attempting illegal actions (tapping elements, i.e. access to unauthorized e-shops accounts) • Public administration (e.g. altered evidences / frauds) • Parts of Body or Tattoo identification (Lee, Jin, Jain & Tong, 2012)
Politics		• Political propaganda and public opinion manipulation (i.e. tampered audio, image and video content used for propaganda during election campaigns) (Krawetz, 2007)
National Security		• Analysis of news alerts and generally informing streams for detecting true emergency situations • Altered audiovisual content for military purposes (e.g. forge military threads, demonstrate untrue fighting superiority, etc.)

by the collaboration of ICT experts, digital literacy educators, professional journalists, scientists and researchers that work on the various aspects of media veracity. Understanding that the anticipated cross-media verification progress is subjected to the fruitful cooperation of all these multidisciplinary specialists, sufficient technological and theoretical background is needed to all parties to be able to understand and communicate with each other.

Looking at the examples listed in Table 1, there are situations where the searched evidence lays in the meaning, the context or even the empathy of the associated messages, so that their evaluation by humans is necessary. In other circumstances, algorithmic solutions can bring forward automations in revealing possible inconsistencies within the digital data (and metadata). In all cases, authenticity for media is an end to itself and someone should be aware of information validation principles to comprehend the context of misinformation. The same applies to the understanding of the technological capabilities and limitations regarding the tampering of multimedia and generally digital content, which are the means and the sources of "digital forgery". This is also profoundly affected by the rapidly transforming media landscape, with the technological advances being reflected in the appearance of new forms of mass communication and digital journalism, sometimes creating uncertainties or even suspicions to the audience regarding their real purpose. Finally, the proposed cross-modal veracity framework should follow the foundations of multi-channel publishing and storytelling (i.e. cross-/ trans-media), thus enlightening interesting aspects and the useful attributes of using multiple media. All these parameters and factors are thoroughly analyzed in focused /distinctive chapters in this book, aiming at providing the necessary knowledge and practical skills towards the materialization of the envisioned multimodal verification integration.

Issues, Controversies, Problems: Digital Journalism Forms and Authentication Needs

Based on the preceding analysis, contemporary informing architectures rely on the engagement of multiple publishing channels, containing information in the form of multimodal media assets (Dimoulas et al., 2014; Veglis et al., 2016). The availability of multiple media with various favored content entities has increased the competition between the media organizations. The effort to gain journalistic exclusivity and highly-rated popularity results in the uncontrolled propagation of unverified content and stories, whereas intentional information tampering is very likely. These unwanted effects are also fueled by the massive availability of tools easing digital content processing, even for the average user, as well as by the biased and/or sensationalized attitudes of media organizations and journalists. It is well known that journalistic analysis behind a story is most of the time subjective or even opinionated (i.e. due to the personal beliefs of the journalist /writer, the associated experience and the momentary point of view, the tendency to line up to the preferences of the targeted audience, etc.). While this is somewhat fair and actually expected by the public, there are also cases where content alteration aims at severely changing the meaning of a story-article, with the intension of misinforming the public about the associated event. Although digital text can be easily modified, such kind of altering is expected by the end users and can be easily revealed (as already implied), so that the text content alone does not provide evidence of originality (Dimoulas et al., 2014, 2018; Katsaounidou, 2016; Katsaounidou & Dimoulas, 2018; Siapera & Veglis, 2012; Silverman, 2013; Veglis et al., 2016).

Nowadays, new forms of text-based social networking, such as short messaging –SMS (i.e. Twitter) and related commenting utilities, have overwhelmed the "digital news landscape", thus resurfacing textual communication services. Along with them, unwanted forgery products also appear (i.e. machine-generated text messages and comments), requiring dedicated verification treatment through proper detection and interpretation of the associated textual inconsistencies. Hence, authentication mechanisms have been implemented to detect fake social media accounts and for the recognition of unexpected text syntaxes, pointing out artificially composed messages (Ho & Li, 2015; Katsaounidou & Dimoulas, 2018). Furthermore, tampering attacks regularly deal with the accompanying multimedia assets, such as photos, audio and video recordings, which usually supplement the associated news stories. For instance, recalling that photos have been extensively used as proofing evidence, even in traditional news reporting, image forgery is placed among the top-listed content tampering cases. Apart from their popularity and the power of the visual media (in terms of vividness, representativeness and attractiveness), the high rate of photo treatment can also be justified on the availability of user-friendly digital image capturing and processing tools. For the same reason, audio and video manipulation is more demanding, therefore more difficult to apply, requiring dedicated tools and expertise. Image and generally multimedia verification rely on context-aware inspection practices that are conducted by experts, which are usually combined with subjective evaluation reports of multiple users, provided through crowd computing frameworks. Moreover, content-based semantic analysis algorithms have been developed to automatically detect inconsistencies in the encoded image, text, audio and video streams, which can then be used as verification assistants. However, despite all this undisputed research progress, a well-tested universal procedure that can be used in practice for media authentication purposes is not yet available (Farid, 2009; Gupta, Cho, & Kuo, 2012; Ho & Li, 2015;

Katsaounidou, 2016; Katsaounidou & Dimoulas, 2018; Pantti & Sirén, 2015; Pasquini et al., 2015; Silverman, 2013).

SOLUTIONS AND RECOMMENDATIONS

Deployment of Cross-Media Authentication Strategies

Significant progress has been achieved in the development of authentication techniques and practices, during the last years. In fact, related research on digital forensics is still ongoing with even higher rates. However, it has been proved that the higher the sophistication of the implemented techniques is, the more are the requirements for an in-depth understanding of digital media technology, or even for some basic comprehension of the underlying verification algorithms (Katsaounidou, 2016). Moreover, what is still missing is a reliable, straightforward and convenient tool that could be easily used by journalists and social media users in their everyday fact-checking needs. Clearly, the fact that multiple content modalities co-exist along with different doctoring operations and a wide variety of inspection and validation techniques does not favor the integration and unification of an easy-to-use universal solution (Katsaounidou, 2016; Katsaounidou & Dimoulas, 2018). On the other hand, the availability of different content versions, which are associated with the corresponding publishing and storytelling channels, allows for further evaluation of their inconsistencies, towards the implementation of cross-modal veracity solutions. Specifically, the same way that cross-media correlation mechanisms are used for content understanding purposes (Lu et al., 2016), innovative multimodal authentication services can be launched to correlate informing streams between the various sources and dissemination paths, so as to assist in revealing potential manipulation actions.

Figure 2 provides an overview of the current news verification approaches with their relation to the different publishing channels and the envisioned cross-media authentication integration. In this context, the used "cross-media" term has a more enhanced meaning, incorporating all the aspects of cross- and trans-media storytelling, as well as the diversity of content modalities and the corresponding evaluation methods, applied by both humans and machines. As it is depicted in the diagram, the proposed framework attempts to provide new cross-validation means, adapted to the layered nature of multiple media (top center block), which have been elaborated as the outcome of the continuously transforming media landscape (top left block). Hence, the prevention of content tampering and misinformation propagation (top right block) is targeted through the materialization of dedicated monitoring and controlling mechanisms, which form the core of the proposed model (placed at the center of the diagram). The presented modular architecture (bottom side blocks) has been enabled to address the multi-factored nature of veracity, driven by the essence of authenticity and its importance in the journalism profession (i.e. "authenticity for media is an end in itself", bottom left block). As already implied, both human-applied practices and algorithm-driven assisted authentication solutions are taken into consideration (bottom blocks, in the middle). Furthermore, added value services concerning system maintenance, users' training, collaborative support and troubleshooting dissemination have been included as important system components (bottom right block). Overall, it is expected that the proposed architecture would facilitate both cross-media publishing and veracity needs through fully- and semi-automated mechanisms, supported by machines and groups of media experts (of various kinds). It is important to mention that most of the terms above (used both in the presented block diagram and in the previously noted definitions), are also reflected in the titles of the associated chapters, aiming at enlightening the various aspects of the discussed problem and its recommended solutions.

CONCLUSION

The current chapter attempts an overview of the media veracity problem and its relation to multi-channel publishing and storytelling paradigms, presenting the main idea and motivation behind the cross-modal verification target. In this context, the concise architecture of the prototype cross-media authentication model is wireframed, whereas basic definitions and background of all the involved matters are briefly discussed. Specifically, the purpose of the present (in this chapter) material is to provide a smooth "Introduction to cross-media authentication and verification", helping the reader in understanding the basics of content tampering and forgery detection processes, as well as their association to multiple media and cross-validation techniques. Based on this, the analysis that is attempted in the following chapters could be more easily comprehended, especially by the average reader.

Figure 2. The proposed cross-media authentication framework and its relation to all the involved cross-modal publishing and veracity aspects

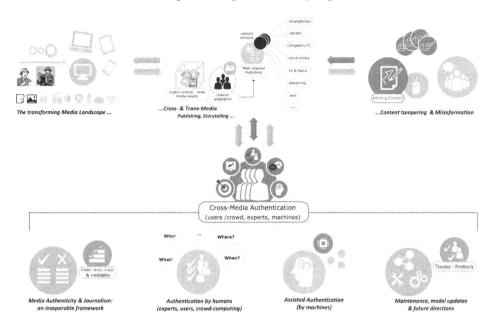

In specific, the basic media theory is initially presented, followed by its elaboration and adaptation to the cases of multiple channels, including the recent "digital genres". Traditional Journalism principles, concerning cross-validation of events and articles, are discussed, indicating the difficulties and particularities that are encountered in today's news ecosystem, which is rapidly transforming. Hence, the need to continually adapt to the new trends is pointed out, which is thought as very crucial, considering the essence of authenticity in news reporting. Except from the human-adopted practices, technological tools and algorithmic procedures are currently implemented for assisting journalists in the increased demands for evaluating the originality of documents and stories. Therefore, the necessity for combining all the available veracity methods and practices is brought to the readers' attention, along with the needs to continually deploy support, training and digital literacy strategies. In this context, the proposed model is sub-structured to several layers, i.e. journalistic, social, ethical, legal, technological, operational, educational, etc., which are going to be thoroughly analyzed in the subsequent chapters. These perspectives will permit an in-depth comprehension of the problem, envisioning the adoption, development and integration of multiple approaches /modalities, towards prospect cross-modal veracity solutions.

REFERENCES

Dimoulas, C., Veglis, A., & Kalliris, G. (2014). Application of Mobile Cloud-Based Technologies. In J. Rodrigues, K. Lin, & J. Lloret (Eds.), *Mobile Networks and Cloud Computing Convergence for Progressive Services and Applications* (pp. 320–343). Hershey, PA: Information Science Reference. doi:10.4018/978-1-4666-4781-7.ch017

Dimoulas, C., Veglis, A., & Kalliris, G. (2015). Audiovisual hypermedia in the semantic Web. In M. Khosrow-Pour (Ed.), *Encyclopedia of Information Science and Technology* (3rd ed.; pp. 7594–7604). Hershey, PA: Information Science Reference. doi:10.4018/978-1-4666-5888-2.ch748

Dimoulas, C. A., & Symeonidis, A. L. (2015). Syncing shared multimedia through audiovisual bimodal segmentation. *IEEE MultiMedia, 22*(3), 26–42. doi:10.1109/MMUL.2015.33

Dimoulas, C. A., Veglis, A. A., & Kalliris, G. (2018). Semantically Enhanced Authoring of Shared Media. In Encyclopedia of Information Science and Technology, Fourth Edition (pp. 6476-6487). IGI Global. doi:10.4018/978-1-5225-2255-3.ch562

Farid, H. (2004). *Creating and detecting doctored and virtual images: Implications to the child pornography prevention act.* Department of Computer Science, Dartmouth College, TR2004-518, 13.

Farid, H. (2006, September). Exposing digital forgeries in scientific images. In *Proceedings of the 8th workshop on Multimedia and security* (pp. 29-36). ACM.

Farid, H. (2009). Image forgery detection. *IEEE Signal Processing Magazine, 26*(2), 16–25. doi:10.1109/MSP.2008.931079

Gupta, S., Cho, S., & Kuo, C. C. J. (2012). Current developments and future trends in audio authentication. *IEEE MultiMedia, 19*(1), 50–59. doi:10.1109/MMUL.2011.74

Ho, A. T., & Li, S. (Eds.). (2015). *Handbook of digital forensics of multimedia data and devices.* John Wiley & Sons. doi:10.1002/9781118705773

Kalliris, G., & Dimoulas, C. (2009, May). Audiovisual content management issues for the new media environment. *Proceedings of the International Conference on New Media and Information: Convergences and Divergences.*

Katsaounidou, A. (2016). *Content authenticity issues: detection (and validation) techniques of untruthful news stories from humans and machine* (Unpublished Master Thesis). Post-Graduate Program of the School of Journalism and Mass Communications, Aristotle University of Thessaloniki.

Katsaounidou, A. N., & Dimoulas, C. A. (2018). Integrating Content Authentication Support in Media Services. In Encyclopedia of Information Science and Technology, Fourth Edition (pp. 2908-2919). IGI Global. doi:10.4018/978-1-5225-2255-3.ch254

Kotsakis, R., Kalliris, G., & Dimoulas, C. (2012). Investigation of broadcast-audio semantic analysis scenarios employing radio-programme-adaptive pattern classification. *Speech Communication, 54*(6), 743–762. doi:10.1016/j.specom.2012.01.004

Krawetz, N., & Solutions, H. F. (2007). *A Picture's Worth...* Black Hat Briefings.

Lee, J., Jain, A., & Tong, W. (2012). Image retrieval in forensics: Tattoo image database application. *IEEE MultiMedia, 19*(1), 40–49. doi:10.1109/MMUL.2011.59

Lu, T., Jin, Y., Su, F., Shivakumara, P., & Tan, C. L. (2015). Content-oriented multimedia document understanding through cross-media correlation. *Multimedia Tools and Applications, 74*(18), 8105–8135. doi:10.100711042-014-2044-9

Lyu, S., Rockmore, D., & Farid, H. (2004). A digital technique for art authentication. *Proceedings of the National Academy of Sciences of the United States of America, 101*(49), 17006–17010. doi:10.1073/pnas.0406398101 PMID:15563599

Matsiola, M., Dimoulas, C. A., Kalliris, G., & Veglis, A. A. (2015). Augmenting user interaction experience through embedded multimodal media agents in social networks. In Social media and the transformation of interaction in society (pp. 188-209). IGI Global. doi:10.4018/978-1-4666-8556-7.ch010

Memon, N. A., & Gilani, S. A. M. (2008, December). NROI watermarking of medical images for content authentication. In *Multitopic Conference, 2008. INMIC 2008. IEEE International* (pp. 106-110). IEEE. 10.1109/INMIC.2008.4777717

Pantti, M., & Sirén, S. (2015). The fragility of photo-truth: Verification of amateur images in Finnish newsrooms. *Digital Journalism, 3*(4), 495-512.

Pasquini, C., Brunetta, C., Vinci, A. F., Conotter, V., & Boato, G. (2015, June). Towards the verification of image integrity in online news. In *Multimedia & Expo Workshops (ICMEW), 2015 IEEE International Conference on* (pp. 1-6). IEEE. 10.1109/ICMEW.2015.7169801

Periaswamy, S., & Farid, H. (2006). Medical image registration with partial data. *Medical Image Analysis, 10*(3), 452–464. doi:10.1016/j.media.2005.03.006 PMID:15979375

Poland, G. A., & Spier, R. (2010). *Fear, misinformation, and innumerates: How the Wakefield paper, the press, and advocacy groups damaged the public health.* Academic Press.

Reich, Z. (2006). The process model of news initiative: Sources lead first, reporters thereafter. *Journalism Studies, 7*(4), 497–514. doi:10.1080/14616700600757928

Satyanarayanan, M., Bahl, P., Caceres, R., & Davies, N. (2009). The case for vm-based cloudlets in mobile computing. *IEEE Pervasive Computing, 8*(4), 14–23. doi:10.1109/MPRV.2009.82

Schetinger, V., Oliveira, M. M., da Silva, R., & Carvalho, T. J. (2015). *Humans are easily fooled by digital images.* arXiv preprint arXiv:1509.05301

Siapera, E., & Veglis, A. (Eds.). (2012). *The handbook of global online journalism.* John Wiley & Sons. doi:10.1002/9781118313978

Silverman, C. (Ed.). (2013). *Verification handbook.* European Journalism Centre.

Silverman, C. (2015). *Lies, Damn Lies, and Viral Content. Tow Center for Digital Journalism (A Tow /Knight Report).* Columbia University Academic Commons. doi:10.7916/D8Q81RHH

Spyridou, L. P., Matsiola, M., Veglis, A., Kalliris, G., & Dimoulas, C. (2013). Journalism in a state of flux: Journalists as agents of technology innovation and emerging news practices. *The International Communication Gazette, 75*(1), 76–98. doi:10.1177/1748048512461763

Veglis, A., Dimoulas, C., & Kalliris, G. (2016). Towards intelligent cross-media publishing: media practices and technology convergence perspectives. In A. Lugmayr & C. Dal Zotto (Eds.), *Media Convergence Handbook-Vol. 1* (pp. 131–150). Springer Berlin Heidelberg. doi:10.1007/978-3-642-54484-2_8

Veglis, A., & Pomportsis, A. (2014). Journalists in the age of ICTs: Work demands and educational needs. *Journalism & Mass Communication Educator*, *69*(1), 61–75. doi:10.1177/1077695813513766

KEY TERMS AND DEFINITIONS

Content Authentication: The process of verifying published content and its multimodal media assets for revealing potential tampering actions, therefore for deciding the authenticity of a story.

Content Tampering: The process of intentionally altering or falsifying digital content, in an effort to make the story more appealing and/or to purposely misinform the public (i.e., as part of a propaganda campaign).

Cross-Media Authentication: A media veracity model that evaluates all the involved modalities across multiple media, so that the inconsistencies between different content version and analysis methods could reveal possible tampering actions.

Chapter 2

Media Authenticity and Journalism:
An Inseparable Framework

ABSTRACT

The evolution of information and communications technologies (ICTs) had a strong positive impact in the media world, and especially in the arrival of the participatory and citizens' journalism paradigms. However, this progress was also marked by the explosion of content tampering and forgery attempts by the dissemination of false informatory data. Verification strategies and initiatives to prevent misinformation were introduced along with the advent of ICTs, aiming at shielding and resurfacing the essence of verification ethics. Based on the principle that information has to be validated before its channeling into journalistic pipelines, the present chapter investigates the trust between news outlets and audience. In specific, the lost "faith" in the media ecosystem is highlighted, focusing on the primary significance that truth holds along the end-to-end newsgathering and publishing processes.

DOI: 10.4018/978-1-5225-5592-6.ch002

INTRODUCTION

In recent years, individuals have been confused about the real purpose of media, partly, due to the fact that the channels of communication between journalists (professionals or citizens) and the audience may propagate misinformation. Indeed, it has been revealed that intended falsification was attempted in many circumstances, purposing to disseminate subjective or opinionated stories (Amarasingam, 2011). There is often a belief that everything is intentionally biased because of the general attitude, which implies that the interpretation of individual cases becomes the rule. As a result, people get disappointed, therefore stop following the associated informing streams, since the provided information is no longer considered useful and necessary. Most journalists claim that truthfulness is the core element of the Journalism vocation, distinguishing news reports from other infotainment or political judgement articles (McNair, 2000). Hence, the notion of "Truth" is assumed to have a central place within the newsgathering and publishing industry.

Journalism holds a fundamental role in the way that people understand what takes place around the world. On one hand, journalists write stories about events that usually occur beyond the physical presence of the citizens, offering the unique accessing medium to the associated information. On the other hand, although reporters are entrusted with the prestige of "experts", they may be biased regarding their judgment about the facts. In the same context, individuals can also influence the content of the news streams or even participate in their formulation. For instance, audience is prone to consume events which appeal to emotions or personal beliefs, offering the opportunity to criticize rather than to applaud. Operating likewise, consumers exert latent pressures on the production of such type of articles. Moreover, end users may shape their received information in many ways, i.e. in order to get informed from specific sources, they customize their favorite pages by connecting informing sites to their social network profiles. Other common practices include the combination of several kinds of devices /access terminals (with their adaptation /customization attributes) and the selection of geographically determined updates, associated with their place of residence or interest. Furthermore, consumers can shape news items by interacting with nonlinear storytelling tools and applications (Thurman, 2015).

Human civilization intensely depends on information transmission (Lewandowsky, 2012).

Through the history of human civilization, there have been eight epochal transformations in communication that, in their way, were no less profound and transformative than what we are experiencing now: from cave drawings to oral language, the written word to the printing press, the telegraph to the radio, broadcast television to cable, and now the Internet. (Kovach, 2011, p. 18)

In addition,

It is not an exaggeration to say that the future of modern society and the stability of its inner life depend to a large extent on the maintenance of the equilibrium between the strength of the techniques of communication and the capacity of the individual's own reaction. (McLuhan, 1994, p. 27)

Each new path of communication, after a required adaptation period, evolves the way of exchanging information to simpler, more textured and more meaningful patterns. Contemporary difficulties that arise due to this incomplete maturity process are related to the uncontrolled spread of diverse or even contradictory informing streams, which have to be cross-validated. Typical examples are the misleading Websites, pursuing to misinform individuals about autism-related vaccination, by guiding them not to immune their children, a practice which can result in severe social consequences (Larson, Cooper, Eskola, Katz, & Ratzan, 2011; Poland & Spier, 2010; Ratzan, 2010). Given that an operational democracy depends on an educated and well-informed population (Kuklinski, Quirk, Jerit, Schwieder, & Rich, 2000), fact-checking procedures are considered essential to avoid the consequences of decisions based on incorrect beliefs and ambiguous claims. It turns out that media authenticity continues to represent an inherent principle of Journalism, with the constant need of being redefined to match the respective social, economic and technological framework.

MEDIA AUTHENTICITY: THE COST OF MISINFORMATION TO SOCIETY

The Lost Trust in New Media: Issues, Controversies, Problems

Traditionally, the audience has had partial capability to influence the production of informatory assets or interact with the creators of the source messages. Today, individuals are creating and exchanging User Generated Content (UGC), turning themselves into news producers and/or citizen journalists who connect and collaborate with other networked participants. This is favored by the nature of Social Networking Sites (SNSs), which "are defined by the characteristics of participation, openness, conversation, community, and connectivity" (Hermida 2012, p. 311). Therefore, *SNSs* become "a source for news media to fill the news vacuum" (Torres & Hermida, 2016 p. 2; Bruno, 2011; Ha & James, 1998; Harrison & Barthel, 2009; Hermida, 2012; Kaplan & Haenlein, 2010). Journalists were always responsible for performing cross-validation tasks, acting as "Gatekeepers" who have access to all sources, while also possessing the required experience and knowledge to verify information accuracy. Gatekeeping represents a consistent and imperative journalistic practice that is almost as old as Journalism, so it does need to continuously adapt to the appearing challenges. Hence, the need for redefining fact-checking emerges, as the traditional approaches might be somewhat obsolete in todays' digital informing landscape. A well-known model that attempts to interpret the bidirectional relationship between audience members and "media" has been suggested by Shoemaker and Vos (2009). Figure 1 depicts an updated version of the associated flow diagram by adding cross-media technologies, utilized in the massive and rapid channeling of information. In this context, all the involved parts have the ability of acting synergistically towards the reconstruction and evaluation of news items, giving them enhanced importance (Thurman, 2015).

Nowadays, the above model cannot be examined irrelevantly of the increasing influence of social media as news providers; the most critical issue is the danger that false stories rely on emotion and become as popular and widespread as the real ones. Changes in journalistic gatekeeping routines were taking place at a time when old-style print and broadcast information suppliers were making attempts to develop new online assets, expanding into geographically wider international markets and inventing novel approaches of

Figure 1. Involved channels in the gatekeeping process: an update to the Shoemaker and Vos (2009) model

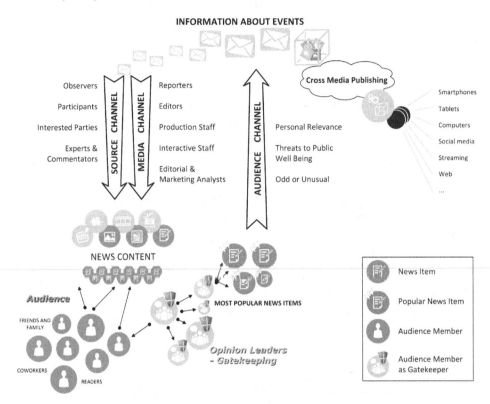

financial gain (Thurman, 2015). In a period that confidence in Journalism is continuously decreasing, the emergence of the so-called Post-Truth Journalism comes to confirm the technology sceptics' point of view, concerning the harmful impact that Internet causes on the field, thus setting the media itself at the center of the public debate. The Oxford Dictionary highlighted the term "post-truth" as the word of the year for 2016, describing it as "an adjective defined, as relating to or denoting circumstances in which objective facts are less influential in shaping public opinion that appeals to emotion and personal belief" (Oxford Dictionaries I English, 2017). Examples of false news, widely propagated within social networks, can be detected in all countries (on both serious occasions /news-stories and gossip-related /lifestyle infotainment streams). A typical story broke out recently in Sweden with reference point to Prime Minister Stefan Leven and a wristwatch of outstanding value. This post was shared on Facebook about 1,000 times and provoked about 2,000 reactions. Eventually, the article turned out to be inaccurate, firstly, because the wristwatch was not that valuable and furthermore, because it was given to the Prime Minister as a gift (Digiday, 2017). Fake-news is not a current trend, but the digital world has become the appropriate arena for their spreading. Hence, in the context of SNSs the uploaded content often does not have professional framing, so it is not clear if the narrative is an expression of opinion, analysis or news. In this increasingly participative environment, we no longer have to talk about separating roles between producers and consumers, but about participants interacting with each other under new rules that no one yet understands (Jenkins, 2006). Due to the spread of UGC and SNSs, Journalism has turned its attention to the users of these new services, thus forming the so-called "new media". It is no coincidence that thirteen years after the launching of the first and most popular social networking platform –Facebook (2004)– even more Internet users in many countries worldwide consider SNSs as a necessary news source (Thurman, 2015). This tendency occurs in a "digital" and "ubiquitous" society, where the media world is experiencing a credibility crisis, while technology is evolving in a fearful frame of adverse impact on the quality of the provided information.

According to a survey conducted by the European Broadcasting Union (EBU) (2016), a scenery of decreasing public confidence in the mass communication channels is observed in Europe, as depicted in Figure 2. By 2015, the general trust had fallen across the range of all informing means. The associated reliability index is slightly deteriorated in Internet and Social Networks, while the faith in Television and Radio reduced even more. However, for Europeans, the mainstream media (Radio, TV) are still the most trustworthy, in contrary to the written press and online news-sites, which present higher levels of unfaithfulness. Equally significant is considered the fact that, radio has found to be the most reliable medium in 20 countries, whereas television holds such lead in 13 countries.

Likewise, based on a longitudinal study, Americans' confidence in media capacity to "broadcast the news completely, accurately and fairly" present declining tendency during the last fifteen years. As Figure 3 presents, the level of trust is steadily below 50% since 2007, whereas the highest measure (72%) was recorded in 1976. The lowest rate is observed in 2015, with only 32% of Americans declaring that they have "Great deal/ Fair amount trust in media". This image of citizens' decreasing entrustment is found in all ages groups, and especially among young people (18-49 years old), where the associated percentage scores are even lower (Gallup, 2017).

Figure 2. Evolution of the Net Trust Index in the European Union (2011-2015)
Source: EBU (2016)

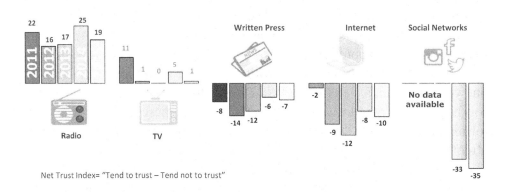

EVOLUTION OF THE NET TRUST INDEX IN THE EU (2011-2015)

Net Trust Index= "Tend to trust – Tend not to trust"

Figure 3. Americans' trust in the Mass Media
(Gallup, 2017)

Americans' Trust in the Mass Media

Question: *In general, how much trust and confidence do you have in the mass media -such as newspapers, TV, radio- when it comes to reporting the news fully, accurately and fairly- a great deal, a fair amount, not very much or none at all.*

%Great deal/ Fair amount

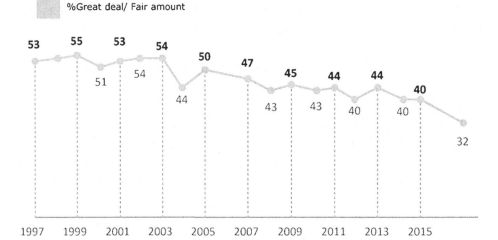

The above discussed crisis of press credibility towards the, as well as the fear of an adverse impact of new technologies on the provided information, are justified if someone takes into account the quality of the news that are shaped and shared through the available channels. For instance, just like every year, 2016 was characterized by stunning international events that took place, related to the refugee crisis, terrorist attacks in Europe, Donald Trump's election, British decision to leave the European Union (Brexit) and the death of many celebrities. These stories were disseminated and became "viral" in social networking platforms. It goes without saying that the latter (i.e. SNSs) have claimed and won their value in the battle of informing, gaining ground from traditional media that gradually lost their power. On the contrary, this superiority appears to be quite weakened in 2017, where audience presents a more cautious attitude (as depicted in Figure 4). The spread of misinformation seems to form a primary reason why individuals all over the world are more suspicious about the role of SNSs. Given the low popularity and trustworthiness of traditional media, the emergence of "fake-news" emanates from the remaining forms of Online Journalism, somewhat confirming those who worry about the harmful impact of the Internet in the news agenda. In a related survey of Reuters Institute, conducted in 36 countries across all continents with the participation of 70,000 content consumers, only a quarter (24%) of respondents answered that SNSs helped in distinguishing reality from fiction (Newman, Fletcher, Kalogeropoulos, Levy & Nielsen, 2017). At the same time, a 40% voted in favor of "News Media" (i.e. the traditional news reporting agencies), with the majority of the interviewees (54%) admitting the exploration of SNSs as informing sources (although with reduced use of Facebook). Overall, while the mainstream informing channels have lost significant portion of their credibility and dominance in the transformed landscape of mass communications, the space left is not credited to the newfangled online services.

Does the Power of Social Networks Become a Weakness?

SNSs are now indissolubly linked to Journalism, shaping a new form of producing content (by both professional journalists and the audience), that is connected on the personal interest in information rather than its objective value; therefore, it is characterized by a more personalized and individualized view of the events. Apart from the roles of readers and UGC contributors, users also operate as "friends" and "followers", grouped around specific

Figure 4. Percentage of audience agreeing that News Media (i.e. traditional news-reporting agencies) and Social Media help in successfully separating the facts from fiction
(Newman, et al., 2017)

Question: *Please indicate your level of agreement with the following statements-*
The media does a good job in helping separate fact from fiction. Base total sample in each country

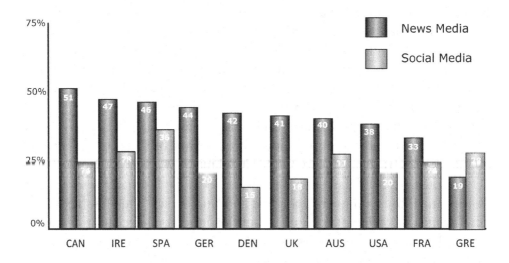

subjects, opinion leaders and other individuals, thus facilitating the rapid propagation of posts and shares (Siapera, 2012). Hence, with the advent of SNSs, Journalism has become "quicker" regarding the amount of news spread. However, many people claim that this is the reason for losing control over informatory streams, due to their unprocessed dissemination without the required journalistic crosschecking. Gowing (2009) discusses about the tyranny of live newscasting, which makes it very difficult for a professional broadcaster to choose whether it is appropriate to transmit information that is incomplete or, perhaps, not 100% confirmed. Overall, reporters are required to find the balance between quickness and truthfulness, within being meticulous and exhaustive or just interesting (Meyer, 2009).

Another essential principle of making journalism refers to objectivity, meaning that media professionals should leave their personal opinion outside their reporting (Hermida, 2012). However, the features and culture of SNSs give individuals the opportunity to express (in written) their thoughts or feelings about an event, with the purpose of sharing it publicly. At the beginning of 2000, the discussion over objectivity and subjectivity was detected in the example of blogs. Those days, similar controversies were triggered with the rise of Twitter and Facebook (Hermida, 2012), which have been used as tools for manipulating public opinion, based on a recent study (Woolley & Howard, 2017). This survey was part of the University of Oxford Computational Propaganda Research Project and it was conducted in nine different countries (Brazil, Canada, China, Germany, Poland, Ukraine, Russia, Taiwan, and USA). According to Professor Philip Howard, "the lies, trash and misinformation" of traditional propaganda are widespread on the Internet and particularly on Facebook and Twitter. Again, it is shown that the decentralized nature of SNSs, besides the provided immediacy in the newsgathering tasks, also offers a fertile ground for information forgery and propagation of untrue stories.

As the British Guardian reports (Hern, 2017), SNSs form a field of political struggle, dominated by the spread of false news, the creation of bogus accounts and the use of automated bots, purposing to promote and reproduce publications in favor of a public figure, i.e. to increase the popularity of a politician. In the USA, similar practices were /are followed by creating more attractive profiles of (political) candidates, a phenomenon that led to the illusion of popularity. Based on the associated study, it has been found that the online endorsement for a candidate can "enhance actual support through the habit of reading public posts in favor of a person", i.e. Donald Trump used Twitter as a central medium of communication in the elections, provoking voters to pay attention. According to Sam Woolley, director of the Research of the Computational Propaganda Project, these procedures lead to the "constructed consensus" effect, which is contradictory to fundamental principles of Journalism, such as objectivity and truthfulness. Consequently, although SNSs currently represent the primary source of news, it seems that skepticism over their role and proper use in informing services is somewhat justified, while it steadily increases. The potential enormous participation with unlimited freedom over content production and propagation might finally have a backfiring result on media authenticity. By all means, it is concluded that principles, practices and tools of information verification need to be reconsidered and redeployed as the only viable solution for recovering the lost trust in the journalistic industry.

SOLUTIONS AND RECOMMENDATIONS

Information Verification Principles, Practices and Tools

The necessity for cross-validation arises from the fact that inaccuracies can be induced in both the news sources and the journalistic shaping /narration, where subjectivity, bias, intentional or mistaken transfer of falsified facts might occur. The principles of classical media gatekeeping should apply here, suggesting that any of today's informative streams, considered as equivalent to the roles of old-time traditional press or broadcasted publications, should be treated with the utmost skepticism. Contemporary differences and difficulties that are encountered at present-day are related to the uncontrollable nature of the digital communications landscape, where Internet services and SNSs have prevailed as reporting /infotainment means, therefore making it impossible to monitor and evaluate the vast amount of the disseminated data. The decentralized, participating and collaborative character of those informing networks implies that every node should be part of the necessary distributed evaluation. Thus, individuals have to act as citizen gatekeepers (in analogy to the citizens' Journalism paradigm), performing their own fact-checking duties, in conjunction with the corresponding news-content consumption, contribution and propagation actions. Consequently, the majority of the efforts being made in developing practices and platforms, purposing on verification, are centered on the cultivation of the necessary audit skills (Katsaounidou & Dimoulas, 2018). However, distinguishing between what is true or lie is not only a critical judgment, so it needs to be surrounded by knowhow, experience, techniques and well-tested best practices. This section summarizes the desired knowledge and skills, which Internet users need to possess for ensuring the credibility of online reporting. Precaution or defending arrangements, that popular news outlets make to protect themselves from misinformation, are regarded as equally significant for compiling an integrated framework for fighting against media forgery.

Over the last two decades, World Wide Web has been introduced into people's lives as an essential, if not necessary, communication tool. As a result, Internet users browse more information than they may actually need, which is not necessarily useful, since there is no assurance regarding the accuracy of the corresponding content. For instance, different websites often provide contradictory data, thus the emerging challenge, faced by individuals, is to detect and classify trustworthy sources. Online verification is a compound procedure, implemented through traditional journalistic practices and live tools, purposing to evaluate the originality of the associated informatory streams and documents. Despite the exponential progress of ICTs and their enhanced computing facilities (including quality assessment automations), the human factor holds an essential role in the process of media authenticity, through the utilization of mature time-established techniques. The combination of the above two mentioned approaches is somewhat equivalent to the four-basic factor model, usually involved in typical news-checking and cross-validating scenarios (Figure 5). Hence, concatenating all these different certification perspectives is very likely to lead to the best possible confirmation results, while deciding on journalistic credibility and reliability.

Full Fact[1], the UK's independent fact checking charity, has also established a related four-stage inspection model, claiming that the inner processes remain intact, either when they are applied by humans or when executed by machines (Figure 6). The procedure begins with the *monitoring* of all the associated public data, moves to the *searching* for specific information, then is *checking* the required material about a claim or an event, and finally concluding in *decision taking* about a news item /claim.

Figure 5. The four basic factors of verification strategies
(Silverman, 2013)

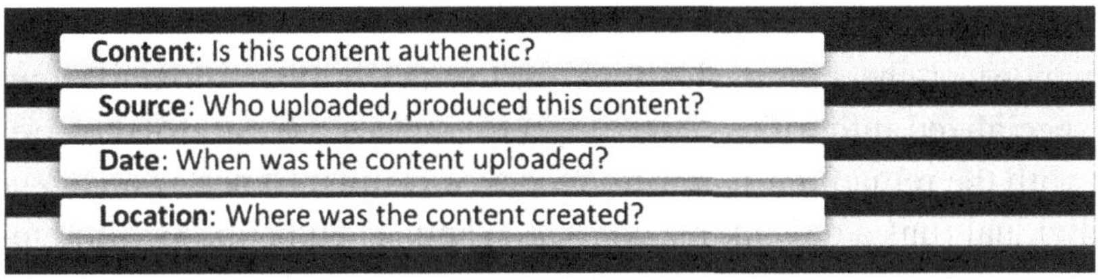

Content: Is this content authentic?
Source: Who uploaded, produced this content?
Date: When was the content uploaded?
Location: Where was the content created?

Figure 6. The four-stage fact checking process by Full Fact Organization
(Babakar & Moy, 2016)

Monitoring
Search information
Check-information
Decision taking

To detect and fight fake-news, mainstream and online channels have begun to develop strategies to secure both their products and audiences from falsified information. The verification process is divided into the accuracy inspection of the content itself and the credibility validation of the associated news sources. On a second level, the reliability of the stories depends on the multimedia evidence that is used to reinforce the value of the presented events. Aiming at deciding whether the articles are trustful or not, two essential measures are introduced: the credibility of the publisher and the authenticity of the documents. One action that has been taken for solving specific aspects of the problem is the enlisting of the International Fact Checking Network (IFCN), a branch of the Journalism research organization Poynter (Wendling, 2017). The purpose of this utility is to hold information about the history of specific informing pages and agencies, concerning their involvement in ambiguous reports that proved to be inaccurate. In the same context, records /log files regarding specific rumors or hoaxes are also kept, targeting to reveal potential reappearance of such topics with similar /untrue framing. The effort is supported by the collaboration of journalists /media professionals and authenticity specialists /experts, employed by press corporations like the Washington Post and the debunking sites Snopes.com, FactCheck.org, Politifact.com, etc. Among the cooperating parties is also listed Google, the largest and most popular online search engine, assisting people by displaying useful information of linked posts, created by publishers, editors and (teams of) external analysts. The so-called "Google Fact Check" service isolates articles that include fact-checking evaluations (performed by related organizations and other specialized authorities), inserting a summarized version of these reports along with the remaining searched /retrieved results. Hence, if an agency or an individual runs a debunking site that examines authenticity "statements" made by thirds, then, "Claim Review", a structured data element is included in the respective webpage and, as a result, the page appears in search lists for that "statement" (Google Developers, 2018).

Facebook has been launched special purpose partnerships with Snopes, Associated Press, FactCheck.org, Politifact and ABC News over the past few months to stop the propagation of fake-news. The goal is to post warnings in news feeds, purposing on limiting and halting the efforts of those who spread rumors, hoaxes or jokes. The process is designed as follows: Facebook enables readers to execute a series of event control services, which are based on the partnerships mentioned above, aiming at alerting users about the potential falsified articles. For this reason, related metadata labeling will be applied with the aid of algorithms or through crowdsourcing mechanisms, taking advantage of the received feedback. If collaborating organizations confirm a news item as fake, Facebook will be informed through a dedicated reporting site and will post a warning notice stating that the narrative "is being challenged by one or more event control agencies". The announcement will also be framed by a hyperlink, either in the news feed or in the page where the story was composed, especially when the user intends to share the hyperlink. Due to the worry caused by the evolving phenomenon of tampered information, there will be many browser extensions or message Bots that will have been performing cross-event processes by the end of 2017 (Schaedel, 2018).

Twitter, with its blue "verified" sign, provides details about the authenticity of a public-interest account. In the same context, various newspaper publishers have implemented related strategies in their online versions, aiming at detecting and fighting misinformation spread by investigating the truth or accuracy of the content. One such service that has been developed in Sweden, posts a double hyperlink at the bottom of each page, with the following functions: the first link asks the public to declare any inaccuracies about the fact that is highlighted in the report and the other allows the user to share the article, within the regulations of the formula (Southern, 2017). In addition, Washington Post attempted to test President Donald Trump's tweets by utilizing an automated system through a new extension to the web browser called "Real Donald Context" (Bump, 2016). The number of such applications as the above, including robotic methods to cross-check the information, is expected to be increased soon. Furthermore, the French newspaper Le Monde has already established a search engine to help readers check the accuracy of political statements. Having set up a specialized group of 13 people called "Les Decoders", Le Monde seeks to combat the distressing phenomenon of false news dissemination, providing a web extension called "Decodex" (Wendling, 2017). Likewise, BBC has launched the so-called "Reality Check team" in the editorial room to combat misinformation (Jackson, 2017). The work of the group is to collect stories that are either not cross-checked or formatted to look real and then, through appropriate research, to "demystify" them by writing penetrating articles and publishing videos in the special section. Finally, BBC attempts to launch the "slower news" idea, using exhaustive analysis and expertise to help the public better understand the contextual framework of the stories, such as the latest political incidents (i.e. Brexit) that appeared in the United Kingdom (Jackson, 2017).

As already implied, various kinds of such authenticity evaluation tools continuously enter the market, purposing to fight fake-news and misinforming propagation. However, the majority of the users is not always aware of the appearance or the proper functioning of such services. It is expected that after putting these utilities into testing for an adequate period, the acquired experience and the exploited feedback will propel the implementation of more prosperous solutions in the future.

CONCLUSION

The evolution of ICTs brought forward many changes in the news business, across the end-to-end sides of production and consumption. The media ecosystem is under continuous and rapid transformations, where Internet and SNNs have prevailed as the most popular informing means, resulting in the domination of the Digital and Online Journalism services. As aptly pointed out by Rochlin (2017, p. 13): "We are currently witnessing a war of information. This war is being fought on an electronic battlefield, and is using clicks as ammunition". Despite this heavy impact of technology and the widespread use of social networks, professionals of digital outlets are not worried about the future of their work. An adverse side effect is located in the uncontrollable nature of information propagation, where intentionally falsified content and messages can easily be disseminated, and accepted as accurate by the broader audience, which implicates further harmful consequences in the society. Nevertheless, the overwhelming majority of publishers believe that fake-news is not a threat to their product, but rather a powerful incentive, causing to became conspicuous and to emerge qualitative Journalism (Newman, 2017). Their optimistic attitude might be attributed to the rapid rise of initiatives, which are purposing to prevent spreading of untrue stories. Indeed, during the last years, there is a systematic research effort, where the Digital Forensics field has been significantly elaborated in the journalistic domain, aiming at helping in news authentication. However, the developed tools and practices have not yet reached the required maturity, to deal decisively with this phenomenon. Additionally, these newfangled utilities are unknown both to the general public and the experts of the field, issue that further deteriorates their practical usefulness (Katsaounidou & Dimoulas, 2018).

Despite the increased ICTs capabilities in implementing automated systems to rank documents in terms of their quality and originality (i.e. absence of tampering trails), the human intervention remains important, if not imperative. In today's digital communications landscape, with the presence of multiple informing channels, propagation paths and sources, cross-modal authentication and verification practices seem to be the only viable solution. In analogy to the participatory journalism, the notion of citizen gatekeepers has already surfaced, implying that every user, acting as engaged interactor /consumer or even as content contributor and disseminator, is obliged to perform fact-checking duties. Dedicated knowledge and skills are essential in this new role, in which the importance of literacy and critical thinking has increased. Thus, academics, librarians, educators and media professionals need to collaborate towards the elimination of these know-how inadequacies, accomplishing a crucial mission in confronting misinformation (Rochlin, 2017). There is no objection that this battle should be combatted with applicable tools and technological means that will assist individuals in their own "personal fights". For this reason, along with the advances of computing systems and services, the research community should bend on the practical needs to assess the credibility of informative data, while users should be trained and supported on how to use the invented methods or protocols (Berghel, 2017; Katsaounidou & Dimoulas, 2018). The unquestionable fact is that fake-news cannot be stopped, but they can only be confronted with digital literacy on the matters (Rochlin, 2017). Out of the contents and the outline, visualized in the present chapter, it is attempted to come an understanding that will ease the way forward, for better managing the fluid identity of the information and for supporting quality journalism. After all, it has been proven that media authenticity and journalism do form an inseparable framework.

REFERENCES

Amarasingam, A. (Ed.). (2011). *The Stewart/Colbert effect: Essays on the real impacts of fake news*. McFarland.

Babakar, M., & Moy, W. (2016). The State of Automated Factchecking. *Full Fact*. Retrieved from https://fullfact.org/blog/2016/aug/automated-factchecking/

Berghel, H. (2017). Lies, Damn Lies, and Fake News. *Computer*, *50*(2), 80–85. doi:10.1109/MC.2017.56

Bruno, N. (2011). Tweet first, verify later? How real-time information is changing the coverage of worldwide crisis events. Oxford, UK: Reuters Institute for the Study of Journalism, University of Oxford.

Bump, P. (2016). Now you can fact-check Donald Trump's tweets–in the tweets themselves. *Washington Post, 16.*

Digiday. (2017). *How Sweden is fighting fake news - Digiday.* Retrieved from https://digiday.com/uk/fake-news-in-sweden/

EBU. (2016). *European Broadcasting Union's Annual Report for 2015-2016.* Retrieved from https://www.ebu.ch/files/live/sites/ebu/files/Publications/ EBU-Annual-Report-15-16_EN.pdf

EBU. (2016). *Trust in Media 2016,* Retrieved from https://www.ebu.ch/files/ live/sites/ebu/files/Publications/EBU-MIS - Trust in Media 2016.pdf

Gallup, I. (2017). *Americans' Trust in Mass Media Sinks to New Low.* Gallup. com. Retrieved from http.//www.gallup.com/poll/195542/americans-trust-mass-media-sinks-new-low.aspx

García de Torres, E., & Hermida, A. (2017). The Social Reporter in Action: An analysis of the practice and discourse of Andy Carvin. *Journalism Practice, 11*(2-3), 177–194. doi:10.1080/17512786.2016.1245110

Google Developers. (2017). *Fact Checks | Search | Google Developers.* Retrieved from https://developers.google.com/search/docs/data-types/ factcheck

Gowing, N. (2009). *"Skyful of Lies" and Black Swans: The new tyranny of shifting information power in crises.* Reuters Institute for the Study of Journalism.

Graves, L., & Cherubini, F. (2016). *The rise of fact-checking sites in Europe.* Academic Press.

Ha, L., & James, E. L. (1998). Interactivity reexamined: A baseline analysis of early business web sites. *Journal of Broadcasting & Electronic Media, 42*(4), 457–474. doi:10.1080/08838159809364462

Harrison, T. M., & Barthel, B. (2009). Wielding new media in Web 2.0: Exploring the history of engagement with the collaborative construction of media products. *New Media & Society, 11*(1-2), 155–178. doi:10.1177/1461444808099580

Hermida, A. (2012). Social journalism: Exploring how social media is shaping journalism. The handbook of global online journalism, 309-328.

Hern, A. (2017). Facebook and Twitter are being used to manipulate public opinion – report. *The Guardian.* Retrieved on August 29, 2017 from https://www.theguardian.com/technology/2017/jun/19/social-media-proganda-manipulating-public-opinion-bots-accounts-facebook-twitter

Jackson, J. (2017). BBC sets up team to debunk fake news. *The Guardian.* Retrieved from https://www.theguardian.com/media/2017/jan/12/bbc-sets-up-team-to-debunk-fake-news

Jenkins, H. (2006). *Convergence Culture: Where Old and New Media Collid.* Click Nothing. Retrieved from http://books.google.com/books?id=RlRVNikT06YC&pgis=1

Kaplan, A. M., & Haenlein, M. (2010). Users of the world, unite! The challenges and opportunities of Social Media. *Business Horizons, 53*(1), 59–68. doi:10.1016/j.bushor.2009.09.003

Katsaounidou, A. N., & Dimoulas, C. A. (2018). Integrating Content Authentication Support in Media Services. In Encyclopedia of Information Science and Technology, Fourth Edition (pp. 2908-2919). IGI Global. doi:10.4018/978-1-5225-2255-3.ch254

Kovach, B., & Rosenstiel, T. (2011). *Blur: How to know what's true in the age of information overload.* Bloomsbury Publishing USA.

Kuklinski, J. H., Quirk, P. J., Jerit, J., Schwieder, D., & Rich, R. F. (2000). Misinformation and the currency of democratic citizenship. *The Journal of Politics, 62*(3), 790–816. doi:10.1111/0022-3816.00033

Larson, H. J., Cooper, L. Z., Eskola, J., Katz, S. L., & Ratzan, S. (2011). Addressing the vaccine confidence gap. *Lancet, 378*(9790), 526–535. doi:10.1016/S0140-6736(11)60678-8 PMID:21664679

Lewandowsky, S., Ecker, U. K., Seifert, C. M., Schwarz, N., & Cook, J. (2012). Misinformation and its correction: Continued influence and successful debiasing. *Psychological Science in the Public Interest, 13*(3), 106–131. doi:10.1177/1529100612451018 PMID:26173286

McLuhan, M. (1994). *Understanding media: The extensions of man.* MIT Press.

McNair, B. (2000). *Journalism and democracy*. London: Routledge.

Metzger, M. J. (2007). Making sense of credibility on the Web: Models for evaluating online information and recommendations for future research. *Journal of the Association for Information Science and Technology, 58*(13), 2078–2091.

Meyer, P. (2009). *The vanishing newspaper: Saving journalism in the information age*. University of Missouri Press.

Newman, N. (2017). *Journalism, Media, and Technology Trends and Predictions 2017*. Academic Press.

Newman, N., Fletcher, R., Kalogeropoulos, A., Levy, D. A., & Nielsen, R. K. (2017). *Reuters institute digital news report 2017*. Reuters.

Oxford Dictionaries | English. (2017). *Word of the Year 2016 is...*. Retrieved from https://en.oxforddictionaries.com/word-of-the-year/word-of-the-year-2016

Parker, R., & Ratzan, S. C. (2010). Health literacy: A second decade of distinction for Americans. *Journal of Health Communication, 15*(S2), 20–33. doi:10.1080/10810730.2010.501094 PMID:20845190

Poland, G. A., & Spier, R. (2010). *Fear, misinformation, and innumerates: how the Wakefield paper, the press, and advocacy groups damaged the public health*. Academic Press.

Rochlin, N. (2017). Fake news: Belief in post-truth. *Library Hi Tech, 35*(3), 386–392. doi:10.1108/LHT-03-2017-0062

Schaedel, S. (2018). *How to Flag Fake News on Facebook - FactCheck.org*. Retrieved 21 January 2018, from https://www.factcheck.org/2017/07/flag-fake-news-facebook/

Shoemaker, P. J., & Vos, T. (2009). *Gatekeeping theory*. Routledge.

Siapera, E. (2012). Forms of online journalism and politics. The handbook of global online journalism, 155-175.

Silverman, C. (Ed.). (2013). *Verification handbook*. European Journalism Centre.

Swift, A. (2016). Americans' trust in mass media sinks to new low. Gallup.

Thurman, N. (2015). *Journalism, gatekeeping, and interactivity*. Academic Press.

Wendling, M. (2017). *Solutions that can stop fake news spreading - BBC News*. Retrieved from http://www.bbc.com/news/blogs-trending-38769996

Woolley, S. C., & Howard, P. N. (2017). *Computational propaganda worldwide: Executive summary*. Academic Press.

KEY TERMS AND DEFINITIONS

Authentication Strategies: Strategies which investigate the truth of events and facts, as well as user and account identity, web pages accuracy, and multimedia content data integrity.

(Automated) Bot: An internet bot, also known as web robot, www robot or simply bot, is a software application that runs automated tasks over the Internet. Bots perform tasks that are both simple and structurally repetitive, at a much higher rate than would be possible for a human alone.

Bogus Accounts: Counterfeit or fake, not genuine accounts of social media.

Constructed Consensus: A process in which the online behavior leads to similar behaviors in the real world e.g. online support for a candidate can enhance actual support through the habit of reading public posts in favor of a person.

Debunking Websites: Websites have taken up the task of spreading awareness against rumors by presenting evidence and hard facts (e.g., Snopes. com, FactCheck.org, Politifact.com, etc.).

Digitalization: Integration of digital technologies into everyday life by the digitization of everything that can be digitized.

Net Trust Index: The net trust index makes it possible to rank the countries according to their level of trust in media, and also to compare the levels of trust across different types of media. It can be a positive value, meaning that on the whole, citizens tend to trust the given medium, or a negative value, which means that generally, citizens tend not to trust it.

Slow News: A new "movement" in Journalism claiming that speed is the fundamental issue of reliability and suggests in-depth and expertise analysis in order to provide accurate information and help the public understand the facts.

ENDNOTE

[1]   https://fullfact.org/

Chapter 3
The Transforming Media Landscape

ABSTRACT

During the last decades, the digital revolution that we have all experienced through the widespread deployment of information and communication technologies (ICTs) has multilaterally influenced individual's perception about significant aspects of everyday life. Among others, the massive adoption of internet technologies and the transition to the Web 2.0/3.0 paradigms (and beyond) have shaped a dynamically changing media environment. As a result, new forms of journalism and mass communication have been launched and are currently available, promoting the so-called citizen and participatory journalism models, where user generated content (UGC) is dominant. The arising issue is that part of the propagated information may be subjective, manipulated, and/or unreliable, which is further deteriorated by the lack of confidence of many average users within the new digital environment. The present chapter attempts to enlighten the correlations between the rapidly transforming media landscape and its unwanted effect on news and content tampering.

DOI: 10.4018/978-1-5225-5592-6.ch003

INTRODUCTION

Historically, technological advances have always affected human life and especially the professional and social activities that were /are related to the associated evolution. We have witnessed such an intensive impact in our everyday habits due to the digital revolution that took place during the last decades. This transformation was dominated by the remarkable progress, achieved in Information and Communication Technologies (ICTs), resulting in the introduction and extensive use of novel mediated communication tools (Kalliris & Dimoulas, 2009; Siapera & Veglis, 2012). In particular, the widespread adoption of Internet technologies and the transition from the primitive Web 1.0 initiative to Web 2.0 and Web 3.0 eras (and beyond), drastically altered (and continues to alter) the "user's access to information" scenarios (Aghaei, Nematbakhsh, & Farsani, 2012; Dimoulas, Veglis, & Kalliris, 2014, 2015, 2018; Matsiola, Dimoulas, Kalliris, & Veglis, 2015). The proliferation of manageable multimedia capturing, processing and sharing tools engaged people to be actively involved in the news production and consumption processes. As a result, new forms of Digital Journalism and Mass Communications are continuously launched and elaborated, advancing contemporary media services. Among others, easier information exchange is favored by the efficient collaboration between remotely-located users, groups, professionals and experts of various kinds, therefore promoting pluralism and diversity with timely- and geographically-boundless news coverage (i.e. without time and/or location restrictions). Along with the contemporary journalism technologies (i.e. robot-, drone-, immersive-journalism, etc.), new digital storytelling potentials also appear, aiming at offering enhanced capabilities of content capturing, processing automation and augmented user interaction (Chamberlain, 2017; Coddington, 2015; Dimoulas, 2015; Dimoulas et al., 2014a, 2015, 2018; Gynnild, 2014; Ntalakas, Dimoulas, Kalliris, & Veglis, 2017; Tremayne & Clark, 2014; Veglis, Dimoulas, & Kalliris, 2016).

On the other hand, in order for the new capabilities to be fully exploited, some minimum "digital skills" and knowhow are necessary, for both news producers and consumers. While reasonable, this fact provokes /triggers a negative attitude on the part of a number of media organizations, journalists and users, who prefer the traditional ways of informing. For instance, professional journalists may get anxiety, regarding their working future, considering that job offer might severely decrease, due to the automation, provided by algorithmic journalism. Similar effects might have the exponential growth of the User Generated Content (UGC), contributed within the citizens' journalism paradigm. Moreover, quite a few practical, ethical and legal issues usually come into sight when a new trend enters the market, as it happens with almost all the aforementioned genres of Digital Journalism (Dörr, 2015; Dörr & Hollnbuchner, 2017; Haim & Graefe, 2017; Johnston, 2016; Linden, 2016; Montal & Reich, 2016). Another arising matter is that part of the news data, contributed by users or machines, is exposed to manipulation and tampering actions that can be easily imposed for intentionally opinionating, sensationalizing and misleading the public. Consequently, content verification processes are even more critical for validating the reliability and authenticity of the associated stories, where related difficulties are further intensified by the implied digital literacy prerequisites (Katsaounidou, 2016; Katsaounidou & Dimoulas, 2018). Besides, the continually changing (therefore being unstable) environment of ICTs and mass communication services requires for training and persistent support actions, which could help informing users and professionals in fast adapting to contemporary trends and challenges (such as forgery detection). The current chapter attempts to enlighten all these aspects of the rapidly transforming media landscape, emphasizing on the unwanted effects of news and content tampering that deteriorate the credibility of journalistic organizations and overall lead to lack of trust in the news industry. Among others, arising technological capabilities, regarding the implementation of novel and more sophisticated information authentication techniques, will be outlined as potential promising solutions, analyzing advantages and shortcomings of their associated attributes.

THE TRANSFORMING MEDIA LANDSCAPE

Background: Digital Media Technology Breakthroughs

Looking back at the beginning of the media revolution, it all started with the breakthrough of digital technology and the development of cost-effective computing systems with constantly increasing processing capabilities (i.e. personal computers and dedicated computing servers), which also initiated the digitization of the newsroom. Computerized editorial systems revolutionized newspaper production and publishing, which, with the arrival of the World Wide Web, brought forward the electronic /online news editions that complemented print and analogue media (i.e. newspapers, radio and TV news). However, the real progress to the contemporary digital environment actually began with the transition from Web 1.0 to Web 2.0, and continued with the gradual implementation of the succeeded models (Web 2.5, 3.0, 4.0), towards the materialization of the so-called "Internet of Thing" envision (Web x.0). As it is depicted in Figure 1, while Web 1.0 was characterized by static content with limited user interaction (restricted in static pages of simple text and still images), both content modalities and interaction mechanisms were enhanced in the Web 2.0 era. Most of all, the number of content providers was significantly increased with the advent of Web 2.0 services (i.e. blogs, wikis, social networking sites in general, etc.), allowing average users to act both as content producers and consumers (Aghaei et al., 2012; Dimoulas et al., 2014a, 2015, 2018; Matsiola et al., 2015; Siapera & Veglis, 2012).

Additional useful attributes, such as mobility, location- and context-awareness, personalization and multilevel adaptation, are being progressively ingested, offering flexibility with literately unconstrained "access to information". These elements are dominant in today's Symbiotic Web (Web 2^+/2.5), while they are continuously augmented with more sophisticated functionalities of smart processing and management automation. Indeed, huge volumes of data are daily produced by innumerous users, a fact that requires increased storage capacities and, mostly, efficient content management mechanisms (Kalliris & Dimoulas, 2009). Furthermore, the semantics behind a story (i.e. topic, meaning, empathy, etc.) are now considered as very important and challenging, pointing in the direction of the Semantic Web, which emerged as the next big thing (Web 3.0). Semantic processing is quite demanding, but also extremely expedient for both content understanding and media management purposes (i.e. opinion and sentiment recognition, content-based searching and retrieval, data summarization, visualization, interpretation, etc.). Hence, machine learning and intelligent processing algorithms possess a key role in the semantic world of Web 3.0 and Web 4.0. The latter is known as the Intelligent Web and is expected to integrate agents and advanced intelligent systems into the next generation semantic services (Aghaei et al., 2012; Matsiola et al., 2015). At the same time, hardware evolution increased the capacity of the media storage (though lowering their costs), thus helping in facing the associated storage demands. Cloud computing (CC) systems have also been promoted for archiving solutions, favoring network-centric collaboration and documentation, while ensuring data safety and integrity. Moreover, mobile cloud computing (MCC) services allow for computationally heavy applications to run on resource-limited mobile devices, thus extending mobile capabilities to pervasive and ubiquitous processing frameworks. In this

Figure 1. Digital media technology breakthroughs and associated progress in journalism

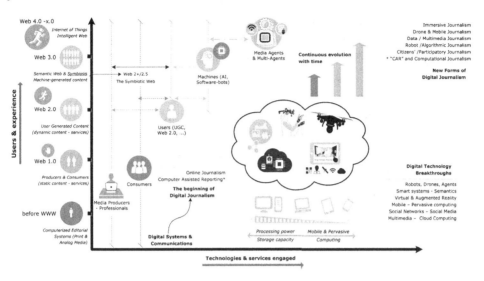

context, the outmost ambition of the "Internet of things" is to provide such semantically-enhanced interconnection with all possible electronic devices that are used in everyday human life (Aghaei et al., 2012; Dimoulas et al., 2014a; 2015; 2018; Dimoulas, Kalliris, Chatzara, Tsipas, & Papanikolaou, 2014; Dimoulas & Symeonidis, 2015; Kotsakis, Kalliris, & Dimoulas, 2012; Matsiola et al., 2015; Papadopoulos, Cesar, Shamma, & Kelliher, 2015).

Apparently, most of the above progress has already been reflected in the media world and the various "models" of Digital Journalism (e.g. Data, Computational and Multimedia Journalism, Robot and Drone Journalism, Immersive Journalism and others), which are depicted in Figure 1 and are further analyzed in the next sections (Álvarez, 2017; Bull, 2010; Coddington, 2015; Ntalakas et al., 2017, Veglis & Bratsas, 2017a; 2017b). An indicative review of a yearly progress (from 2015 to 2016) brings forward some useful conclusions, foreseeing the most important future expectations. For instance, the year 2015 can be characterized as "the year of distributed content", where auto-play videos and animated User Interfaces (UIs) intensified their presence (Newman, 2016). New interaction mechanisms were launched, such as the "3D touch" by Apple, while waterproof and foldable mobile phones made their appearance, along with the first sights of wireless charging. Mobile network speeds were further increased with the transition to 4G technology, also extending the available mobile storytelling capabilities. At the same time, avatars, media agents and multi-agents have been elaborated as virtual user assistants, augmenting the associated human-machine interaction (HMI) experience. In addition, data summarization and mush-up services have extended the utilization of "push notifications and glanceable content", where smart-watches and wearable sensors can find their place. The above trends, combined with the advances of Virtual and Augmented Reality (VR, AR), resulted in the so-called "Zero UI" idea, where media producers are required to make their content available, not just for multiple screens, but even for no screens. With the beginning of 2016, it is foreseen that the aforementioned multisensory technologies could lead into new journalistic services, within the envisioned "Internet of Things" conception. Similarly, it is expected that immersive storytelling will continue to emerge, taking advantage of the contemporary virtual reality technologies (i.e. navigation through aerial views, panoramas, AR, gigapixel imaging, etc.), as well as of the upcoming next-generation drones and mobile systems (Dimoulas, 2015; Dimoulas et al., 2014b; Matsiola et al., 2015; Newman, 2016; Ntalakas et al., 2017; Pavlik & Bridges, 2013).

Digital Journalism Models: Issues, Controversies, Problems

As already stated, most of the conducted digital technology breakthroughs have their reflection in the formulation of new forms and models of Digital Journalism. The remarkable speed of the technological progress resulted in the corresponding fast transformation of the media world, where overlapping or oven confusion between the different definitions was rather unavoidable. Hence, several difficulties appear, regarding the right conception of the various new fields, bringing forward further complications and problems on the proper use of the associated services. These inconveniences concern all the involved parties, namely professional journalists and news producers, content contributors and participating users, average /ordinary users or news consumers. Along with the controversies that usually emerge when a new technology enters the market, the above matters deteriorate the full potentials of the newly surfaced services, diminishing the prospects for extended real-world practice and testing, which otherwise could lead to constructive evaluation and feedback with possible useful updates. Considering that technological advances in digital media continue to evolve even at higher rates, it is vital for someone involved in the news business to comprehend existing services and their corresponding terminology, before being able to cope with the forthcoming tools. Among others, these shortcomings affect cross-media publishing and verification practices, making users more susceptible to forgery attacks, thus weakening the chances of thorough, versatile and unbiased informing. On the contrary, there are challenging opportunities located in the innovative character of the up-to-date /upcoming journalism "products", which could be exploited towards the implementation of integrated and unified information authentication strategies (Bull, 2010; Ho & Li, 2015; Johnston, 2016; Katsaounidou & Dimoulas, 2018; Lu, Jin, Su, Shivakumara, & Tan, 2015; Silverman, 2013; Spyridou, Matsiola, Veglis, Kalliris, & Dimoulas, 2013; Veglis et al., 2016).

Figure 2 attempts to depict the most important genres of Journalism that have been formed with the advent and the widespread domination of digital technology, thus portraying a kind of taxonomy of the associated tools and media services. From a linguistic point of view, Digital Journalism refers to the implementation of digital technology for the collection, publishing and consumption of news, therefore along the end-to-end chain of the journalistic profession. In that principle, it stands as the main root of all the newfangled models that followed. Although the term is often ascribed as a synonym to Online Journalism in the related bibliography, in the current chapter (and for the rest of the book) the more strict terminology will be used, which slightly differentiates the two disciplines. In specific, Digital Journalism has a more generic meaning that academically encapsulates all the digital media sub-cases, where news is produced, managed and disseminated through digital means, having the form of multimodal assets (text, image, audio, video, etc.). On the other hand, online Journalism has a somewhat narrower focus, emphasizing on the distribution of the news stories through the Web, as clearly indicated by the associated "online" adjective. Another possible way of discrimination between the two terms relies on the fact that Online Journalism holds only the second half of the whole process (the publishing and dissemination part), so that it can be viewed as a supplemental task to Computer Assisted Reporting (CAR). The later describes the prerequisite work of gathering and writing news reports with the help of computers, the origin of which is dated back in the early 50s (Coddington, 2015; Dimoulas, 2019; Johnston, 2016; Siapera & Veglis, 2013; Spyridoy et al., 2013).

Figure 2. Representation of the various forms of Digital Journalism, based on their time-entrance (starting point), their relation to the Web eras and the involved technologies

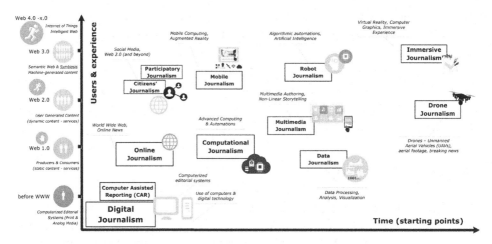

Closely related to CAR is Computational Journalism, which has been surfaced as a recent model /definition, implying that more sophisticated processing can be now applied in the newsgathering, shaping and publishing tasks. For instance, Artificial Intelligent (AI) and Natural Language Processing (NLP) algorithms can be exploited for information searching and retrieval, automated news alerts, topic detection, story classification, semantic conceptualization, sentiment and opinion extraction, computer-assisted authentication and others. In this context, dedicated management and recommendation techniques can be deployed for automating all the tasks of the news reporting chain, often without any involvement or engagement of the human factor. Such kind of automated tools forms the sub-section of the so-called Robot Journalism (also known as Automated and Algorithmic Journalism), where the headlines or even the entire news articles are created by computer programs (often called "Web-bots" and "Internet-bots"). Furthermore, the programing of the media channel and the time-slots that the gathered information is pushed online can be decided by these "software robots" or simply "bots". Overall, Robot Journalism describes the processes of gathering and publishing news information with minimum or complete absence of human interventions (i.e. semi- or fully-automated news reporting). No doubt, this type of algorithmic automation provokes many ethical and legal questions, including possible oppositions to the ideology of Journalism, which usually results in lack of trust in the associated news stories by the public (Montal & Reich, 2016). Likewise, it can raise concerns regarding the working future of "human reporters", who might be thought as redundant, an anxiety that is likely to shape a fighting /defending attitude by the journalists. On the other hand, it is not clear whether human-reported news is preferred over automated ones, an issue that seems to depend on many different aspects, i.e. content and story types, users' profiles and preferences, etc. (Haim & Graefe, 2017). In all cases, professionals can take advantage of the offered automation tools, by exploiting them as useful information alerting and gathering means, also having the choice of reinventing and enriching the human aspects of making journalism (Bull, 2010; Coddington, 2015; Dimoulas, 2018; 2019; Dörr, 2015; Dörr & Hollnbuchner, 2017; Johnston, 2016; Linden, 2016, 2017; Montal & Reich, 2016; Siapera & Veglis, 2013; Symeonidis & Mitkas, 2006; Van Dalen, 2012).

Extending the above, apart from media professionals and "machines", average users can now have the role of citizen journalists, through feedback /commenting and UGC contribution actions. Hence, the forms of Citizens' and Participatory Journalism have flourished with the advent of social networks (Web 2.0 and beyond). While many researchers use the two terms as synonyms, again, small variations can be found in their strict definitions. Particularly, in the Participatory Journalism scenario, people can be part of the news collection, contribution, sharing and commenting processes, however, under the authority of a professional media organization. In the citizens' journalism case, users can act as information providers or commenters, autonomously (i.e. without any professional guidance or control). Both two paradigms met an exponential growth with the advancement of mobile computing devices (i.e. smartphones and tablets), which offer in-built Internet /networking connections with convenient audiovisual capturing capabilities, thus allowing the involved participants to produce and consume news independently of time and place. Computational power and storage limitations are dealt with the technological evolution of the new-generation processing (and storage) units, as well as with the use of contemporary CC and MCC services. Moreover, new utilities of pervasive and ubiquitous computing became available, incorporating context- and location-awareness attributes, semantically enhanced services and AR applications. Consequently, the predominant role of pervasive communication in today's ubiquitous society also fueled Mobile Journalism, offering new ways of making journalism. Indeed, mobile devices have become the natural extension of journalists and their audience (i.e. users) in their everyday informing needs, revolutionizing news production and consumption ends. However, there are still remaining practical issues, such as the lack of full-scale interoperability and platform independence concerning hardware, operating systems and applications, as well as the need for increased reliability, trust and privacy, for both users and mobile terminals (Álvarez, 2017; Dimoulas et al., 2014a; Pavlik & Bridges, 2013; Rodríguez & Freire, 2017; Vázquez & Pérez, 2017; Veglis et al., 2016).

As already mentioned, the exchanged "online news information" usually has the form of multimodal assets (combinations of text, images, audio and video), which can run almost identically in mobile and desktop systems. Moreover, multimedia authoring can be applied for engaging nonlinear storytelling mechanisms with enhanced UI, thus offering rich-media experience, aligned to the aims of Multimedia Journalism. Besides vividness and active user engagement, the new genre also gave users the opportunity to have access to the involved digital documents, which can be treated as proof evidence of the associated news stories. In this context, multiple publishing channels are usually implicated for unfolding the storytelling, either in parallel (cross-media) or through trans-media concepts. Again, correlations between the different content entities and the associated transmitting channels can be useful in revealing potential information tampering actions. However, inconveniences do remain, with most important the appearance of strong heterogeneity among the different nonlinear navigation mechanisms and the corresponding interaction technologies, which can further create operating difficulties and lack of confidence to the average user (Bull, 2010; Dimoulas, 2015, 2019; Dimoulas et al., 2014a, 2015, 2018; Ho & Li, 2015; Lu et al., 2015; Thomee et al., 2016; Veglis et al., 2016).

An extension to the previous example is the Data Journalism specialty, where data accompanying a story are processed, analyzed and visualized for creating storytelling products. For instance, photos and videos can be shared through online repositories, thus providing new ways of unfolding nonlinear narrations. Data journalism brought forward another innovative way of storytelling through the use of digital content, where arithmetic sequences, multimedia assets, geographical and time-related information, infographics and big-data repositories can be involved. The success of the assembled news-tales relies on the availability of applicable data, their efficient statistical analysis and visualization. This data-driven approach shares some common characteristics with the previously described genres (i.e. Computational and Robot Journalism, CAR, etc.), with the addition that the human factor favors the appliance of investigative processes (precision journalism). As in the case of multimedia news reporting, the presented information can be used as evident proof documents of the associated stories, where forgery attempts can be revealed. However, Data Journalism is a relatively new discipline, represented by a limited number of participating users and journalists, so that it hasn't reached the required maturity level yet, on the broad scale. Thus, further progress and real-world practice are needed for facing the arising difficulties, before the true potentials of this interdisciplinary field could be fully exploited (Thomee et al., 2016; Vázquez & Pérez, 2017; Veglis & Bratsas, 2017a, 2017b).

Drone Journalism represents another ongoing media paradigm that favors mobility and rapid news coverage, in which drones, and generally Unmanned Aerial Vehicles (UAV), are engaged as means of newsgathering, in a diverse range of journalism and mass communication scenarios. Specifically, drones can "collect" photos, video and other data (i.e. from temperature and humidity sensors, GPS/location, etc.), even in places where ground access is not feasible (e.g. due to natural/geographical obstacles, unsafe or hazardous environment, etc.). The gathered information can be pushed into multiple publishing channels, while it can be further utilized in the aforementioned contemporary forms of journalism. For instance, photos and video can be treated as media assets in Multimedia Journalism; number sequences, acquired by various sensors, can be additionally exploited in Data Journalism; their combination can provide context- and location-aware information, therefore AR-data (and metadata) that are best suited for Mobile or Immersive Journalism, etc. (Chamberlain, 2017; Gynnild, 2014; Ntalakas et al., 2017). Regarding the last example, immersive storytelling is another innovating trend that is based on VR, 3D computer graphics and gaming technologies, aiming at creating first-person experiences by posing the audience into the (virtual) world of the news-story. In this context, drones are very useful in collecting aerial shooting with possible 360° coverage angles and at different scales, thus producing panoramas, 3D images/videos and gigapixel imaging products (i.e. multiple images covering the events/scenes of interest at different scales, while preserving high resolution). Hence, in combination with other capturing means (i.e. satellite photos, ground footage, etc.) and 3D gaming techniques (i.e. 3D-modelled characters, synthetic/virtual environments, interaction mechanisms, etc.), photorealistic motion sequences can be created and embedded in Immersive Journalism services (De la Peña et al., 2010; Ntalakas et al., 2017; Seijo, 2017).

As in all previous forms, both these two ongoing journalism frameworks feature certain advantages and disadvantages. For instance, drones and UAVs are quite convenient and have low-cost (at least, when compared to other aerial means), while they offer flexibility regarding mobility and information gathering capabilities. On the contrary, the running distances and the maximum time of flight are very short, at the moment (unless high-end expensive equipment is used). Moreover, a universal regulatory framework is still missing, so that different certifications are required worldwide for the candidate journalists and users who want to fly these machines as pilots in command. Most of all, legal and moral implications, related to journalism ethics, as well as safety, privacy and security concerns need to be properly faced and settled. Similar criticism is encountered regarding the case of Immersive Journalism. While VR techniques aim at causing empathy to stimulate the feelings of the news readers, there is a discussion about the ethical limits of these storytelling approaches. For instance, unfitting footage, containing scenes of violence, cannot be utilized in immersive news stories that are addressed to all ages. In addition, the adopted gamification mechanisms might fail to deliver the emotions and the essence of the real events (e.g. someone might take serious wild actions for a game). The final results are strongly depended on the appropriateness and the quality of the produced services, thus requiring dedicated know-how and experience of both the engaged users and the media professionals (not only for the Immersive and Drone Journalism, but almost across the entire range of the aforementioned journalistic models). In every case, the lack of confidence in the use of the new tools also deteriorates the trust to the associated journalism products, leaving the audience more vulnerable to potential misinformation actions. Hence, the continuous training and support of all the involved parties seem to be the solution to their digital media literacy, therefore to the unwanted uncertainty effects of the rapid media transformations (Katsaounidou & Dimoulas, 2018; Katsaounidou, 2016; Linden, 2016, 2017; Matsiola et al., 2015; Ntalakas et al., 2017; Seijo, 2017; Veglis et al., 2016).

SOLUTIONS AND RECOMMENDATIONS

Digital Literacy and Continuous Support for Fast Adapting to the New Trends

Based on the preceding analysis, most of the contemporary genres of Digital Journalism promise to deliver specific conveniences and benefits, the same time that they seem to suffer from some unwanted and rather unavoidable shortcomings. For instance, there is a contradictory argumentation regarding the consequences of Robot Journalism, which is considered both a savior and a threat to human journalists (Linden, 2017). In the former case, the offered automation is (positively) judged of being assistive to media professionals, in receiving alerts while gathering news information. The already implied automation anxiety is justified in the second case, since it results in the formation of a defensive attitude, caused by the expected decrease of job offers due to the applied automations (Linden, 2016, 2017). Likewise, drones may replace human reporters, but they can also ensure healthier and less dangerous working conditions (e.g. when covering a civil disaster, a conflict in a war zone and, generally, in cases that news scenes are located in hazardous environments). Moreover, drones allow faster responding to breaking news events, while, in most cases, offer higher quality footage, provided by the aerial coverage (Chamberlain, 2017; Gynnild, 2014; Ntalakas et al., 2017). Similar advantages and disadvantages can be found in all the discussed media models. For example, specific digital skills and knowhow are demanded by journalists (and users) to take full advantage of Immersive and Multimedia Journalism. The same applies to the cases of Robot and Data Journalism, where a familiarization with computer software and data processing algorithms is rather necessary. Overall, the rapid technological changes redefine the core skills of human journalists, requiring a kind of turn to computational and algorithmic thinking; they are also challenging them to improve themselves at the things that humans can do better than machines and algorithms, such as in writings more appealing and humane news articles (De la Peña et al., 2010; Linden, 2016, 2017; Montal & Reich, 2016; Van Dalen, 2012).

It can be foreseen that most of these new forms of journalism will further evolve and, in many cases, will probably dominate the news market, in the near feature. As it has been cleverly argued for the case of Algorithmic Journalism, "what can be automated will be automated" (Van Dalen, 2012). Considering that the skills and specialties of news producers and consumers are continuously redefined, all participating actors have to be informed and/or trained, in order to find their place in the rapidly transforming media landscape. Otherwise, the power of the new services will remain in the hands of the elite groups and experts, worsening, even more, the conditions for diverse, objective and timely informing. Apart from the roles of the involved journalists, news-reporting organizations and contributing users, misinforming capabilities could be further extended through the power of the newfangled journalism forms. Again, the lack of trust to the "fresh products" makes even more possible the appearance of the unwanted content forgery and falsification effects. Recollecting the practical and legal questions regarding these digital media trends, the absence of related regulatory frameworks and/or ethical codes (basically in Drone, Robot and Immersive Journalism), as well as the concerns of privacy, security and safety (mostly in Drone Journalism), decelerate the paces of the anticipated progress. Therefore, there is an urgent need to proceed with the decisive and convincing accommodation of these matters, the settlement of which seems to be crucial. In other words, it is vital to practice and evaluate the newly surfaced informing services in real-world scenarios, so that potential weaknesses and problems would be detected, analyzed and eventually resolved. In this context, digital media literacy and continuous support actions are anticipated as the fitting solutions for testing and improving these novel models, which would be beneficial for all professionals, average/ordinary users and the society, as a whole (Katsaounidou & Dimoulas, 2018; Katsaounidou, 2016; Linden, 2016, 2017; Lu et al., 2015; Matsiola et al., 2015; Ntalakas et al., 2017; Seijo, 2017; Veglis et al., 2016).

Figure 3 presents the basic architecture of a model, founded in the principles of ensuring digital media literacy with continuous support, which intends to help users for fast adapting to the needs of the rapidly transforming media environment. The proposed solution aims at exploiting the true potentials of the latest and upcoming informing services, incorporating training sessions, users' validation and feedback that could drive to further improvements and updates to the corresponding machinery. It also promotes the close (though distant) collaboration between professionals /journalists, ordinary people / news consumers and experts of various kinds. Specifically, when a newfangled media product enters the market, screening processes will be initiated to analyze its features, indicating potential functional difficulties. Both trainers (experts) and trainees (users) can trigger the initiation of learning sessions and on demand support, which can be deployed under the control of specialized authorities, as well as through news-group discussions and crowd computing approaches. In the latter case, direct communication and cooperation between various groups of users and specialists can take place for recommending possible solutions and getting feedback, as soon as a new matter arises. In this manner, proper documentation of the troubleshooting actions and the associated updates result in gain and dissemination of firsthand knowledge, indicating the adoption of the tested best practices.

It is important to re-emphasize that there are possible forgery detection mechanisms, which can be found in the differentiations encountered in the same story between the different media channels or forms. In addition, many of the presented trends favor the transparency of the published news articles through the principles of investigative and precision journalism. For instance, this

Figure 3. The proposed continuous support and digital literacy model for fast adapting to the new media trends

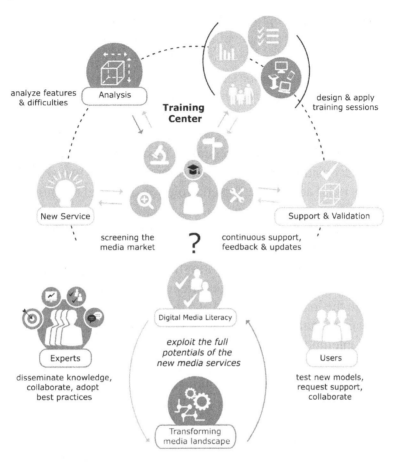

applies when the involved data repositories and/or the associated automation algorithms are open /publicly available for evaluation and testing (i.e. in the cases of Data, Multimedia and Robot Journalism); also, by releasing instant and multi-angled footage from the (breaking) news scenes, so that it could be accessed by the inquiring or engaging users (i.e. with the help of Drone and Mobile Journalism products). In this direction, integrated cross-modal authentication strategies could be developed by combining the advantages of all the contemporary mediated communication models, so as to face the challenges of forgery detection and misinformation prevention. It turns out that the rapidly progressing media environment can be beneficial to the news authentication needs, subjected to careful planning, implementation and support of the proposed cross-media solutions.

CONCLUSION

The present chapter attempts to provide an overview of the current status in the digital media landscape, unveiling the dynamics behind its remarkably rapid transformation. Major technological breakthroughs in the fields of journalism and communications are outlined as the necessary background for realizing the achieved evolution. Modern forms of digital media are listed along with their main functional attributes, the involved technologies and the potential weaknesses that need to be addressed. The relation of the conducted analysis to the problem of misinformation, therefore to the necessity for reconsidering cross-validation procedures, is two-folded. Firstly, the extremely rapid and uninterrupted evolution of digital technologies, with their reflection on the appearance of novel informing services, result in a very unstable environment, causing discomfort, anxiety or even defending attitude to the audience. Among others, suspicions regarding the validity of the collected and presented information streams might appear because of the missing (or incomprehensible) transparency, thus further deteriorating the lack of trust to the journalistic world and the news business. Secondly, due to the deficient understanding and comprehension of the operating mechanisms behind the contemporary tools, their power cannot be fully exploited in the direction of objective and unbiased journalism, which would help in fighting misinformation. In the opposite direction, when this communication power is restricted in the hands of limited people and elite groups, its exclusive misuse could act in favor of falsification propagation and fake news dissemination. Based on this, the importance of digital literacy is justified, resulting in the recommendation of a collaborative training and continuous support model. It is also argued that the proper design and development of such a solution will allow further exploration of the real potentials of the new trends, which can be positively deployed towards the desired integration of cross-media authentication.

REFERENCES

Aghaei, S., Nematbakhsh, M. A., & Farsani, H. K. (2012). Evolution of the world wide web: From WEB 1.0 TO WEB 4.0. *International Journal of Web & Semantic Technology*, *3*(1), 1–10. doi:10.5121/ijwest.2012.3101

Álvarez, M. V. (2017). The Future of Video-Journalism: Mobiles. In *Media and Metamedia Management* (pp. 463–469). Springer International Publishing. doi:10.1007/978-3-319-46068-0_61

Bull, A. (2010). *Multimedia journalism: A practical guide*. Routledge.

Chamberlain, P. (2017). *Drones and Journalism*. Taylor & Francis.

Coddington, M. (2015). Clarifying journalism's quantitative turn: A typology for evaluating data journalism, computational journalism, and computer-assisted reporting. *Digital Journalism*, *3*(3), 331–348. doi:10.1080/216708 11.2014.976400

De la Peña, N., Weil, P., Llobera, J., Giannopoulos, E., Pomés, A., Spanlang, B., ... Slater, M. (2010). Immersive journalism: Immersive virtual reality for the first-person experience of news. *Presence (Cambridge, Mass.)*, *19*(4), 291–301. doi:10.1162/PRES_a_00005

Dimoulas, A. C. (2015). *Multimedia authoring and management technologies: non-linear storytelling in the new digital media*. Athens: Association of Greek Academic Libraries. Retrieved from https://repository.kallipos.gr/handle/11419/4343 (in Greek)

Dimoulas, C., Veglis, A., & Kalliris, G. (2014). Application of Mobile Cloud-Based Technologies. In J. Rodrigues, K. Lin, & J. Lloret (Eds.), *Mobile Networks and Cloud Computing Convergence for Progressive Services and Applications* (pp. 320–343). Hershey, PA: Information Science Reference. doi:10.4018/978-1-4666-4781-7.ch017

Dimoulas, C., Veglis, A., & Kalliris, G. (2015). Audiovisual hypermedia in the semantic Web. In M. Khosrow-Pour (Ed.), *Encyclopedia of Information Science and Technology* (3rd ed.; pp. 7594–7604). Hershey, PA: Information Science Reference. doi:10.4018/978-1-4666-5888-2.ch748

Dimoulas, C. A. (2018). Machine Learning. In B. Arrigo (Ed.), The SAGE Encyclopedia of Surveillance, Security, and Privacy. Golson Media. (forthcoming)

Dimoulas, C. A. (2019). Multimedia. In D. Merskin & J. G. Golson (Eds.), The SAGE International Encyclopedia of Mass Media and Society. SAGE. (forthcoming)

Dimoulas, C. A., Kalliris, G. M., Chatzara, E. G., Tsipas, N. K., & Papanikolaou, G. V. (2014). Audiovisual production, restoration-archiving and content management methods to preserve local tradition and folkloric heritage. *Journal of Cultural Heritage*, *15*(3), 234–241. doi:10.1016/j.culher.2013.05.003

Dimoulas, C. A., & Symeonidis, A. L. (2015). Syncing shared multimedia through audiovisual bimodal segmentation. *IEEE MultiMedia*, *22*(3), 26–42. doi:10.1109/MMUL.2015.33

Dimoulas, C. A., Veglis, A. A., & Kalliris, G. (2018). Semantically Enhanced Authoring of Shared Media. In Encyclopedia of Information Science and Technology, Fourth Edition (pp. 6476-6487). IGI Global. doi:10.4018/978-1-5225-2255-3.ch562

Dörr, K. N. (2015). Mapping the field of Algorithmic Journalism. *Digital Journalism*, *4*(6), 700–722. doi:10.1080/21670811.2015.1096748

Dörr, K. N., & Hollnbuchner, K. (2017). Ethical Challenges of Algorithmic Journalism. *Digital Journalism*, *5*(4), 404–419. doi:10.1080/21670811.2016.1167612

Gynnild, A. (2014). The robot eye witness: extending visual journalism through drone surveillance. *Digital Journalism, 2*(3), 334-343.

Haim, M., & Graefe, A. (2017). *Automated News: Better than expected?* Digital Journalism.

Ho, A. T., & Li, S. (Eds.). (2015). *Handbook of Digital Forensics of Multimedia Data and Devices*. John Wiley & Sons. doi:10.1002/9781118705773

Johnston, L. (2016). Social News= Journalism Evolution? How the integration of UGC into newswork helps and hinders the role of the journalist. *Digital Journalism*, *4*(7), 899–909. doi:10.1080/21670811.2016.1168709

Kalliris, G., & Dimoulas, C. (2009, May). Audiovisual content management issues for the new media environment. *Proceedings of the International Conference on New Media and Information: Convergences and Divergences.*

Katsaounidou, A. (2016). *Content authenticity issues: detection (and validation) techniques of untruthful news stories from humans and machines* (Unpublished Master Thesis). Post-Graduate Program of the School of Journalism and Mass Communications, Aristotle University of Thessaloniki. (in Greek)

Katsaounidou, A. N., & Dimoulas, C. A. (2018). Integrating Content Authentication Support in Media Services. In Encyclopedia of Information Science and Technology, Fourth Edition (pp. 2908-2919). IGI Global. doi:10.4018/978-1-5225-2255-3.ch254

Kotsakis, R., Kalliris, G., & Dimoulas, C. (2012). Investigation of broadcast-audio semantic analysis scenarios employing radio-programme-adaptive pattern classification. *Speech Communication, 54*(6), 743–762. doi:10.1016/j.specom.2012.01.004

Linden, C. G. (2016). Decades of Automation in the Newsroom: Why are there still so many jobs in journalism? *Digital Journalism, 5*(2), 123–140. doi:10.1080/21670811.2016.1160791

Linden, C. G. (2017). Algorithms for journalism: The future of news work. *The Journal of Media Innovations, 4*(1), 60–76. doi:10.5617/jmi.v4i1.2420

Lu, T., Jin, Y., Su, F., Shivakumara, P., & Tan, C. L. (2015). Content-oriented multimedia document understanding through cross-media correlation. *Multimedia Tools and Applications, 74*(18), 8105–8135. doi:10.100711042-014-2044-9

Matsiola, M., Dimoulas, C. A., Kalliris, G., & Veglis, A. A. (2015). Augmenting user interaction experience through embedded multimodal media agents in social networks. In Social media and the transformation of interaction in society (pp. 188-209). IGI Global. doi:10.4018/978-1-4666-8556-7.ch010

Montal, T., & Reich, Z. (2016). *I, Robot. You, Journalist. Who is the Author? Authorship, bylines and full disclosure in automated journalism.* Digital Journalism.

Newman, N. (2016). *Journalism, media and technology predictions 2016.* Retrieved on May 1,2017 from https://ora.ox.ac.uk/objects/uuid:f15fac34-bafb-4883-898c-a53ade027e32

Ntalakas, A., Dimoulas, C. A., Kalliris, G., & Veglis, A. (2017). Drone journalism: Generating immersive experiences. *Journal of Media Critiques, 3*(11), 187–199. doi:10.17349/jmc117317

Papadopoulos, S., Cesar, P., Shamma, D. A., & Kelliher, S. (Eds.). (2015). Special issue on Social Multimedia and Storytelling. MultiMedia IEEE, 22(3), 10-65.

Pavlik, J. V., & Bridges, F. (2013). The emergence of augmented reality (AR) as a storytelling medium in journalism. *Journalism & Communication Monographs*, *15*(1), 4–59. doi:10.1177/1522637912470819

Rodríguez, A. S., & Freire, F. C. (2017). Reports in and from Smartphones: A New Way of Doing Journalism. In Media and Metamedia Management (pp. 479-490). Springer International Publishing.

Seijo, S. P. (2017). Immersive Journalism: From Audience to First-Person Experience of News. In Media and Metamedia Management (pp. 113-119). Springer International Publishing.

Siapera, E., & Veglis, A. (Eds.). (2012). *The handbook of global online journalism*. John Wiley & Sons. doi:10.1002/9781118313978

Silverman, C. (Ed.). (2013). *Verification handbook*. European Journalism Centre.

Spyridou, L. P., Matsiola, M., Veglis, A., Kalliris, G., & Dimoulas, C. (2013). Journalism in a state of flux: Journalists as agents of technology innovation and emerging news practices. *The International Communication Gazette*, *75*(1), 76–98. doi:10.1177/1748048512461763

Symeonidis, A. L., & Mitkas, P. A. (2006). *Agent intelligence through data mining* (Vol. 14). Springer Science & Business Media.

Thomee, B., Shamma, D. A., Friedland, G., Elizalde, B., Ni, K., Poland, D., ... Li, L. J. (2016). YFCC100M: The new data in multimedia research. *Communications of the ACM*, *59*(2), 64–73. doi:10.1145/2812802

Tremayne, M., & Clark, A. (2014). New perspectives from the sky: Unmanned aerial vehicles and journalism. *Digital Journalism, 2*(2), 232-246.

Van Dalen, A. (2012). The algorithms behind the headlines: How machine-written news redefines the core skills of human journalists. *Journalism Practice*, *6*(5-6), 648–658. doi:10.1080/17512786.2012.667268

Vázquez, A. I. R., & Pérez, X. S. (2017). Trends in Journalism for Metamedia of Connectivity and Mobility. In *Media and Metamedia Management* (pp. 457–462). Springer International Publishing. doi:10.1007/978-3-319-46068-0_60

Veglis, A., & Bratsas, C. (2017). Reporters in the age of data journalism. *Journal of Applied Journalism & Media Studies, 6*(2), 225–244. doi:10.1386/ajms.6.2.225_1

Veglis, A., & Bratsas, C. (2017). Towards a taxonomy of data journalism. *Journal of Media Critiques, 3*(11), 109–121. doi:10.17349/jmc117309

Veglis, A., Dimoulas, C., & Kalliris, G. (2016). Towards intelligent cross-media publishing: media practices and technology convergence perspectives. In A. Lugmayr & C. Dal Zotto (Eds.), *Media Convergence Handbook-Vol. 1* (pp. 131–150). Springer Berlin Heidelberg. doi:10.1007/978-3-642-54484-2_8

KEY TERMS AND DEFINITIONS

Citizens' Journalism: Form of journalism where ordinary citizens can act as news providers/publishers, without any professional guidance or control (autonomously). It is also called "public" or "participatory" journalism, although slight differences can be found in the second term, which implies the control of the whole news reporting process by an authoring professional media organization.

Computational Journalism: A contemporary model of digital journalism that uses computing systems (not necessarily personal computers) for the processes of news gathering, shaping and publishing. The difference with the preceding Computer Assisted Reporting lays in the principle that more sophisticated computations can be now applied for automating the aforementioned media tasks, taking advantage of contemporary Artificial Intelligent (AI) and Natural Language Processing (NLP) algorithms, as well as of intelligent content management and (semantic) analysis techniques.

Computer-Assisted Reporting (CAR): A news reporting model that utilizes computers for assisting the tasks of data collection and analysis, which correspond to the necessary information for writing news articles. While there is an overlapping with data and computational journalism, these three terms are not synonyms, since they have distinct differences. Besides, the origins of computer-assisted reporting are dated back in the early '50s, while the other two trends models are more recent.

Digital Journalism: In linguistic terms, Digital Journalism refers to the implementation of digital technology for the collection, publishing and consumption of news, therefore along the end-to-end chain of journalistic processes. Although the term is often ascribed as a synonym to Online Journalism in related bibliography, the strict definition slightly differentiates the two disciplines. Specifically, Digital Journalism is a more generic term that academically encapsulates all the digital media sub-cases, where news are produced, managed and disseminated through digital means. Hence, it stands as the main root of all the newfangled models that followed.

Digital Literacy: A set of competencies and skills that are required in order for someone to comprehend and fully exploit information and communication technologies in today's digital world. Digital literacy describes a contemporary need for digital knowledge and knowhow. It is considered as the successor of the previous "Computer literacy" term, since, apart from traditional computers and software, new mobile devices and web applications are currently in use (e.g., smartphones, tablets, laptops, smart-watches, cloud computing services, and others).

Drone Journalism: An ongoing media paradigm that utilizes drones, and generally Unmanned Aerial Vehicles (UAV), as means of news-gathering, in a diverse range of journalism and mass communication scenarios. Drone journalism favors mobility and rapid news coverage, where drones can "collect" photos, video and other data, even in places where ground access is not feasible (e.g., due to natural /geographical obstacles, unsafe or hazardous environment, etc.).

Immersive Journalism: A recent trend in the broader field of Digital Journalism that is based on the use of Virtual Reality (VR) with 3D computer graphics and gaming technologies, aiming at creating first-person experiences, by immersing the audience into the (virtual) world of the news story.

Mobile Journalism: A new way of making journalism, using mobile computing terminals (mostly tablets and smartphones), which have become the natural extension of journalists and users in their everyday communication needs. The new capabilities of pervasive and ubiquitous computing that are currently available allow for the incorporation of innovative context- and location-aware attributes, supplementing augmented reality (AR) and semantically-enhanced services. Overall, the predominance of mobile computing models in today's ubiquitous society has revolutionized news production and consumption ends, while further progress is expected in the near future (i.e. with the materialization of the "Internet of things" envision).

Multimedia Journalism: A form of digital journalism that combines all the contemporary forms of digital media (text, images, audio, video, etc.), along with multimedia authoring and nonlinear storytelling mechanisms. Multiple publishing channels are usually engaged for unfolding the storytelling, either in parallel (cross-media) or thru trans-media concepts, thus favoring vividness and rich-media experience with more active user participation.

Online Journalism: A form of Digital Journalism where the news reports are made available online (i.e., they are disseminated through the web). Although the term is often ascribed as a synonym to Digital Journalism, Online Journalism has a somewhat narrower meaning, emphasizing on the news publishing and dissemination part, as clearly indicated by the associated "online" adjective.

Participatory Journalism: A journalism paradigm where users can be involved in the processes of news collection, contribution, sharing and commenting, usually under the authority of a professional media organization. The last part of the previous sentence indicates the slight difference to Citizens' Journalism, despite the fact that a lot of people consider the two terms as synonyms.

Robot Journalism: A contemporary trend in Digital Journalism describing the processes of gathering and publishing news information with minimum or complete absence of human interventions (i.e. semi- or fully-automated news reporting). In Robot Journalism (also called Automated or Algorithmic Journalism) the gathered information is pushed online by computer programs known as "software robots" or simply "bots", which can assemble and eventually create the headlines or even the entire news articles. This software usually runs in the form of web services, so that they are also encountered with the names "Web-bots" and "Internet-bots."

Chapter 4
Misinformation via Tampered Multimedia Content

ABSTRACT

The present chapter investigates the use of multiple resources/modalities (text, audio, images, video, etc.) as evidence in journalism (i.e., documenting the associated articles). Indeed, multimedia assets are essential components of the professional news coverage, considering their ability to captivate enormous and complex amounts of data more rapidly (than reading the elongated plain text). Hence, the narration becomes vivid, representative, and attractive, while answering all the involved "questions" that surround a report (i.e., who, what, where, when, why, the so-called five Ws of journalism). However, their proofing attributes can be used in the reverse order (i.e., for applying content tampering), thus creating falsified documents to support and propagate untrue stories. Nowadays, user-friendly tools facilitate textual and audiovisual editing operations, easing the forgery processes even for the average user. This chapter analyzes the role of rich media in engaging infotainment services and their side effects in misinformation propagation.

DOI: 10.4018/978-1-5225-5592-6.ch004

INTRODUCTION

Journalism is and has been theorized, researched, studied and criticized worldwide by people coming from a wide variety of disciplines. (Deuze, 2005, p. 2)

The divergences between modern forms of Journalism and the other genres of public communication are gradually vanishing, due to the dominance of the Internet and Social Networking Sites (SNSs) in the new media landscape (Deuze, 2008). In this context, multimedia resources have claimed and gained a key role along the end-to-end chain of informing, favoring audience engagement through more vivid, representative and attractive storytelling, while also serving proof evidence in supporting the truthfulness of the presented stories. On the other hand, the availability of digital information processing tools, offered through user-friendly software, web and/or Cloud Computing (CC) services, have facilitated the editing of textual and audiovisual modalities, even by the non-experts or through everyday used mobile devices, like smartphones and tablets (Dimoulas, Veglis, & Kalliris, 2014, 2015, 2018; Katsaounidou & Dimoulas, 2018). Hence, content tampering can be easily deployed as part of intentional falsification and forgery attempts. The epidemic effects of disinformation are considered among the latest adverse reactions of the ongoing media ecosystem transformation, where Internet alters everything. In a related report, the World Economic Forum has stated that the "massive digital misinformation" is one of the foremost dangers for the present civilization (Howell, 2013). Purposing on producing articles about events, facts and people, journalists utilize all the applicable assets, which may be people (witnesses, experts), press issues (newspapers, magazines, etc.) or other records that provide related insights. However, besides the genuine use of the data surrounding a publication, ambiguous journalistic coverage with doctored images or other falsified documents is always possible. Therefore, being informed by reliable sources is not such self-evident and becomes more challenging in present days, since fake-news and their consequences arise a lot of disputes. Correspondingly, news and media organizations are judged on the truthfulness and credibility of the disseminated information, which must be accurately-sourced, checked and verified, transparent and unmistakable, strengthened by convincing proofs and arguments (Brewer, 2017).

The massive adaptation of social media and microblogging platforms on the World Wide Web offers non-stop and disintermediated news distribution from producers to consumers, revolutionizing the way that audiences become up-to-date and form their opinion (Del Vicario et al., 2016). Nowadays, contemporary Journalism practices differ from their predecessors, taking advantage of the most significant feature of the Internet, which is the feasibility to syndicate several media elements seamlessly. These capabilities equip the online-publishers with useful authoring services, helping them to tell stories in novel intriguing ways, by combining text, links, graphics, video, audio in rich interactions, therefore overcoming presentation inadequacies /limitations of traditional print and broadcast channels (Foust, 2017). Additionally, material that originates from users (User Generated Contend-UGC) contributes to the journalistic product, often leading to spread and consumption of non-professionally edited information, where traditional gatekeeping procedures are gradually vanishing. According to Wardle (2017), to understand the current information ecosystem, we need to break it down to three elements: the various sorts of content that are being produced and propagated, the "whys and wherefores" of those who create this material and the methods through which the material is being disseminated. These three perspectives represent the principal components of digital storytelling, which, along with the use and misuse of multimedia, outline the main subject of the current chapter.

CONTENT AS EVIDENCE IN NEWS: MULTIMEDIA JOURNALISM

Media Tampering and Misinformation: Issues, Controversies, Problems

The evolution of Information and Communication Technologies (ICTs) and the low cost of portable devices (i.e. smartphones, tablets and laptops) have fueled the proliferation of UGC, thus facilitating the transition to the so-called Web 2.0 era (Dimoulas et al., 2014; Dimoulas & Symeonidis, 2015; Kotsakis, Kalliris, & Dimoulas, 2012; Spyridou, Matsiola, Veglis, Kalliris, & Dimoulas, 2013). The overwhelming adoption of ICTs allows digitization, distance computing /telecollaboration and, of course, informing globalization, resulting in the change of work patterns. An example somewhat indicative of this new situation is that the old saying "a story travelled around the world" has been recently rephrased to "a story travelled around the Internet" (Katsaounidou & Dimoulas, 2018). While the daily agenda has become global and is characterized by common headlines in many countries, local individuals are "recruited" as reporters, since they are aware of what is happening around their "neighborhood", detecting and covering local news more efficiently (Rosales, 2006). Overall, a lot of time has been spent for cultivating different forms of Journalism, in response to the new context that the Internet brought forward. Specifically, along with the development of Web 2.0, we have witnessed the explosive growth of web services that offer rich-media experience (in terms of both multimodal resources /assets and enhanced interaction), usually referred as networked multimedia or hypermedia (Dimoulas et al., 2015; Wang, Li, & Tang, 2017). As a result, the genre of Multimedia Journalism has also surfaced, emphasizing on users' engagement through the non-linear storytelling and interfacing nodes. New elements, such as temporal and geolocation tags, have been introduced to accompany the narration of events, taking place at any time or location worldwide, where the utilization of multiple types of digital material has become the commonplace (i.e. text, images, audio, videos, etc.). Again, these new trends are facilitated by the extensive use of mobile computing terminals, featuring inherent networking and audiovisual capturing capabilities, hence they are regularly utilized in posts and shares of infotainment character, purposing to inform the audience. Therefore, Journalism 2.0 was emerged (in analogy to Web 2.0), incorporating the citizens' involvement in the news reporting tasks (and their overall activities of commenting /interacting, i.e. participatory and citizens' journalism paradigms). Considering that Internet provides unlimited space, where there is always room for everyone to produce and distribute content, a side effect is that people face vast quantities of information, becoming confused about its integrity /validation.

Many news-sites offer the opportunity to their readers to post stories about their communities, personal interests or beliefs, as long as they do not raise legal and ethical complications. These articles, submitted by citizen journalists and broadly Web 2.0 /UGC contributing users, are received by the editors, who push them to be published /online, after their evaluation concerning credibility, readability or even popularity potentials. Most of the times, a screening procedure is conducted by humans /experts and usually assisted by related systems, aiming at distinguishing the unreliable contributors. Moreover, bloggers, hosted by the corresponding servers /web environments, submit their reports or comments on almost any topic (e.g. politics, economy, entertainment, social gossip, etc.). Besides "observing" and broadcasting, blogs offer connection to news, documents, pictures, interactive media, pages and graphics, pointing to associated sources and links for further reading. At this point, traditional cross-validation models become deficient or inapplicable, resulting in necessary changes in the well-known "gatekeeping" processes. Although the latter term is frequently quoted, a definition is still required: "Gatekeepers are reputational intermediaries who provide verification and certification services to media investors" (Coffee, 2002).

As already supported, ICTs have altered the communication landscape over the years, introducing new ways of assembling and transmitting information. Indeed, the most important factors related to the "lack of trust" phenomenon are the social processes, involved in the violent radicalization and the vehement adoption of technology breakthroughs, which are also indicated in Figure 1 (Katsaounidou & Dimoulas, 2018; Thurman, 2015). In specific, hardware and software evolution contributed to the transformation of the media ecosystem

Figure 1. The elements of misinformation and their relation to social processes, associated with the violent radicalization and the vehement adoption of technology breakthroughs

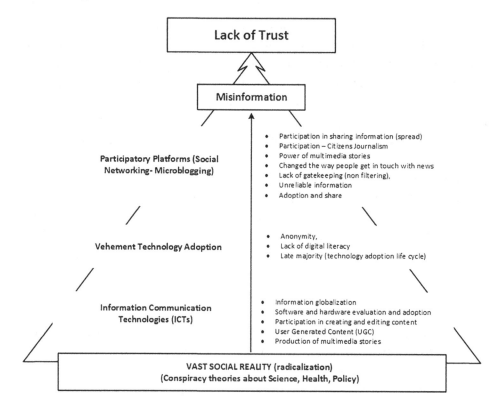

in its present digital and highly multidisciplinary form. Hardware refers to physical devices associated with computing tasks, which can be found in many shapes, sizes, speeds and prices. Both their computational and operational capacities are continually elaborating, in parallel with the high-tech race, thus offering new capabilities to the users, including the processes of creating, shaping and broadcasting UGC streams. Mobile phones and other small-sized and low-cost digital equipment (i.e. photo-/video-cameras, voice recorders /microphones, etc.) can be easily utilized by average users for content production purposes, i.e. in capturing a newsworthy event. Instant editing and sharing of this audiovisual footage is possible by running mobile applications or dedicated CC services, while the use of computers (desktop and portable) offers further processing and publishing options that can size-up to the professional online reporting utilities. For instance, web and multimedia authoring tools, combined with popular commercial software and free /open source solutions, can be conveniently functioned by the non-experts in their audio, image and video projects (e.g. Wix, Webbly, WordPress and other online HTML-5 editors; Adobe Audition, Audacity, etc. for sound processing; iMovie, Windows movie maker, Adobe Premiere, Sony Vegas, etc. for video editing; Adobe Photoshop, Gimp, etc. for photo and image processing and others). Additionally, specific social networking environments (i.e. Facebook, Twitter, YouTube, Vimeo, Ustream, etc.), that often outperform the usage and popularity ratings of other Web 2.0 products (e.g. blogs), do favor and promote the dissemination of such multimodal material, which can describe and visualize events in a more direct and communicative manner (Dimoulas, 2015; Dimoulas et al., 2014; Spyridou et al., 2013). However, along with the presentation and operation expediencies, these platforms also have a negative effect in the formulation of the present uncontrollable nature of informing, where the risk of disinformation is always present. As appositely pointed out by Berghel (2017) "Social networks are frequently used to spread false rumors, calumnious stories, and propaganda because they offer extensive reach and minimal filtering". Given the aforementioned vehement adoption of technology, along with the attributes that favor immature or even irresponsible users' behavior (i.e. anonymity, digital illiteracy, inadequate and/or inappropriate censorship, etc.), the vast sociopolitical reality offers fertile ground to grow fake-news and conspiracy theories, i.e. regarding science, health, policy, etc. After all, it is a political matter, since nothing noteworthy would have happened without the formulated seedbed for emerging intentional falsification and propaganda undertakings.

The Power of Multimedia

The term multimedia refers to the multimodal presentation of information through the exploitation of many different media, such as text, images, animations, audio and video, using various user interfaces and human machine interaction mechanisms. Nowadays, multimedia stand as the most common and most popular mediated communication paradigm, enabling users to communicate with "machines" (and with each other) through the combination of textual and audiovisual information, in a variety of versatile non-linear narrative scenarios. This kind of "messaging" is closer to the archetypal audiovisual presentation and perception of information that human beings have been accustomed to be taught and informed, to discuss and debate, to learn and generally to communicate, so that multimedia are considered to be more informative and vivid compared to other documents. (Dimoulas, 2019)

Each type of the primary content components (text, photos /graphics, audio and video) features different communicative characteristics, i.e. presentation advantages or data processing and analysis demands. Text is an assembled representation of characters, numbers and symbols, standing as the least demanding resource of all digital media entities. With the introduction of linking mechanisms (i.e. hypertext) and visualization "instructions" (i.e. markup signs), which launched with the advent of the Hypertext Markup Language (HTML), the textual material can be displayed in many sizes, styles or other format options, thus extending its online usefulness on more appealing /nonlinear storylines. Graphics can include vector images, photographs, illustrations, artworks and other visual assets, helping to illustrate a concept or to provide a more pleasing, exciting and emotional experience for the reader. Photos and overall imaging means are both compelling and effective, because of their vividness, the ability to provoke reactions and to recall memories. Audio has the potential to equally support supplementary /decorative and informative operations, providing more profound insights into the world of a story, thus enhancing the associated narrations and the users' experience. Finally, movie files concatenate all the above informing attributes and can convey a significant amount of data in thicker and more robust demonstrations, in which audiovisual and textual entities can be overlaid. For this reason, video is considered to be the denser and more compact communicative medium, i.e. due to the high volumes of the carried informatory streams, making it also the most demanding and technologically complex element. Hence, combining all the aforementioned factors, it can be claimed that multimedia can encode, carry and project information in much more efficient and attractive manners, thus turning them into a valuable storytelling instrument for engaging the audience and attracting the consumers' interest. The rapidly gained popularity of this multimodal framework made its utilization the most straightforward way for individuals, in their newsgathering and publishing tasks (Bull, 2010; Dimoulas, 2015; 2019; Dimoulas et al., 2014, 2015, 2018; Papadopoulos, Cesar, Shamma, & Kelliher, 2015; Spyridou et al., 2013; Vaughan, 2014; Veglis, Dimoulas, & Kalliris, 2016).

Extending the previous remarks, the domination of audiovisual assets is verified by the corresponding media analytics, i.e. by measuring the rate of the different types of the transferred information. According to the Visual Networking Index of Cisco (2017), every day, more than seven billion videos are shared through Facebook and YouTube, while the associated network load is estimated to reach 82 percent of all IP traffic, by 2019. The same reports also predict that, by 2021, more than 5 million years will be required to watch the total video material that will go across global networks monthly. Thus, it is no coincidence that many popular SNSs are primarily visual-oriented (i.e. Instagram, Pinterest, Tumblr, Snapchat, etc.), even Facebook and Twitter, which were created to rely solely on text at their beginning. Large-scale functional and algorithmic changes in the Facebook environment force publishers to intensify the frequency of posts that involve motion-pictures and animations, as a strategy for increasing the popularity and reproduction rates of their content. Moreover, video subtitling is possible, ensuring that the delivered "messages" can be still understood, even if the sound is turned off, i.e. in the default setting when scrolling down the news feeds. Similar turn to multimedia resources is observed in the Twitter paradigm, with visually-framed tweets to reach an average of more than 35% re-tweets, whereas infographics and quotes are being some of the most commonly met image types (Ellering, 2017).

Given the maximum 280 characters tweeting limitation, the strategy of re-directing followers to external sources allows for encompassing additional /linked information by adopting the well-established practices of hypertext and hypermedia. Furthermore, in cases that textual streams are supplemented by pictures, the attributes of vividness and representativeness are induced, thus helping people to quickly understand the context behind of a story, without the need of reading elongated reports. Indicative of the significance of the visualized data is the well-known idiom supporting that "A picture is worth a thousand words", which was recently updated to "A minute of video is worth 1.8 million words". The latter phrase is attributed to the researcher Dr James McQuivey, who combined the initial statement of Barnard with arithmetic calculations with putting into equation typical digitization parameters. In specific, he multiplied "one thousand words" per image with "30 frames per second" that a video commonly contains, and then again with "60 seconds that a minute contains" concluding that "A minute of video is worth 1.8 million words". While the above phrase is a figure of speech that should not be taken literally, still, it can be illustrative of the exponential increase of the involved volume of informatory pieces, which can be interpreted in terms of pixels, bits, demanded bitrate, etc. (Alton, 2017; Webb, 2017).

Another interesting perceptive, somewhat complementary and/or parallel to the above remarks, is related to the imaging processing capabilities of the human vision system. According to Marieb & Hoehn (2007), nearly half of the human brain is involved in visual administering, while seventy percent of all sensory receptors are situated in the eyes. The human mind can identify and pass-on the imaging data more rapidly, in a more adequate and everlasting way, compared to the printed or vocal counterparts (Dur, 2014; Yuvaraj, 2017), hence an optical scene can be perceived faster than one-tenth of a second (Semetko & Scammell, 2012). In fact, related studies have shown that articles which encompass visualizations get ninety-four percent more readership and popularity than those with plain text (Shah, 2017). These remarks justify the reason that nowadays, where technology can support the demanding processing load with the associated increased transmission rates (i.e. high bitrates), the media landscape has become primarily visual. The remaining modalities can also be part of the audiovisual projection and reproduction, composing a more complex and rich mediated communication experience, which gets closer and closer to the natural stimulus encountered in the world. On the contrary, manipulated images, sounds and videos can produce and reproduce falsified streams for disinformation purposes. Contemporary publishing technologies offer to news organizations the opportunity to create content once and make it available on multiple channels and devices, i.e. through the paradigms of cross- and trans-media publishing (Veglis, 2007; 2012; Veglis et al., 2016). Furthermore, consumers, contributing users and citizen journalists are very likely to interact with the disseminated forgeries, with a big chance of further propelling their widespread propagation, either unintentionally or purposely. Consequently, the amazing dynamics of massive content sharing, along with the considerable threat of multimedia tampering foment the danger that inaccurate stories, relying on prejudice, personal beliefs and emotions, to become equally or even more popular and believable than the real events.

Who Is Shaping the Lies End-Users Consume in Media Ecosystem?

In a workshop held by Reuters in February 2017, the discussion was about the number of the different kinds of "fake-news", the seriousness of the situation and the research strategies, deployed for addressing the problem and its consequences. From the discussions, it has been concluded that despite journalists' efforts and volition to cross-check their reports, news-articles that contain errors are frequently published and propagated. From a political perspective, on many occasions, connotations cannot be avoided, since false information is produced with specific strategic intent. Trying to understand what drives those who create or reproduce falsified stories for misinformation purposes, Marwick and Lewis in their report "Media manipulation and disinformation online" (2017), catalog several classes based on manipulators' political beliefs and ideological orientations. In general, the lines between groups and individuals that create and propagate inaccurate content are blurry. However, there are some well-defined patterns, related to the motives of the involved actuators, such as the "Internet Bogus Accounts" and the "Gamergates". In the former case, "forgery administrators" systematically entice people to cause emotional reactions, while in the latter, they withhold the profiles of "highly politicized" or "hobbyists", usually united by their mutual advocation in computer games. "Hate Groups", "Ideologues" and "Hyper-Partisan News Networks" form additional categories, consisted of xenophobe or white supremacist crowds with increased reflectiveness, which use the Internet to engage new supporters. "Opinion Leaders and Massive Influencers", described as ideologue and conspiracy "truth-seekers", perform a key-role in the manipulation of the public opinion, by manufacturing and disseminating untrue informatory posts, the so-called "trolls", from which, they are also known as "trollers" (Marwick & Lewis, 2017). Melissa Zimdars, an assistant professor of media and communication studies at Merrimack College, has set up a page, containing the most popular unreliable news sites, inviting users to complement this record, by incorporating further related links (i.e. their URL addresses). The list includes eleven paradigms /classifications of misinforming websites, presented and explained in Table 1, thus serving as a kind of "bibliography" of fake-news sources (Zimdars, 2016).

Table 1. Overview of Melissa Zimdars' unreliable news sites categories

Fake News	News sites generate and share information by altering real events.
Satire Sources	Sources use comicality, sarcasm, exaggeration, ridicule, and fallacious information to state their opinion on contemporary events
Extreme Bias Sources	Outlets may rely on propaganda, decontextualized information, and opinions distorted as facts from a particular point of view (e.g. political)
Conspiracy Theory Websites	Websites promote weird conspiracy theories.
Rumor Mill Websites	Sources specialized in rumors, scandals, insinuations, and unverified statements.
State News Sources	Outlets operating under government authorization, in order to spread propagation at repressive states.
Junk Science Sources	Websites promote practices that are considered unscientific, metaphysics, naturalistic delusions, and other scientifically ambiguous claims.
Hate News	Outlets promote racism, misogyny, homophobia, and other forms of social discrimination with the purpose to strengthen social marginalization
Clickbait Sources	News sites which provide generally credible content using exaggerated, misleading, or questionable headlines, social media descriptions, and/or images
Proceed With Caution	Sources which may be credible but whose reports require additional verification.
Political Websites	Outlets which provide generally verifiable information in support of certain points of view or political orientations.

The above categorization helps us to understand the ways and the reasons that tampered content is shared on the Internet. Moreover, Prof. Zimdars mentions the credible sources that generate and share confirmed or validated stories in harmony with the traditional and ethical reporting practices. Apart from that, the most useful remark that Zimdars (2016) provided to the audience is the fact that, even trustful sources often count on "clickbait-style" titles or sometimes make mistakes. It turns out that, no news organization is ideal, justifying the necessity of multiple sources of information, which a correct news consumption model entails (Rochlin, 2017). Unfortunately, there are plenty of dedicated web-pages, providing users with tools and methods to generate and disseminate their own fake stories. In his article "Caveat Lector: Fake News as Folklore", Frank (2015) divides these websites to "Generators", "Cloners", "Wishful Thinkers", "Citizen Satirists" and "Enables". However, most of the examples that are listed as indicatives of his adopted classification are no longer active. The most interesting point is the easiness with which, an individual can create and publish falsified informatory items, incorporating tampered multimedia assets. Among others, *fodey.com*, a "newspaper clipping generator", provides an automated procedure for directed news production. Users are only required to write down the name of a newspaper (existent or invented), the time and the title of the report, to fill in the main text box, where the (impersonated) story is imported and then to "push" the "Generate!" button. Trying to become more believable, the so-called Cloners-websites, like the *breakyourownnews.com*, copy the design of a legitimate media organization, allowing users to upload pictures, write the headlines or even shape a phony image, to be regarded as the screen capture of a real TV news-broadcasting show. Finally, fewer web platforms target the cultivation of conspiracy theories from nonprofessional filmmakers, who can publish their treachery documentaries, avoiding the traditional journalistic gatekeeping. A recent example is the theory that *"the world is flat"*, which is supported by videos uploaded to YouTube platform. The proponents of this belief have gone so far as to organize the first Flat Earth International Conference[1] (FEIC2017), which took place on November 9-10, 2017 in Raleigh, North Carolina ("Flat Earth International Conference 2017", 2018).

Extending the preceding analysis, representative /indicative forgery examples are given, to have a better picture about the mechanisms behind the creation and propagation of untrue content. The year 2017 will possibly remain in history as the year of the frauds, ranging, from star and personality deaths to unscientific delusions and politics (Novak, 2017). The USA presidential election had cast a spotlight on fake-news sites that traffic in misinformation, also blamed for the election of Donald Trump as president (Hunt, 2016). One of the most popular occasions involving inaccurate information is the theory known as Pizzagate, a story about a proprietor of a restaurant in Washington, whom conspiracy theory websites centered him at the spot of a pedophile scandal (Kang, 2017). News outlets and radical circles of Twitter and Facebook propagated conspiracy theories claiming that Hillary Clinton was involved in this case. These assertions were reproduced by a series of cloners-sources (designed to look like mainstream media channels), which published outrageous doctored content to enhance their profit, i.e. through advertising (Marwick & Lewis, 2017). Schemers' statements were reinforced when WikiLeaks revealed hacked emails from Hillary Clinton's campaign, in specific, with the detection of a message associating Clinton's fundraising to the place. The above event forms an excellent incident to understand how fake-news can cause severe and "very" real consequences. Once this (untrue) story was spread, the restaurant owner and his employees became the targets of continual annoyance, receiving murder warnings and other threats of ferocity. Violence has not remained at a verbal level or abuse over SNSs, the moment that a man entered the restaurant carrying a weapon, to examine the place by himself (he shot, but no one was debilitated) (Lipton, 2016). The guy had browsed some reports on the topic, repeatedly listening to radio shows which promoted the hypothesis. The publicity of the "scandal" guided people "in the garden" of the White House to press the authorities for further research (Marwick & Lewis, 2017). The most ironic part is that many of the protestors expressed the complaint that the dominant press and journalistic corporations were not concerned about their worries and they did not report on the story with the seriousness it deserved (Miller, 2017).

Propaganda is a conscious attempt to persuade a person in accepting a conviction imprecisely. Typically, authoritarian regimes that do not have citizens' consent resort to this technique to manipulate the audience and ensure that will stay in power. In order to influence public opinion, the targeted dissemination of beliefs can take place through a variety of methods, such as speeches (talks, lectures, conferences, news agencies, government statements), written discourse (notices, letters, books), as well as via the use of any form of art (theater, cinema, painting and literature). Nowadays, to attain such objectives, the potential influencers take advantage of the power of both SNSs /web services and their multimedia engaging attributes. Another example, clearly illustrating the strength that audiovisual narratives /communication campaigns hold in shaping people's beliefs, is related to the USA elections and, in specific, the rumors implying that Hillary Clinton was concealing severe health difficulties (Cheadle, 2016; Marwick & Lewis, 2017). Based on the exploitation of doctored photographs, a common practice for weakening political opponents, in 2016, bloggers began distributing inaccuracies about Hillary's physical, mental and cognitive health, circulating that she suffered from several serious illnesses (seizure attacks, Parkinson's disease and dementia). The theory relied on "visual pieces of evidence" and mainly on videos, i.e. "The Truth About Hillary's Bizarre Behavior" (6.127.238 views). Figure 2 depicts two imaging examples, sourced from the article entitled "Hillary Clinton's Entire Staff Say They Have Pneumonia: Cover up Begins -Voters Don't Believe Pneumonia Claims". This material has been published along with additional "proofing documents", i.e. more photos, doctors' diagnoses and other experts' statements for convincing the audience. Overall, the related hashtag "#HackingHillary" was spread through Twitter, being augmented by "Opinion Leaders and Massive Influencers", celebrities and public figures. Thus, it became a trending topic, which was displayed to users of Twitter influencing their response actions (Dourish, 2016; Watson, 2016; Feldman, 2016; Marwick & Lewis, 2017).

As already mentioned, falsified images frequently become viral, not only for political reasons but just to honor an artist or to comment /criticize the emergence of a social event. For instance, after the death of Lemmy (Motorhead), at the period when the famous music icon David Bowie also passed away, the Internet was floated with an unbelievable number of related images, spread around as a tribute to these two idols. A characteristic example is depicted in Figure 3 (left), in which the two artists have been photographed together. However, according to Getty Images (Novak, 2017), the original picture of Lemmy is taken in June 1972, presenting him with his "French girlfriend" (Figure 3, right). Based on the above documentation of the manipulators' motives, it can be concluded that misinformation is an intricate and politically sensitive issue, the importance of which can be understood only with the examination of indicative exposed cases (i.e. debunked rumors). Clearly, the above three examples of inaccurate /untrue posts became viral, partly due to the lack of the individuals' awareness, illustrating that education and media literacy form critical factors for preventing disinformation. Considering that the stemming flow of fake-news depends on the collective decisions of millions of individual users, whose choices around clicking and sharing determine its spread, the audience must become more discerning and suspicious regarding the trustworthiness of online reports (Reuters Institute, 2017).

Figure 2. Inaccurately framed images implying that Hillary Clinton could not climb up common stairs on her own in February 2016 (left), with a photo-collage (right) "proofing" the symptoms of her sickness
(Chang, 2016)

Figure 3. The manufactured photo of David Bowie with Lemmy from Motorhead (left). The original picture posed him with his French girlfriend (right)
Photo by Jorgen Angel /Redferns, Source: Getty Images.

SOLUTIONS AND RECOMMENDATIONS

Informing Awareness, Cultivation and Literacy

Historically, images (and broader audiovisual /multimedia assets) have been extensively used to convince readers about the truth of the surrounding reports, serving as witnesses /proofing evident documents. However, the possibility of altering visual material, which appeared almost together with the invention and use of the photography, eroded this trust. Before the digital age, "scams" required the knowledge of complicated and time-consuming techniques of the "dark room", with the associated infrastructures. Today, the evolution of ICTs has provided the tools, so that anyone with elementary skills and knowledge on computers, can modify pictures, using powerful and easy to access digital image processing software (i.e. free /online, inexpensive). While the initial purpose of those services was not to facilitate information manipulation and forgery, this option has become very popular, and it is applied by many users, seeking for fun in the news spread (i.e. trolling) or aspiring to propagandize about specific topics of interest. Consequently, sophisticated counterfeits tend to be produced (and reproduced) with shocking frequency recently, thus reducing the people's "good faith" in what they see. Doctorate /altered photos appear with exponentially increasing rates in almost all publication categories, such as traditional media, scientific journals, political campaigns, fashion- and lifestyle-related magazines, as well as in more severe cases of national security and in the courts, thus having a significant impact on many aspects of human life. The continuously increasing digital storage and computational power capacities, extended the processing (and tampering) capabilities in other more demanding content entities, like sound, video and their use in virtual worlds and immersive environments. The communicative power of the new means makes the storytelling more fascinating, engaging the audience in more intense and dynamic participating interactions, so the offered advantages can be exploited in favor of the unpleasing phenomenon of fake-news propagation. In addition, the latest trends and the appearance of associated genres of journalism deteriorate even more the confidence of the average citizens (i.e. concerning the use of the newfangled informing utilities), resulting in the further lack of trust and/or the adoption of a defending stand against the news-world.

The presented examples and the analysis that followed provide some useful insights regarding the cause, the mechanisms and, most of all, the recommended solutions towards facing fake-news. In the long run, education and media literacy would form the essential factors in the battle against this unwanted phenomenon. Know-how is considered very important for being informed about the problem itself and its potential answers, for which many different approaches, procedural routines and algorithmic techniques need to be integrated, formalized and orchestrated in multiple layers (i.e. journalistic, operational, social, ethical, technological, educational, regulatory, etc.). Examining this issue from a theoretical /journalistic point of view, chapter 2 focuses on the essence of authenticity and the corresponding gatekeeping models that every individual, involved in the news consumption and contribution processes, should be aware of. The technological perspective implies the need for continuous adaptation to the new services, aiming at excluding ourselves from being outsiders in the swiftly transformed ecosystem of digital communications, aspects that are thoroughly reviewed in chapter 3. The present chapter discusses the power of multimedia and their potentials in undesirable misuse, related to misinformation, concluding that almost all the actions we perform online are useful, exciting and amusing, but there are always steps we can follow to improve the experience and to act more responsibly. The fact is that SNSs cannot behave like judges of what is fake or real, true or false and censor all the information, arising worries about particular defending actions, i.e. the creation of blacklists (Jarvis, 2016). Hence, chapter 5 investigates the involvement of citizens in veracity procedures (i.e. rational judgment, criticism, physical presence, etc.) and the adopted cross-validation best-practices from a human-centered perspective. Many people are concerned about certain decisions, which devalue specific news providers, sometimes excluding them unwarrantably due to the unavoidable subjectivity or bias of the evaluators. Considering the massiveness of the informatory streams that are daily exchanged and the subsequent practical difficulties, content searching and managing procedures with the use of related automation algorithms are pursued, which is thought as a step forward, toward censorship. Indeed, algorithmic methods and tools are elaborated continuously, aiming at helping average users and media professionals securing themselves against disinformation. Chapter 6 demystifies the principles of these assisted authentication strategies, which are deployed with the purpose to minimize the needed time for revealing possible forgeries and for reducing the spread of non-validated reports.

Overall, many researchers, academics and specialists that work in the fields of journalism and mass communications have been already convinced that social media must exert more active censorship rules, strengthening a related regulatory framework in favor of their members, especially those with remarkable roles in the public life. For instance, while established media companies are often punished, when they make errors or fail to check facts, producers and disseminators of untrue stories usually operate under the cover of the anonymity, so their misinformation reporting activity has typically no consequences (Reuters Institute, 2017). Higher agreement exists about the importance of revealing the motivations of fake-news providers and, moreover, of addressing the matter, by integrating all the available defending means towards decisive collaborative solutions. An indicative example of this effort is the proposed cross-media authentication and verification model, which stands as the core objective of this book and is thoroughly analyzed in chapter 8, in functional, technological and humanoid /ethical level. Returning to the title of the present section, informing awareness, cultivation and literacy are required with respect to all the implicated factors: i.e. knowing the problem itself and its dimensions, the new technological capabilities, the demanded responsibility in consuming and sharing ambiguous news reports, the best-practices adopted by humans, who perform gatekeeping operations and, the possibility of utilizing cross-modal assisting authentication tools.

CONCLUSION

The present chapter focuses on multimedia tampering, dealing with the problem of "digital shaping", which can be utilized for intentionally falsifying documents that accompany a news report. ICT evolution has increased the associated processing capacities, which have been expedited by the remarkable progress of (mobile) computing systems, regarding both hardware and software developments. Online tools and user-friendly services allow the efficacious execution of demanding content altering operations, that can be easily performed almost by everyone. In fact, these capabilities have extended the simple cases of textual altering to the more advanced doctoring of audiovisual assets, which usually frame written articles as proofing facts of the corresponding stories. Moreover, authoring of nonlinear narratives with enhanced interactions attempts to engage the audience by offering more appealing and rich storytelling experiences, in which, forgery attacks can more easily pass-by unnoticed. The chapter outlines the relationship between multimedia resources, its widespread utilization and propagation by individuals and the potential dissemination of unverified events, lacking the necessary journalistic cross-validation and/or gatekeeping. Such changes have influenced professional newsgathering and coverage practices, resulting in a significant rise in the creation and spread of misleading information. No doubt, the present period may be easily characterized as the era of fake-news and contradictory arguments, since data is being generated and transmitted at dizzying speeds, taking advantage of the thousands connected devices that individuals use every day. A noteworthy remark that can be borrowed for consolidating the previous assumption is the fact that, the world internet population has grown 7,5% since 2016, currently representing 3.7 billion, people who generate 2.5 quintillion bytes of data each day ("Data Never Sleeps 5.0," 2018).

The characteristics of the above setting have transformed the current international reality, with an adverse side effect on the massive propagation of ambiguous informing streams, that cannot be validated in real time through traditional gatekeeping approaches. It cannot be a coincidence that administration initiatives, aimed at stopping the distribution of false stories, are announced throughout the world. For instance, the French president has declared as an urgent priority of his government the adoption of a new regulatory framework fighting fake-news laws. Furthermore, United Kingdom has announced the establishment of a dedicated national security authority to deal with disinformation (Walker, 2018; Chrisafis, 2018). These policies may highlight the gravity of the situation, but the practical aspects of this phenomenon are very complicated, requiring for cross-modal, more complex and cooperative confronting strategies. Among the most challenging difficulties that modern societies have to face, is dealing with the problem of "multimedia manipulation", which, in some degree, is the root or the fuel of the misinforming actions. Besides the technical, algorithmic, operational and journalistic perspectives, the anticipated solutions should rely on the cultivation of informing awareness attitudes and digital media literacy. Illustrative examples that were presented in the previous sections of this chapter and the subsequent argumentation, which they triggered, rather advocated the above necessity. In this digital epoch, individuals have separate responsibility for collecting, analyzing, checking and validating information, an ascertainment that seems to converge to the famous equation, coined by Francis Bacon in 1597, stating that "knowledge is power".

REFERENCES

Alton, L. (2017). *A One Minute Video Is Worth 1.8M Words: Content Marketing's Newest Weapon*. Available at: https://www.business.com/articles/a-one-minute-video-is-worth-1-8m-words-contentmarketings-newest-weapon/

Berghel, H. (2017). Lies, Damn Lies, and Fake News. *Computer*, *50*(2), 80–85. doi:10.1109/MC.2017.56

BrewerD. (2017). *Accuracy in journalism*. Available at: http://www.mediahelpingmedia.org/training-resources/editorial-ethics/237-the-importance-of-accuracy-in-journalism

Bull, A. (2010). *Multimedia journalism: a practical guide*. Routledge.

Chang, S. (2017). *Hillary Clinton's Entire Staff Say They Have Pneumonia: Coverup Begins*. Available at: http://www.theimproper.com/141737/hillary-clinton-staff-claim-pneumonia-coverup-begins/

Cheadle, H. (2017). *How Conspiracy Theories About Hillary Clinton's Health Went Mainstream*. Available at: https://www.vice.com/en_us/article/wdbdvn/hillarys-health-conspiracy-theory

Chrisafis, A. (2018). Emmanuel Macron promises ban on fake news during elections. *The Guardian*. Retrieved 26 January 2018, from https://www.theguardian.com/world/2018/jan/03/emmanuel-macron-ban-fake-news-french-president

Cisco. (2017). *The Zettabyte Era: Trends and Analysis*. White paper. Available at: https://www.cisco.com/c/en/us/solutions/collateral/service-provider/visual-networking-index-vni/vni-hyperconnectivity-wp.html

Coffee, J. C. Jr. (2002). Understanding Enron: It's About the Gatekeepers, Stupid. *Business Lawyer*, 1403–1420.

Data Never Sleeps 5.0 | Domo. (2018). Retrieved 26 January 2018, from https://www.domo.com/learn/data-never-sleeps-5

Del Vicario, M., Bessi, A., Zollo, F., Petroni, F., Scala, A., Caldarelli, G., ... Quattrociocchi, W. (2016). The spreading of misinformation online. *Proceedings of the National Academy of Sciences of the United States of America, 113*(3), 554–559. doi:10.1073/pnas.1517441113 PMID:26729863

Deuze, M. (2005). What is journalism? Professional identity and ideology of journalists reconsidered. *Journalism, 6*(4), 442–464. doi:10.1177/1464884905056815

Deuze, M., (2008). Understanding journalism as newswork: How it changes, and how it remains the same. *Westminster Papers in Communication and Culture, 5*(2).

Dimoulas, A. C. (2015). Multimedia authoring and management technologies: non-linear storytelling in the new digital media. Athens: Association of Greek Academic Libraries.

Dimoulas, A. C. (2015). *Multimedia authoring and management technologies: non-linear storytelling in the new digital media*. Athens: Association of Greek Academic Libraries. Available online https://repository.kallipos.gr/handle/11419/4343 (in Greek)

Dimoulas, C., Veglis, A., & Kalliris, G. (2014). Application of Mobile Cloud-Based Technologies. In J. Rodrigues, K. Lin, & J. Lloret (Eds.), *Mobile Networks and Cloud Computing Convergence for Progressive Services and Applications* (pp. 320–343). Hershey, PA: Information Science Reference. doi:10.4018/978-1-4666-4781-7.ch017

Dimoulas, C., Veglis, A., & Kalliris, G. (2014). Application of Mobile Cloud-Based Technologies. In J. Rodrigues, K. Lin, & J. Lloret (Eds.), *Mobile Networks and Cloud Computing Convergence for Progressive Services and Applications* (pp. 320–343). Hershey, PA: Information Science Reference. doi:10.4018/978-1-4666-4781-7.ch017

Dimoulas, C., Veglis, A., & Kalliris, G. (2015). Audiovisual hypermedia in the semantic Web. In M. Khosrow-Pour (Ed.), *Encyclopedia of Information Science and Technology* (3rd ed.; pp. 7594–7604). Hershey, PA: Information Science Reference. doi:10.4018/978-1-4666-5888-2.ch748

Dimoulas, C. A. (2019). Multimedia. In D. Merskin & J. G. Golson (Eds.), The SAGE International Encyclopedia of Mass Media and Society. SAGE. (forthcoming)

Dimoulas, C. A., & Symeonidis, A. L. (2015). Syncing shared multimedia through audiovisual bimodal segmentation. *IEEE MultiMedia*, *22*(3), 26–42. doi:10.1109/MMUL.2015.33

Dimoulas, C. A., Veglis, A. A., & Kalliris, G. (2018). Semantically Enhanced Authoring of Shared Media. In Encyclopedia of Information Science and Technology, Fourth Edition (pp. 6476-6487). IGI Global. doi:10.4018/978-1-5225-2255-3.ch562

Dimoulas, C. A., Veglis, A. A., & Kalliris, G. (2018). Semantically Enhanced Authoring of Shared Media. In Encyclopedia of Information Science and Technology, Fourth Edition (pp. 6476-6487). IGI Global. doi:10.4018/978-1-5225-2255-3.ch562

Dourish, P. (2016). Algorithms and their others: Algorithmic culture in context. *Big Data & Society*, *3*(2). doi:10.1177/2053951716665128

Dur, B.İ.U., Filipczak-Bialkowska, A., Bresciani, S., Ge, J., Niu, Y., & Othman, A. (2014). Interactive infographics on the internet. *Online Journal of Art and Design, 2*(4).

Durkin, J. (2017). *Drudge Report Lead Story Shows Hillary Clinton Falling… in Photo From Six Months Ago*. Available at: https://www.mediaite.com/online/drudge-report-lead-story-shows-hillary-clinton-falling-in-photo-from-six-months-ago/

Ellering, N. (2017). *30 Social Media Engagement Tactics That Will Boost Shares And Conversions*. Available at: https://coschedule.com/blog/social-media-engagement-tactics/

Feldman, J. (2017). *#HackingHillary Tops Twitter Trends as Clinton Dismisses Health 'Conspiracy Theories'*. Available at: https://www.mediaite.com/online/hackinghillary-tops-twitter-trends-as-clinton-dismisses-health-conspiracy-theories/

Flat Earth International Conference 2017. (2018). Retrieved 26 January 2018, from http://fe2017.com/

Foust, J. (2017). *Online journalism: principles and practices of news for the Web*. Taylor & Francis.

Frank, R. (2015). Caveat Lector: Fake News as Folklore. *Journal of American Folklore*, *128*(509), 315–332. doi:10.5406/jamerfolk.128.509.0315

Howell, L. (2013). Digital wildfires in a hyperconnected world. *WEF Report*, *3*, 15–94.

Hunt, E. (2016). What is fake-news? How to spot it and what you can do to stop it. *The Guardian*. Available at: https://www.theguardian.com/media/2016/dec/18/what-is-fake-news-pizzagate

Jarvis, J. (2016). *A Call for Cooperation Against Fake News – Whither news? – Medium*. Available at: https://medium.com/whither-news/a-call-for-cooperation-against-fake-news-d7d94bb6e0d4

Kang, C. (2017). *Fake News Onslaught Targets Pizzeria as Nest of Child-Trafficking*. Available at: https://www.nytimes.com/2016/11/21/technology/fact-check-this-pizzeria-is-not-a-child-trafficking-site.html?mcubz=3

Katsaounidou, A. N., & Dimoulas, C. A. (2018). Integrating Content Authentication Support in Media Services. In Encyclopedia of Information Science and Technology, Fourth Edition (pp. 2908-2919). IGI Global. doi:10.4018/978-1-5225-2255-3.ch254

Lipton, E. (2016). *Man Motivated by 'Pizzagate' Conspiracy Theory Arrested in Washington Gunfire*. Available at: https://www.nytimes.com/2016/12/05/us/pizzagate-comet-ping-pong-edgar-maddison-welch.html?mcubz=3

Ljung, A., & Wahlforss, E. (2008). *People, Profiles and Trust: On interpersonal trust in web-mediated social spaces*. Lulu.com.

Marieb, E. N., & Hoehn, K. (2007). *Human anatomy & physiology*. Pearson Education.

Marwick, A., & Lewis, R. (2017). *Media manipulation and disinformation online*. Data & Society.

Matsiola, M., Dimoulas, C. A., Kalliris, G., & Veglis, A. A. (2015). Augmenting user interaction experience through embedded multimodal media agents in social networks. In *Social media and the transformation of interaction in society* (pp. 188–209). IGI Global. doi:10.4018/978-1-4666-8556-7.ch010

Miller, M. (2017). *Protesters outside White House demand 'Pizzagate' investigation*. Available at: https://www.washingtonpost.com/news/local/wp/2017/03/25/protesters-outside-white-house-demand-pizzagate-investigation/?utm_term=.0ce71d6b4873

Novak, M. (2017). *69 Viral Images From 2016 That Were Totally Fake*. Available at: https://www.gizmodo.com.au/2016/12/69-viral-images-from-2016-that-were-totally-fake/

Papadopoulos, S., Cesar, P., Shamma, D. A., & Kelliher, S. (Eds.). (2015). Special issue on Social Multimedia and Storytelling. MultiMedia IEEE, 22(3), 10-65.

Reuters Institute. (2017). *RISJ Review | Reuters Institute for the Study of Journalism*. Available at: http://reutersinstitute.politics.ox.ac.uk/risj-review/how-can-we-combat-fake-news-%E2%80%93-role-platforms-media-literacy-and-journalism

Rochlin, N. (2017). Fake news: Belief in post-truth. *Library Hi Tech, 35*(3), 386–392. doi:10.1108/LHT-03-2017-0062

Rosales, R.G. (2006). *The elements of online journalism*. iUniverse.

Semetko, H. A., & Scammell, M. (Eds.). (2012). *The Sage handbook of political communication*. Sage Publications. doi:10.4135/9781446201015

Shah, A. (2017). *Why We Prefer Pictures: It's the Way That We're Wired - The Shutterstock Blog*. Available at: https://www.shutterstock.com/blog/why-we-prefer-pictures-its-the-way-that-youre-wired

Thurman, N. (2015). *Journalism, gatekeeping, and interactivity*. Academic Press.

Vaughan, T. (2014). *Multimedia: making it work* (9th ed.). McGraw-Hill Osborne Media.

Veglis, A. (2007). Cross-media publishing by US newspapers. *The Journal of Electronic Publishing: JEP*, *10*(2). doi:10.3998/3336451.0010.211

Veglis, A. (2012). Journalism and Cross-Media Publishing: The Case of Greece. The handbook of global online journalism, 209-230.

Veglis, A., Dimoulas, C., & Kalliris, G. (2016). Towards intelligent cross-media publishing: media practices and technology convergence perspectives. In A. Lugmayr & C. Dal Zotto (Eds.), *Media Convergence Handbook-Vol. 1* (pp. 131–150). Springer Berlin Heidelberg. doi:10.1007/978-3-642-54484-2_8

Walker, P. (2018). New national security unit set up to tackle fake news in UK. *The Guardian*. Retrieved 26 January 2018, from https://www.theguardian.com/politics/2018/jan/23/new-national-security-unit-will-tackle-spread-of-fake-news-in-uk

Wang, X., Li, Z., & Tang, J. (2017). Multimedia news QA: Extraction and visualization integration with multiple-source information. *Image and Vision Computing*, *60*, 162–170. doi:10.1016/j.imavis.2017.01.004

Wardle, C. (2017). *Launching our new Chrome extension NewsCheck*. Available at: https://firstdraftnews.com/launching-new-chrome-extension-newscheck/

Watson, P. (2017). *The Truth About Hillary's Bizarre Behavior*. Available at: https://www.youtube.com/watch?v=OqbDBRWb63s

Webb, J. (2017). *Information Technology Whitepaper*. Academic Press.

Weigel, D. (2016). In prime time, Sean Hannity carries out a Clinton medical 'investigation'. *Washington Post*. Available at: https://www.washingtonpost.com/news/post-politics/wp/2016/08/11/in-prime-time-sean-hannity-carries-out-a-clinton-medical-investigation/?utm_term=.1b819c2468b7

YouTube. (2017). *Hillary Clinton Proves She's in Good Health.* Available at: https://www.youtube.com/watch?v=Kt22Y9-dfNk

Yuvaraj, M. (2017). Infographics: Tools for designing, visualizing data and storytelling in libraries. *Library Hi Tech News, 34*(5), 6–9. doi:10.1108/LHTN-01-2017-0004

Zimdars, M. (2016). *False, misleading, clickbait-y, and satirical "news" sources.* Google Docs.

ENDNOTE

[1]   See http://fe2017.com/

Chapter 5
Authentication by Humans

ABSTRACT

The present chapter investigates the involvement of the human factor in news evaluation procedures. Indeed, the "wise" crowd is an essential component of the verification practices, although there are continuously arising automated processes in the related research field (digital forensics). The idea of validating events using individuals' advantages (rational judgment, criticism, physical presence) is not new, since audience has always influenced the published stories regarding their formulation and perception. It is no coincidence that the term "collective intelligence" has been used for many years. Furthermore, this section of the book attempts to provide an overview of the fact-checking procedures, while utilizing the capabilities of Semantic Web and the developed initiatives around the world regarding authentication. The utmost goal of the chapter is to highlight that people hold a crucial role in in the dissemination of misleading information, but also in detecting, flagging, and debunking.

DOI: 10.4018/978-1-5225-5592-6.ch005

INTRODUCTION

Traditionally, Journalism has constantly included verification processes; for that reason, reporters always had an obligation to crosscheck the stories they published (Kolodzy, 2012). Many may argue that journalists must adapt their traditional work practices to the new digital environment, but things are not quite straightforward. The current digital environment has different characteristics from the media landscape of the 20th century. Speed is an essential factor that dominates the journalistic work, and the variety of contemporary information sources makes the evaluation process very demanding for every media organization (Veglis & Pomportsis, 2014; 2016). The news is produced from various sources in a 24-hour cycle, and all data must be consumed fresh otherwise, they lose their value (Veglis, 2012). This transforming media landscape has positioned media in an extremely vulnerable position.

Due to the need for endless content production, reporters, to succeed the highest "number of clicks", utilize Social Networking Sites (SNSs) as an important information source, in which a significant amount of data is not valid. Considering that every internet user can create and disseminate news items, which can become "viral" (image, video, hashtag, etc.) and lead to coverage from mainstream media (Marwick & Lewis, 2017), anything published online should be questioned. Organizations around the world study the problem by focusing on specific areas or by covering the entire field to reduce misinformation and continuous radicalization, as well as to increase trust in mainstream media. The present chapter aims to point out the need for digital literacy enhancement and to highlight that even, algorithmic and mechanically assisted, solutions must be human-centered, understandable and user-friendly. Data verification and authentication practices, debunking sites and crowdsourcing methodologies are the topics which are discussed.

THE "WISE" CROWD: VERIFICATION COLLABORATIVE PROCEDURES

Verification Can Be a Team Activity: Issues, Controversies, Problems

Public trust has fallen across the range of media and the core reason for this is the existence of the fake-news problem (EBU, 2016). The crisis of credibility towards the press, as well as the fears of an adverse impact of new technologies on the media industry, have resulted in the urgent need for finding solutions to face the problem. The rise of misinformation in the Internet era is presumably caused by the ease of content creation, transmission and access/retrieval. (Zelizer, 2004). This phenomenon is not new, since it appeared, in some form, in the sixth century (Byzantine period). The problem became quite widespread in eighteenth-century London when newspapers started to impact on a broader public (Darnton, 2017). It reached its climax at the beginning of the 21st century (Post-truth era) with the production of fake, semi-false and true but compromising stories. From a theoretical standpoint, Kumar and Geethakumari (2014) utilize the perceptions of cognitive psychology to understand the process of individuals' decision-making. According to them, the cognitive procedure associated with the decision to share stories, involves the response to four main questions: "consistency of message, "the coherency of message", "credibility of source" and "general acceptability of message". Considering that individuals determine their news consumption through filtering and personalization, they never actually browse reports that challenge or contradict to what they already believe (Libicki, 2007). Even more, people believe "kinds of stuff", which reinforce their prior thoughts without questioning them (Lewandowsky, Ecker, Seifert, Schwarz, & Cook, 2012). According to the above perceptions, manipulators usually shape "news evidences" towards specific beliefs, aiming at achieving higher levels of acceptance and widespread dissemination.

An outstanding example of worldwide crowdsourcing investigation is the paradigm related to the leaked "Panama Papers". According to a Wikipedia entry, this case was consisted of about 11.5 million documents that contain financial and client information for more than 214,488 offshore entities. Because of the different kinds of records (printed, manuscript, pdf), participants all over the world converted them into a common format (pdf), in order to conduct optical character recognition (OCR) procedures and extract evidence related to names, ownerships, etc. Journalists from 107 media organizations in 80 countries collaborated for analyzing the documents. After more than a year of examination, the first news stories were published along with a database of interconnected graphs aiming at enhancing the identification of the correlations between the elements more easily. Among others, computer scientists were united towards the popularization of information extraction technology by creating user friendly interfaces, therefore effortless ways for journalists to search the documents. The above paradigm represents an important momentous in terms of transdisciplinary collaboration, use of data and journalism software tools.

Until now, computational approaches coping with the fake-news problem have mainly focused on automated platforms. These tools can label formerly identified counterfeit claims and automatically detect odd articles via natural language processing (NLP) techniques, based on predefined ground truth / databases (Katsaounidou & Dimoulas, 2018). While most of these methods can partially prevent the transmission of fake articles, none of them can perceive the semantic content of them or understand the exact meaning of the text. Consequently, humans continue to perform an important role in the verification processes or serve also as sources of validated information. The most common example, regarding the power of the crowd in providing confirmed data is the case of *"2009 Darpa Network challenge"* and especially the *"Red Balloon Challenge"*, in which vying teams competed in searching for ten weather balloons placed across the entire United States of America. The winning team from MIT found all 10 balloons within 8 hours by using social media to crowdsource the search (Silverman, 2013; Poblet, García-Cuesta, & Casanovas, 2017). The idea of validating news events using the human factor is not new. Lévy (1997) established the term "collective intelligence" targeting to that sometimes, when a group performs successfully a task, it seems intelligent. For instance, the Wikipedia project is often referred as an example of "collaborative knowledge" or to talk about the *"wisdom of crowds"* (Niederer & Van Dijck, 2010). Since Web is considered as a location for peoples' cooperation (Shirky, 2008) and web-based/mobile technologies have expanded crowdsourcing methods, users can easily contribute to crowdsourced verification projects. For example, taking into consideration that Social Networking Sites (SNSs) are the perfect place for information extraction and dissemination, VerI.ly platform was created as the first crowdsourced fact-checking and evidence collection platform, purposing in verifying the available evidences during humanitarian disasters (Poblet, García-Cuesta, & Casanovas, 2017). Its main "raison d'être" is to disprove unverified claims and reveal the truth by calling hundreds of people to contribute different types of evidence such as texts, images, videos, (meta)data collected from mobile position sensors and geo-social check-ins.

There are established methods to exploit social media in the verification process. According to Silverman (2013), the validation of User Generated Content (UGC) in breaking news situations must agree with specific investigative fundamentals, such as "The five W's" (Hart, 1996). Rumors and unconfirmed reports tend to spread rather quickly on social media, thus the crowd can also be part of the solution. In today's interconnected world it is quite natural to create a network of SNSs users (Facebook Groups, Twitter, Google+, etc.), which can be employed to verify an event (Silverman, 2014a). For instance, journalists should contact and discuss with people, consult several and authorized sources, correspond and cooperate with other professionals and familiarize themselves with research processes and techniques. Moreover, media professionals ought to build and sustain a social network of credible sources to be able to monitor social media for current trends. In addition, the existence of this network of interested parties through social media provides new possibilities in the verification process, through utilization of crowdsourcing schemes (Hermida, 2012). Reporters must also be able to use SNSs and Internet tools /services for crosschecking the obtained evidences. Finally, they should exploit the social media connectivity to disseminate their articles (Silverman, 2014b). Such systems must be already established before there is a need for them to be utilized. The challenge to use hundreds of individuals as information providers for events verification, points the finger of responsibility at the users, while also signifies the enormous importance of their mandatory presence in fact-checking procedures.

Algorithmic solutions had not only become part of everyday life, but they are now "objects of public attention, topics of newspaper articles and coffee shop conversations" (Dourish, 2016, p.1). In the last decade, the establishment of online tools, services and browser extensions that deal with the verification problem is widened. However, the tools with "a stand-alone" nature meaning that there is no interconnection between them. The detection of propaganda in large volumes of data is a perplexing task and methods which use Machine Learning (ML) and Natural Language Processing (NLP) techniques has been developed through research programs, attempting to automate the process to a degree (Schifferes et al., 2014; Tzelepis, et al., 2016).

As already mentioned, humans in contrast to machines can perceive data based on logic and observation in this context the field Digital Image Forensics (DIF) encloses an approach which utilizes the humans' abilities as mentioned earlier. For example, objects which are depicted in an image can be used as indicators to determine its location (electrical outlets, language of the signs) and its time of creation (clocks, calendars, other kinds of devices and their operating systems, e.g. smartphones). Among others, some meaningful and detectable by human eye indications are reflections, shadows, people and objects on wrong scale or appearing to be "floating" etc. (Farid, 2009; Redi, Taktak, & Dugelay, 2010; Wen, 2017). In this context, Schetinger, Oliveira, da Silva, and Carvalho (2015) conducted a study to evaluate whether people are able to identify doctored images. Although some of the images were not altered in any way, more than half had been spliced (meaning that they were synthesized by multiple photos), involved areas that had been erased, or contained segments that were copied and pasted from the same image. Participants were only able to spot the fakes in a proportion of 47%. Moreover, Katsaounidou (2016) undertook a partly similar survey using crowdsourcing techniques to estimate users' abilities in retrieving valuable information about images consistency. The key/ element element which separates the aforementioned surveys is that in the latter case were included interviews with journalists and experts on image analysis. The scope of the interviews was to seek if the above professionals can comprehend the results which DIF algorithms (analyzed in chapter 6) provide regarding the detection of possible image manipulation. Moreover, participants were able to identify the fakes in a performance rate of 56%, while interviewers found the task rather difficult.

Even though humans do not have the computational or storage capacity of machines they are able to verify all kinds of the provided information, by following a variety of paths. Specifically, individuals can examine the originality of a report by investigating the containing rich media (text, image, sound, video), which offer many opportunities to conduct multilateral fact-checking (i.e. an article which analyses an odd Politician's statement, published via his Twitter account). This article is most likely to embed the tweet itself along with other evidences to strengthen the analysis. First and foremost, the authenticity of the politician's account must be checked (blue verified badge which appears next to the name on an account's profile and next to the account name in search results). Moreover, a common strategy is to cross-check the trustworthiness of the statement among the Politician's SNSs pages (Facebook, Google+, etc.). If the above procedure is not effective, "investigators" must direct their attention to the major challenge; if the tweet is real or fake. A tweet can include multimedia content, physical language, punctuation, hashtags, mentions and external links. In more detail, it can contain question and exclamation marks, pronouns, slang words or words and sad/ happy emoticons that highlight a positive that highlight a positive or negative sentiment. Generally, the usage patterns of the above entities can determine the "character" of the tweet. For example, syntax errors and styles (e.g. size, color, font type /size, etc.), punctuation points (e.g. question/ exclamation marks), lowercase versus capital characters, etc. may indicate that the messages have been artificially generated. Likewise, the frequency of certain words, the statistics of the used terminology or even the structure of the entire vocabulary may imply that the tweet is fake. Except for the above, a user can utilize Google's image archive to dismiss a photo as being fake or out of context in a matter of seconds. These procedures offer the opportunity for users to form a first impression about the validity of the content. However, the last and more important thing to do is to acquire information about the Politician i.e. if the statement is in harmony with the Politician's "path" so far.

Nowadays, the media ecosystem has been dominated by the contemporary forms of Journalism, where Multiple publishing and digital storytelling means/ channels have emerged. Specifically, the cross- and trans-media publishing systems have become an everyday practice for journalists in most professional organizations. Even though that the existence of multiple publishing alternatives facilitates the spread of misleading stories, the availability of differentiated audiovisual material (and overall data) describing a story works also in favor of the authentication. Therefore, end-users are expected to contribute equally to verification activities, participating in crowdsourcing projects, and to towards multimedia authentication. The challenge of addressing the fake-news phenomenon needs to be supported, taking advantage of the information dissemination channels. Table 1 aims to partly visualize what an extended cross-media correlation could be, while listing the most popular publishing channels and associating them with their commonly available entities. As presented in the Table 1, users can look through the channels in order to cross-check the elements of a story/report. For example, when a person reports his /her physical presence to a news event

Table 1. A simple correlation matrix presents the relation between the popular publishing channels and their containing elements; Multimedia (text, audio, image, video), Tags (all applicable metadata), Source (profile, contacts, network, personal, information, bio, account), Links (Urls), Attachments (digital files/ multimedia)

CHANNELS	WWW	E-Mail, Newsletter	Facebook, Google+	Twitter	Instagram, Pinterest, Tumblr	Messenger, Viber, Snapchat, WhatsApp
WWW	Multimedia Links, Tags	Source Text, Links Attachments	Source, Tags, Links, Multimedia	Source, Links	Image Tags	Text, Attachments Links
E-Mail, Newsletter	Source Text, Links Attachments	Multimedia Links, Tags	Source, Tags, Links, Multimedia	Source Text, Links Attachments	Image Tags	Text, Attachments Links
Facebook, Google+	Source, Tags, Links, Multimedia	Source Text, Links Attachments	Multimedia Links, Tags	Source, Links	Image Tags	Text, Attachments Links
Twitter	Source, links	Source Text, Links Attachments	Source, Links	Multimedia Links, Tags	Source, Links Image Tags	Text, Attachments Links
Instagram, Pinterest, Tumblr	Image Tags	Image Tags	Image Tags	Source, Links Image Tags	Multimedia Links, Tags	Text, Attachments Links
Messenger, Viber, Snapchat, WhatsApp	Text, Attachments Links	Text, Attachments Links	Image Tags	Text, Attachments Links	Text, Attachments Links	Multimedia Links, Tags

and presents itself as an eyewitness, the "investigator" can gather geo-data from witness' related accounts on SNSs to be sure that the person was there at the corresponding event.

SOLUTIONS AND RECOMMENDATIONS

Human-Based Prevention Initiatives for Fake News Dissemination

Since 2016, the issue of fake-news attracted the attention of the media organizations as well as public's and there was much debate on the ways in which our society can tackle this problem. The first thing that comes to mind when speaking about rumors, hoaxes, claims, conspiracy theories, propaganda and misinformation is the "debunking sites", such as Snopes.com[1], Buzzfeed. com[2], Politifact.com[3], Factcheck.org[4] and TruthOrfiction.com[5]. The Snopes.

com project, founded by David Mikkelson[6] in 1994, is the initial effort in researching urban legends and today it is the leading fact-checking agency that embraces not only urban legends, but also popular misjudgments, odd news stories, rumors, personalities' gossip etc. It is supported by a small number of researchers and writers dedicated to investigate and analyze claims of various topics. The editorial team usually attempts to contact the source of the rumor (to acquire support information) or individuals and organizations, who might be aware of about or have appropriate expertise on the subject under inspection. Moreover, editors are searching in printed editions (articles, scientific and medical journal articles, books, interview transcripts, statistical sources). The most important element is that all the utilized research material in the investigation is listed in the reference, displayed at the foot of each article so that readers, who wish to verify the accuracy of the information, could check the sources. While most experts seem to agree that the most efficient way to debunk the stories is with the help of such sites, even these services are not useful in case of breaking news, because of the needed time for choosing and inspecting a topic. Moving one-step further, Politifact.com and Snopes.com web sites, based on their experiences, composed their Guides on Fake News Sites/ Hoax Purveyors[7,8] in order to support readers in distinguishing facts from fiction on their social streams.

In January 2016, Reynolds Journalism Institute[9] launched the Trusting News Project[10], with the initial queries: "How do people decide what news is trustworthy?" and "How can journalists influence what users consume and share?". After a year being spent on studying users' reactions to social media, this site is offering guidance on those questions, which are crucial in an scenery where journalists struggle to stand out in a minefield of misinformation (Kearney, 2017). Another effort is made via the the "Public Data Lab[11]", which achieves to simplify research, democratic engagement and public debate around the future of the data society. Its aim is the development and dissemination of innovative research, teaching, design and participation formats for the creation and use of public data. Furthermore, the purpose of "News Integrity Initiative[12]" is the advancement of news literacy, increase of trust in Journalism around the world and better inform the public conversation.

An important development which reflects the significance of the misinformation problem, as mentioned in chapter 2, is the "Google Fact Check[13]". This service identifies articles that include fact checked information by news publishers and fact-checking organizations. The process is designed as follows: if a publisher "owns" a web page (debunking site) that reviews claims, he can include a "ClaimReview" structured data element in his web page which enables Google Search results to show a summarized version of the fact review. It is no coincidence that when a user searches with Google for the first time the search engine provides clearly authoritative results containing fact checking snippets about ambiguous social events. As it was already pointed out, crowdsourcing is a specific financial model in which individuals or organizations use contributions from Internet users to develop needed services or ideas. An interconnected "online" municipality with its members spirited by their passion for objective Journalism, can perform a crucial role in news coverage procedures. An excellent example is the "FirstDraftNews[14]" collaboration, a nonprofit partnership and academic network, aiming to raise awareness and address challenges related to trust and truth. This association is the first of its kind to bring social platforms together with global newsrooms and other industry projects, organizations, research labs, projects and universities. Partners work together to deal with common issues, including ways to streamline the verification process, improve the experience of eyewitnesses and increase news literacy. Among others, "CrossCheck" is a project supported by "FirstDraftNews", a "breathing" work room aiming in investigating if collaborative services are helpful to the public (First Draft, 2017). "FirstDraftNews" is also involved in developing guides for fake-news detection and provides others solutions like "NewsCheck" Chrome extension. That extension allows people to investigate the authenticity of an online image or video by running through a standardized checklist which encourages users to examine material authenticity, creator, time and location. The innovation of the above interactive guide is that the rules are attractively visualized and always available at the browser toolbar.

Another interesting association is the "Poynter International Fact Checking Network[15]" (IFCN). A forum for fact-checkers worldwide hosted by the "Poynter: A global leader in Journalism" which monitors trends in fact checking worldwide published articles, encourages best practices through the fact-checkers' code of principles or projects and provides training in person and online. Finally, the above association performs a crucial function by increasing the impact of fact-checking and also promotes collaborative efforts by funding annual fellowships and a crowdfunding program and by holding an annual "International Fact-Checking Day. Moreover, recent projects have included examination of best practices to determine the future of fact-checking, like training sessions across the United States of America (USA), creation of online courses on fact-checking and weekly fact-checking newsletter. Currently, IFCN cooperates with thirty-four partners and has launched a cooperation as a third-party fact-checker on Facebook.

We believe in giving people a voice and that we cannot become arbiters of truth ourselves, so we're approaching this problem carefully. We've focused our efforts on the worst of the worst, on the clear hoaxes spread by spammers for their own gain, and on engaging both our community and third-party organizations. (Mosseri 2016)

Until now, Facebook users have been able to report a person for fake account /profile, as well as potential inappropriate or even illegal activity (i.e. nudity, sexual harassment [or sexism], hateful language, threats, etc.). However, with the above statement, Adam Mosseri, the Vice President of Facebook, informed the audience about Facebook's commitment to begin solving the issue of fake-news by "activating" also the users. In his announcement he describes four areas, which are some of the first steps they are taking to manage the problem: a) Easier reporting, b) Flagging Stories as Disputed, c) Informed Sharing, d) Disrupting Financial Incentives for Spammers. Moving ahead at the same direction, "Storyful[16]", an award-winning social marketing and news company helps publishers and marketers to find social insights, while using proprietary technology that gathers real-time data from social platforms around the world. "Reveal[17]" from the Center for Investigative Reporting engages and empowers the public, through investigative journalism and groundbreaking storytelling, to spark action, improve lives and protect democracy (Reveal, 2018). "Trust Project[18]" explores how Journalism can stand out from the chaotic crowd and signal its trustworthiness. The project constructs tangible digital strategies to fulfill journalism's basic pledge: to serve society with a truthful, intelligent and comprehensive account of ideas and events. It should be made distinct that the purpose of the above organizations /initiatives reference is to be abundantly clear that multilevel efforts are being made towards resolving the problem. Overall, no matter the attempts mentioned above and the exponential ICTs development regarding the automated opportunities to rank data in terms of its quality, the great merit of media literacy towards impartial, objective and credible Journalism is the core subject at the misinformation issue.

CONCLUSION

The present chapter points out that research and development are important factors for closing current knowledge gaps regarding the misinformation phenomenon. Nowadays, individuals increasingly learn ICT skills informally, and aspects such as critical thinking in the use of new technologies and media, risk awareness, and ethical and legal considerations have received less attention. However, digital literacy has central role as a framework for progressing towards the problem solutions. Moreover, the analysis of news fact-checking /cross-validation practices and verification procedures, focuses on the involvement of the human factor in news evaluation tasks. Additionally, after presenting crowdsourcing strategies, in which individuals or organizations utilize internet users to gather evidence for fact-checking, the chapter concludes with related initiatives on preventing the propagation and dissemination of fake news. As already mentioned, crowdsourcing methods offer unique prospects for society to provide its wisdom to the authentication strategies and furthermore to the fact-checking procedures.

Thousands of propaganda accounts on social networks are spreading all over the world, lies in all languages. False information, photos or videos are purposefully created and spread to confuse or misinform. News, pictures or videos are manipulated to deceive, and old photographs are shared as new. Satire or parody which means no harm can fool people by overflow the media ecosystem. Thus, in recent years, a wide discussion has been conducted regarding the issue of fake-news, its implications and the strategies to deal with this phenomenon. Several initiatives, which attempt to tackle the misinformation problem, have emerged from organizations that explore different aspects of the problem and try to alleviate the crisis. On one hand, maybe the solution is identified at the development of the legal systems for protecting democracy from fake-news, while on the other hand, perhaps the answer can be found by launching new schemes to help people identify real news and filter out fake or falsified content.

REFERENCES

Darnton, R. (2017). The True History of Fake News. *The New York Review of Books*. Available at: http://www.nybooks.com/daily/2017/02/13/the-true-history-of-fake-news/

Dourish, P. (2016). Algorithms and their others: Algorithmic culture in context. *Big Data & Society*, *3*(2). doi:10.1177/2053951716665128

EBU. (2016). *Trust in Media 2016*. Available at: https://www.ebu.ch/files/live/sites/ebu/files/Publications/EBU-MIS - Trust in Media 2016.pdf

Farid, H. (2009). Seeing is not believing. *IEEE Spectrum, 46*(8), 44–51. doi:10.1109/MSPEC.2009.5186556

Hart, G. J. (1996). The five W's: An old tool for the new task of audience analysis. *Technical Communication (Washington), 43*(2), 139–145.

Hermida, A. (2012). Social journalism: Exploring how social media is shaping journalism. The handbook of global online journalism, 309-328.

Katsaounidou, A. (2016). *Content authenticity issues: detection (and validation) techniques of untruthful news stories from humans and machines* (Unpublished Master Thesis). Post-Graduate Program of the School of Journalism and Mass Communications, Aristotle university of Thessaloniki. (in Greek)

Katsaounidou, A. N., & Dimoulas, C. A. (2018). Integrating Content Authentication Support in Media Services. In Encyclopedia of Information Science and Technology, Fourth Edition (pp. 2908-2919). IGI Global. doi:10.4018/978-1-5225-2255-3.ch254

Kearney, M. (2017). *Trusting News Project Report 2017*. Available at: https://www.rjionline.org/reporthtml.html

Kolodzy, J. (2012). *Practicing Convergence Journalism: An Introduction to Cross-Media Storytelling*. Routledge.

Kumar, K. K., & Geethakumari, G. (2014). Detecting Misinformation in online social networks using cognitive psychology. *Human-centric Computing and Information Sciences, 4*(1), 14. doi:10.118613673-014-0014-x

Lévy, P. (1997). *L'intelligence collective: pour une anthropologie du cyberspace*. Paris: La découverte.

Lewandowsky, S., Ecker, U.K., Seifert, C.M., Schwarz, N., & Cook, J. (2012). *Misinformation and its correction continued*. Academic Press.

Libicki, M. C. (2007). *Conquest in cyberspace: national security and information warfare*. Cambridge University Press. doi:10.1017/CBO9780511804250

Marwick, A., & Lewis, R. (2017). Media manipulation and disinformation online. *Data & Society*. Retrieved from https://datasociety.net/pubs/oh/DataAndSociety_MediaManipulationAndDisinformationOnline.pdf

Mikkelson, B., & Mikkelson, D. P. (2004). *Urban legends reference pages.* Academic Press.

Mosseri, A. (2016). *News Feed FYI: Addressing Hoaxes and Fake News.* Retrieved from https://newsroom.fb.com/news/2016/12/news-feed-fyi-addressing-hoaxes-and-fake-news/

Niederer, S., & Van Dijck, J. (2010). Wisdom of the crowd or technicity of content? Wikipedia as a sociotechnical system. *New Media & Society, 12*(8), 1368–1387. doi:10.1177/1461444810365297

Poblet, M., García-Cuesta, E., & Casanovas, P. (2017). Crowdsourcing roles, methods and tools for data-intensive disaster management. *Information Systems Frontiers*, 1–17.

Redi, J. A., Taktak, W., & Dugelay, J. L. (2011). Digital image forensics: A booklet for beginners. *Multimedia Tools and Applications, 51*(1), 133–162. doi:10.1007/11042-010-0620-1

Reveal. (2018). Retrieved 20 January 2018, from http://reveal-mklab.iti.gr/reveal/fake/

Schetinger, V., Oliveira, M. M., da Silva, R., & Carvalho, T. J. (2015). *Humans are easily fooled by digital images.* arXiv preprint arXiv:1509.05301

Schifferes, S., Newman, N., Thurman, N., Corney, D., Goker, A. S., & Martin, C. (2014). Identifying and verifying news through social media: Developing a user-centred tool for professional journalists. *Digital Journalism, 2*(3), 406–418. doi:10.1080/21670811.2014.892747

Shirky, C. (2008). *Here comes everybody: The power of organizing without organizations.* Penguin.

Silverman, C. (Ed.). (2013). *Verification handbook.* European Journalism Centre.

Silverman, C. (Ed.). (2014a). *Verification handbook: a definitive guide to verifying digital content for emergency coverage.* European Journalism Centre.

Silverman, C. (Ed.). (2014b). *Verification handbook: An ultimate guideline on digital age sourcing for emergency coverage.* European Journalism Centre.

Tzelepis, C., Ma, Z., Mezaris, V., Ionescu, B., Kompatsiaris, I., Boato, G., ... Yan, S. (2016). Event-based media processing and analysis: A survey of the literature. *Image and Vision Computing*, *53*, 3–19. doi:10.1016/j.imavis.2016.05.005

Veglis, A. (2012). Journalism and Cross Media Publishing: The case of Greece. In The Wiley-Blackwell Handbook of Online Journalism. Blackwell Publishing.

Veglis, A., & Pomportsis, A. (2012). The e-citizen in the Cyberspace – A Journalism Aspect. *Proc of the 5th International Conference on Information Law and Ethics*, 658-672.

Veglis, A., & Pomportsis, A. (2016). Journalists in the age of ICTs: Work demands and Educational needs. Journalism & Mass Communication Educator, 69(1), 61 – 75.

Weil, T. (2017). *The hidden signs that can reveal a fake photo.* Retrieved 2 December 2017, from http://www.bbc.com/future/story/20170629-the-hidden-signs-that-can-reveal-if-a-photo-is-fake

Zelizer, B. (2004). When Facts, Truth, and Reality Are God-terms: On journalism's uneasy place in cultural studies. *Communication and Critical/Cultural Studies*, *1*(1), 100–119. doi:10.1080/1479142042000180953

KEY TERMS AND DEFINITIONS

Cognitive Psychology: Cognitive psychology is the study of mental processes such as "attention, language use, memory, perception, problem solving, creativity and thinking". Much of the work derived from cognitive psychology has been integrated into various other modern disciplines of psychological study, including educational psychology, social psychology, personality psychology, abnormal psychology, developmental psychology and economics.

Crowdsourcing: It is s a specific sourcing model in which individuals or organizations use contributions from Internet users to obtain needed services or ideas. Crowdsourcing was coined in 2005 as a portmanteau of crowd and outsourcing.

Digital Image Forensics (DIF): This field emerged as a sub-field of Digital Image Processing (DIP), aiming at providing tools for images tampering investigation.

Digital Literacy: Digital literacy is the set of competencies required for full participation in a knowledge society. It includes knowledge, skills and behaviors involving the effective use of digital devices such as smartphones, tablets, laptops and desktop PCs for purposes of communication, expression, collaboration, and advocacy.

Machine Learning (ML): Scientific discipline that investigates algorithms and methods aiming at giving machines the ability to learn from experience (without being explicitly programed), in order to respond autonomously on specific tasks and automate various data-handling processes.

Natural Language Processing (NLP): Scientific discipline utilizing Machine Learning and Computational Linguistics, aiming at giving computers/machines the ability to perceptually interact trough human (natural) languages.

Predefined Ground Truth: Ground truth is a term used in various fields to refer to information provided by direct observation (i.e., empirical evidence) as opposed to information provided by inference.

User-Generated Content (UGC): Any form of content created and shared by users of an online system or service.

"Wise" Crowd: The theory according to which the many are smarter than the few.

ENDNOTES

1   See https://www.snopes.com/
2   See https://www.buzzfeed.com
3   See http://www.politifact.com/
4   See https://www.factcheck.org/
5   See https://www.truthorfiction.com/
6   See https://www.snopes.com/author/snopes/
7   See http://www.politifact.com/punditfact/article/2017/apr/20/politifacts-guide-fake-news-websites-and-what-they/
8   See http://www.snopes.com/2016/01/14/fake-news-sites/
9   See https://www.rjionline.org/
10   See https://trustingnews.org/
11   See http://publicdatalab.org/

[12]   See https://www.journalism.cuny.edu/2017/04/announcing-the-new-integrity-initiative/

[13]   See https://blog.google/products/search/fact-check-now-available-google-search-and-news-around-world/

[14]   See https://firstdraftnews.com/

[15]   See https://www.poynter.org/

[16]   See https://storyful.com/

[17]   See https://www.revealnews.org/

[18]   See http://thetrustproject.org/

Chapter 6
Assisted Authentication

ABSTRACT

The present chapter deals with the issue of information manipulation detection from an algorithmic point of view, examining a variety of authentication methods, which target assisting average users and media professionals to secure themselves from forged content. The specific domain forms a very interesting, highly interdisciplinary research field, where remarkable progress has been conducted during the last years. The chapter outlines the current state of the art, providing an overview of the different modalities, aiming at evaluating the various types of digital data (text, image, audio, video), in conjunction with the associated falsification attacks and the available forensic investigation tools. In the coming years, the problem of fake news is expected to become even more complicated, as journalism is heading towards an era of heightened automation. Overall, it is anticipated that machine-driven verification assistance means can speed up the required validation processes, reducing the spread of unverified reports.

DOI: 10.4018/978-1-5225-5592-6.ch006

INTRODUCTION

Nowadays, Social Networking Sites (SNSs) have become the most dominant place for news origin and propagation. Although journalists have in their availability innumerous ways for verifying SNSs streams, these means also require different competences and expertise (Brandtzaeg, Luders, Spangenberg, Rath-Wiggins, & Folstad, 2016). Subsequently, multimedia evaluation for discovering the evidence of potential tampering has become a significant and currently popular research field among disciplines. The formed domain of Digital Forensics Science (DF /DFS) embraces a broad combination of various technological and methodological approaches. In principle, DFS has been launched for commonly addressing the recovery and investigation of material found in digital devices, often in relation to computer crimes. In recent years, the term is more often attributed to the analysis of the counterfeit instances of individual resources, which is the objective of DF inspections. Indeed, given that most of today's articles are composed by Multimodal Media Assets (MMA), altering operations usually involve all the encountered types of digital assets, i.e. text, images, audio, video, etc. (Dimoulas, Veglis, & Kalliris, 2014; 2015; Katsaounidou, 2016; Katsaounidou & Dimoulas, 2018). Each content entity has distinct communicative and operative characteristics, which are taken into consideration for applying potential forgery actions. Likewise, strategies for verifying the integrity of the different categories also rely on their unique representative features (Katsaounidou & Dimoulas, 2018). Overall, there are two discrete though supplementary issues: integrity and authenticity. Integrity ensures that the involved media components have not been modified, while authenticity refers to the ability to confirm the integrity of the provided information, as a whole.

According to a recent survey (Brandtzaeg et al., 2016), Twitter is the most popular SNS platform, commonly used as informing source. In specific, journalists are trying to stay tuned /up-to-date and aware of the newsworthy events, by monitoring Twitter profiles /posts and the associated breaking news alerts. Various add-on tools have also emerged for helping to organize /structure timelines, keeping track of lists, searches, activities and more (Tame.it, TweetDeck, etc.). On the contrary, Twitter is an excellent example concerning the dissemination of unverified textual streams. With the previous restriction state of the maximum number of one hundred and forty (140) characters, Twitter messages, the so-called tweets, often used to contain odd or fake data to raise interest, attract reactions, provoke retweets /shares, etc. Considering the "computational propaganda", namely the exploitation of algorithms, automations and human curation for purposefully distributing misleading information over SNSs, automated software robots (or just bots) have been used for contaminating public life with artificial affairs (Woolley & Howard, 2017). Hence, machine-operated Twitter profiles are engaged in shaping and publishing auto-generated tweets or links, often conveying ambiguous and inaccurate content. In addition, while the tweeting length limit has been extended to two hundred and eighty (280) characters, Twitter users still re-direct their followers to external sources, very often, pointing to hyperconnected multimedia assets (or even to authored nonlinear hypermedia).

The trustworthiness of audiovisual material has an essential role in many areas: forensic assessment, criminal investigation, surveillance systems, intelligence services, medical imaging and journalism. The "art" of content fakery has a long history. Only a few decades after Niepce generated the first photograph in 1814, images were already being manipulated (Farid, 2008). Forensic audio examination, for example, traces its roots to the 1950s, with the advent of outdoor recording systems (for use outside of the studio). According to Koenig (1990), the Federal Bureau of Investigation (FBI) in the United States has developed expertise in audio forensics since the early 1960s, for the purposes of speech intelligibility enhancement and authentication of recordings. Undoubtedly, the invention of the digitization, the arrival of personal computing systems and the development of dedicated processing software have simplified the data manipulation tasks, even for the non-professionals (Ho & Li, 2015; Katsaounidou, Vryzas, Kotsakis, & Dimoulas, 2016; Katsaounidou & Dimoulas, 2018; Silverman, 2013). In today's digital age, it is possible to quickly alter the information, represented by an image, without leaving apparent traces of tampering (Mahdian & Saic, 2007). Hence, the existence of digital editing tools and overall the evolution in related technology and algorithms have made it more challenging to perform accurate validation of cross-modal sources and documents. For instance, visual objects can be quite easily deleted or inserted in a motion pictures sequence, utilizing frames from other time-instances and/or from entirely different clips/footage. The fact that video forms the most demanding element of mediated communication, helps us realize the challenge that we are facing, as far as the verification of multimedia content is concerned (Al-Sanjary & Sulong, 2015).

MACHINE-DRIVEN FORGERY DETECTION AND ASSISTED AUTHENTICATION

Multimedia Verification Algorithms: Issues, Controversies, Problems

It is admitted that 2015-2016 were the years of audiovisual content, where SNSs responded to the users' growing desire for consuming images and videos, by optimizing related news feed services (Newman, 2016). Specifically, subtitling tools were added, automatic video activation (auto-play) was applied and live video streaming was launched. Purposing to keep-up with the SNSs competition in the news-sourcing dominance and to re-gain a loyal audience engagement, official web pages of the associated journalistic organizations have also invented new mechanisms of events notifications through smart devices. For instance, media agencies progressively invested in "social video" solutions, such as the live streaming facilities that are currently available for serving real-time /synchronous multimedia communications on Facebook, Twitter and YouTube. Considering the popularity of the messaging applications in informing alerts (i.e. Messenger), publishers are also trying to edge into this field for triggering information distribution and public interaction. Hence, automated /robot journalism utilities have emerged and are continually elaborating, such as the case of chatbox messaging platforms (Bock, 2011).

A variety of robot tools are currently used for intelligent content production, fast-packing and publishing of journalistic narratives across different platforms. For example, Wibbitz[1] is an artificial decision-making system that was designed to summarize stories through audiovisual presentations, relying on Machine Learning (ML) and Natural Language Processing (NLP) algorithms. Specifically, Wibbitz parses and harvests textual headlines, keywords and corpora from international news outlets, thus producing mashup videos in seconds. At the same time, newfangled services are continuously entering the market, aiming at helping journalists in monitoring and managing related data streams. For instance, Sam Desk[2], Dataminr[3] and SocialSensor[4] are notable social media management tools, allowing for configuring cross-modal notification services, therefore helping newsroom personnel to detect, classify and rank sources of public informing. Moreover, event tracking and metadata processing utilities can be applied for categorizing, semantically annotating and overall documenting the collected archives, for future utilization and re-use scenarios. Ordering to survive the vast competition, news-casting sites should creatively adopt usable interaction interfaces with enhanced back-end automations. Thereby, in the race to establish their relationship with the audience, major stakeholders like CNN, Wall Street Journal, The Economist and The Guardian have built their own custom front-ends, purposing to serve their distinct demands. Algorithmic Journalism strategies promise smarter and more efficient procedures in the future news battle, however cybernetic methodologies contain certain security risks, including the dissemination of tampered content (Alden, 2013; Dayan & Cohen, 2017; Diplaris et al., 2012; Schwartz, Naaman, & Teodoro, 2015).

In order to get a deeper and clearer picture about the algorithmic aspects of the assisted verification tools, a metaphor will be attempted, attributing science advancements to the growth of trees. Both expand their "vertices" outwardly and not inwardly to their core, so most of the "fertile" and exciting evolutions are detected across several (scientific) branches. For instance, the tremendous progress of the Information and Communication Technologies (ICTs) propelled many other multidisciplinary fields, related to social and humanistic domains. Thus, targeting to prevent the misinformation phenomenon, Journalism has been affected by research initiatives, developments and achievements of many other disciplines. Evolutionary algorithms and architectures of ML and Deep Learning (DL) are listed among the recent scientific trends (Dourish, 2016), which have been deployed to establish methods and technologies for verifying data, concerning their integrity and credibility. On the other hand, the constantly increasing conveniences and capabilities of digital processing allow for easier shaping of online content /news. Therefore, reliability measures /estimations are difficult to be extracted, by both humans and machines. Wardle (2014) supports that automated verification technology guaranteeing perfect scores (100% accurate) does not exist, yet. Nonetheless, remarkable research progress has been succeeded regarding the implementation of fully- and semi-automated authentication algorithms, developed for assisting in the forensic investigation needs (Katsaounidou & Dimoulas, 2018).

Specifically, the purpose of DF techniques is to trace the processing history of a multimedia document, to detect potential manipulation trails and generally to identify all possible forgeries. For example, DL and NLP frameworks are jointly used for contextual analysis of text streams. Hence, detected syntax errors and styles (e.g. size, color, font type /size, etc.), punctuation points (e.g. question /exclamation marks), lowercase versus capital characters, etc. could indicate that the messages have been artificially generated. Likewise, the frequency of some certain words, the statistics of the used terminology or even the structure of the entire vocabulary may form useful metrics for identifying specific writing patterns, which can be associated to humans or machines (Katsaounidou & Dimoulas, 2018). Although the same algorithmic principles (i.e. textual processing /numbering, search /computing of patterns, etc.) are used in most cases, different thresholds and adaptation mechanisms are implicated, depending on the specifications of each particular use-scenario. The configuration of the employed frameworks (i.e. ML /DL architectures and adopted topologies, NLP structures, etc.) can adjust and/or alter the operational attributes of the decision-making systems and the provided outcomes. Taking advantage of the increased computing power and the availability of dedicated datasets, the initial searching utilities of headlines, messages and keywords have been extended to more elongated corpora analyses, web crawling and parsing tasks, and beyond (Bock, 2011; Boididou et al., 2017; Diamantopoulos, Roth, Symeonidis, & Klein, 2017; Mendoza, Poblete, & Castillo, 2010; Roth, Diamantopoulos, Klein, & Symeonidis, 2014; Zubiaga & Ji, 2014). Overall, text-driven processes can extract useful information regarding the origin and the semantics behind the news-stories /articles, as well as correlations with other sources and users, thus providing the "fingerprints" of the associated instances. There are also the active or double-sided approaches (described next), in which the primary /root reports contain "digital signatures" as security measures, that are usually invisible to the consumers, i.e. watermarks, active fingerprints, etc. (Ho & Li, 2015; Katsaounidou & Dimoulas, 2018).

Moving forward to the currently pursued and more demanding cases of audiovisual content (i.e. photos, audio recordings and video sequences), the above-implied categorization exists, classifying the implicated techniques into two major categories: the active and the passive approaches. The former, which enclose digital watermarks, signatures, etc., are further indexed as full-reference (FR) and reduced-reference (RR) methodologies, depending on the types of the provided source material (Mulla & Bevinamarad, 2017). FR is implied when both the original and the tampered versions are fully available to detect manipulations (through direct comparisons), while RR is considered in circumstances that, instead of the previous two sources, tampering is detected by the combination of the available material and the associated signatures. However, the disadvantage of these methods is that they require some processing, during the production, for creating and embedding the distinctive "content signatures", which is not the typical case for the most capturing devices, e.g. the watermarking processes can destroy image quality (Qureshi & Deriche, 2015). In passive or blind procedures, the only available information is the digital item itself, supposed to be the authentic material (Mulla & Bevinamarad, 2017). In these cases, though the tampering is invisible, the researchers assume that altering operations transform the statistical properties of the original media assets /resources, so that proper feature extraction can reveal these changes (Qureshi & Deriche, 2015).

Redi, Taktak and Dugelay (2010) in their manual "A booklet for beginners" define two main strategies of Digital Image Forensics (DIF). The first utilizes "capturing metadata" related to the recording devices (if they are available) and exploits them for detecting potential contradictions. The second group of methods aims at finding semantic manipulation traces, by studying irregularities in the physical image. Hany Farid (2009) classifies these latter techniques into five basic categories, regarding the data they handle:

1. Pixel-based techniques search for cloning, resampling, splicing and general altering processes at the pixel level (i.e. statistical changes in the image histograms, etc.).
2. Format-based techniques evaluate the attributes of the used encoding standards, looking for possible differences in the thresholding levels that are applied during compression (JPEG quantization, double JPEG, JPEG Blocking, etc.).
3. Camera-based techniques search for inconsistencies in the associated capturing patterns, which could be attributed to different devices (i.e. chromatic aberration, color filter array-CFA, camera response, sensor noise, device fingerprints, etc.).
4. Physics-based techniques analyze the three-dimensional interactions between physical objects, lights, and cameras (i.e. 2D/3D light directions).
5. Geometry-based techniques apply image transformations for projecting the visual information into the reconstructed geometrical space, where specific parameters, concerning the relative placements of objects and lens, can be further evaluated (i.e. principal point, metric measurements, etc.).

Moving to the field of audio forensics, their initial /traditional objective was to determine the integrity of the captured /stored sound signals, relying on the analogue magnetic recording footprints (head switching transients, mechanical splices, overdubbing signatures, etc.) (Owen, 1996; Begault, Brustad, & Stanley, 2005; Boss, 2010; Malik, 2013). Other methods monitor the electrical network frequency (ENF) as an identification metric /footprint (Grigoras, 2007; Cooper, 2008). Overall, by utilizing features related to the recording devices or the changes in the situated acoustic environment (background noise inconsistencies, reverberation, etc.), researchers can export interesting conclusions concerning data integrity (Buchholz, Kraetzer, & Dittmann, 2009; Garcia-Romero & Espy-Wilson, 2010; Katsaounidou et al., 2016; Kraetzer, Oermann, Dittmann, & Lang, 2007; Kurniawan, Khalil, & Malik, 2015; Malik, 2013; Malik & Farid, 2010). Nowadays, editing and processing software offer the ability to apply diverse "shaping" operations, without leaving "visual traces". Therefore, recording-based assessment has rather became obsolete, so the investigation of other methods turned out to be a necessity. In specific, novelty detection, pattern analysis and overall semantic processing approaches have emerged, trying to locate unexpected transitions in the appearance of various patterns (i.e. detection of speech, music and noise events, speakers' succession, thematic /emotional categories, etc.). In lower level analysis, waveforms and spectrograms can be used to reveal these irregular altering points (Gupta, Cho, & Kuo, 2012). Another distinguished methodology, initially deployed in the case of photos, is the detection of different compression levels as an indicator of multiple sources, thus leading to the advancement of compression-driven methods (Malik, 2013; Gupta et al., 2012; Ho & Li, 2015). The field of audio forensics requires expertise in a variety of complementary fields, such as acoustics, electroacoustics and digital signal processing. Thus, despite the progress that has been achieved, there is a lack of methods and "real world" tools, available and comprehensible to the non-knowledgeable and not adequately equipped average user.

Currently, research about multimedia tampering detection has turned its focus on digital images and motion pictures. The usefulness of video (i.e. in education, medicine, documentaries, infotainment and many other fields) is directly proportional to its composite nature (i.e. it combines multiple photos /frames and audio tracks), therefore to its enhanced vividness / representativeness, key elements that resemble the natural audiovisual communication of human beings. However, the previous advantages come along with a more demanding character concerning all factors, such as storage demands, encoding and compression complexities, processing difficulties or even computing power that is needed for proper decoding during reproduction /play. These matters can be used to justify the relative delay in the appearance of associated digital forgery operations, as well as on the implementation of the corresponding revealing algorithms. The most popular cases of tampering include frame cropping and repetition of specific scenes, ordering to conceal valuable information (i.e. important visual objects, subtitles and logos that provide the source of the footage, etc.). Video manipulation refers to the change of the content by inserting or hiding items that do not exist in the authentic captures. These "shaping adjustments" are usually applied at different viewing scales, i.e. at scene-, shot-, frame-, block- or pixel-level (Christian & Sheth, 2016). According to Mulla and Bevinamarad (2017) video manipulation strategies can be grouped into the following three categories (Yin & Hong, 2001; Upadhyay & Singh, 2012):

1. Spatial tampering that adds, deletes, crops or replaces image regions and blocks of pixels, at the frame level.
2. Temporal tampering that forgers the frame sequence by adding, deleting, or rearranging the order of the scenes, as depicted in Figure 1.
3. Spatio-temporal tampering that refers to the combination of the above two methods, in which both spatial (image) and temporal (motion) modifications take place.

Besides the above content-based passive approaches, similarly to the photos and audio recordings cases, active /double-sided methods also exist, where camera coding detection can be used for the identification of specific fingerprints that are connected to distinct devices (Hsu, Hung, Lin, & Hsu, 2008). Particularly, source class, like model type, brand, sensor, etc., can be recognized by analyzing the visual content and/or its accompanying metadata, so that capturing signatures are provided. Again, forgery detection alerts are triggered when trails of more than one device are encountered within a single footage, implying that the sequence has been edited with multi-source material (Popescu & Farid, 2005; Kot & Cao, 2013; Al-Sanjary & Sulong, 2015). However, as already explained in the previous categories of photos and audio, "active methods" have some prerequisites that may not always be met, hence, making passive approaches more important and challenging. The argued significance is justified on the global character of their appliance (i.e. they can be utilized in all situations, without requiring extra information besides the stream under examination). Analogously, the claimed interesting and demanding attributes are rationalized to the arisen difficulties, as well as to the anticipated resourcefulness and sophistication of the pursued /under development algorithms. While reviewing the recent scientific publications in this research area, Yang, Huang, and Su (2016) proposed a new technique for detecting frame duplication through similarity analysis, while Saxena, Subramanyam, and Ravi (2016) focused on the temporal localization of copy-paste inpaintings. Su, Huang, and Yang (2015) introduced a compressive sensing procedure for estimating the deletion of moving objects, which are substituted with background information from the surrounding areas. Tralic,

Grgic, and Zovko-Cihlar (2014) presented a method for copy-move frame detection, relying on cellular automata and local binary patterns. This process can additionally find duplicated frames, by inspecting their similarities within the monitoring timeline. Subramanyam & Emmanuel (2013) developed a pixel-wise tampering localization strategy, through the presence of possible double quantization, deriving from dual compression setups. Chao, Jiang, and Sun (2013) have worked on the discovery of inter-frame altering operations, based on the Lucas Kanade optical flow consistency (i.e. frame addition or deletion will affect the motion flow vectors). Kancherla and Mukkamala (2012) used a different predictive approach (Markov models) for the video motion estimation, along with a final ML-based pattern recognition layer. Innumerous other works have been conducted featuring different motivation and emphasis: i.e. on temporal and spatial copy-paste (Subramanyam & Emmanuel, 2012); on blind feature-based assessment and fusion (Goodwin & Chetty, 2011); on motion-compensated edge artifacts inspection at various frames (Su, Zhang, & Liu, 2009), etc. Likewise, correlation approaches, between, either the noise characteristics and residues (Hsu et al., 2008; Kobayashi, Okabe, & Sato, 2009), or the frequency components (Porter, Mirmehdi, & Thomas, 2000), managed to identify a variety of manipulations. In other occasions, the analysis focuses on the differences between interlaced and de-interlaced videos (Wang & Farid, 2007).

Figure 1. Categorization of the encountered multimedia forgery operations for each content type (i.e. text, audio, image, video) and indicative algorithmic verification principles

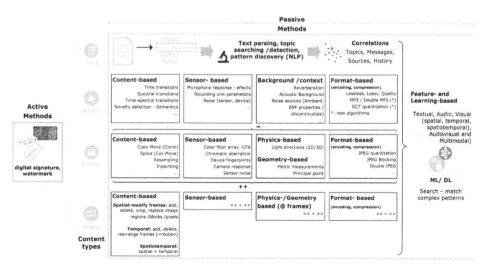

Based on the above review, it becomes clear that the list of the different algorithmic approaches and their configurations with respect to the various multimedia forgeries, is literally endless and goes far back in time (especially for the case of photo forensics). The previously discussed categorization and the main principles of each approach are depicted in Figure 1. The reader who desires a detailed presentation and in-depth comprehension of the different methods can refer to corresponding review articles (Al-Sanjary & Sulong, 2015; Gupta et al., 2012; Mahdian & Saic, 2007; Maher, 2010; Mizher, Ang, Mazhar, & Mizher, 2017; Mulla & Bevinamarad, 2017; Qureshi & Deriche, 2015; Thajeel & Sulong, 2013). Furthermore, from the number and the alternative directions of the published papers, it can be noted that research on these areas is very active, anticipating the realization of far more scientific accomplishments, shortly. On the contrary, along with the technological advancement and the progress of the authentication methods, the field of counter-forensics (or anti-forensics) also evolves, aiming at concealing the forgery tracks, thus making harder the proper forensic investigation (Katsaounidou & Dimoulas, 2018; Stamm, Lin, & Liu, 2012). Overall, it can be supported that, even for the listing and superficial review of the above-outlined categories, essential knowledge and understanding of the underlying technical principles is required for being able to distinguish and/or to interpret the main differences. Similar knowhow is needed for operating such tools, i.e. for properly configuring their working parameters and for elucidating the provided results. Unfortunately, very few of the presented paradigms have turned out to be usable and easy to operate practical applications, whereas the majority of the achieved research outcomes are still of no use for the average journalist. The next section provides an overview of the currently available tools, attempting to indicate their expansion and combined implementation towards integrated and collaborative solutions.

SOLUTIONS AND RECOMMENDATIONS

Automated Verification Toolsets

Considering the current state of real-world services, SNSs seem unable to address the proliferation of misinformation propagation on their platforms substantively. As already supported, the framework for addressing the misinformation phenomenon encloses heavily technical challenges, which are related to the algorithmic perspectives of the involved methods. Thus, along with the journalistic fact-checking, new features need to be discovered for detecting fake content and revealing the truth, aiming at reaching decisive problem-facing towards prosperous solutions. Encompassing all the above approaches (i.e. ML /DL and NLP applied for multilevel pattern recognition and multimedia semantics), cognitive computing takes on as a key-factor, favoring the wanted sophistication and integration. Cognitive apps are platforms focusing on contextual understanding and conceptualization of the various news items, purposing to come to conclusions through logical steps, easily comprehended by human beings. A simple example of such software is the B.S. Detector[5], offered as a browser extension and powered by OpenSources[6], intending to keep and update a professionally curated list of unreliable or otherwise questionable sources. B.S Detector operates as source classifier (i.e. domain name), categorizing the media sites to fake-news, satire, extreme bias, conspiracy theory, rumor mill, state news, junk science, hate group, clickbait, proceed with caution, etc. At this moment, the repository[7] of OpenSources has a tiny number of entries (834), if we consider the billions of sites online. The optimal utilization of the above tool could be ensured by checking and rating, if possible, all the webpages worldwide, a process that is thought as unfeasible, for the time being. Another web-based service is "The Tweet Verification Assistant[8]", a tool that evaluates the veracity of a tweet, by analyzing multiple (textual mainly) parameters, i.e. language, punctuation, number of hashtags, mentions and external links, as well as multimedia content (attached or connected). However, reading and identifying a specific article as fake, does not necessarily entails that all the pieces of information contained to this site are untrue (Fan, 2017). Still, ranking measures and further /optional filtering of the top popular sources (i.e. concerning county /location, topic, etc.) could offer more thorough credibility assessment insights, which may have significant added-value results.

Other browser add-ons are trying to solve misinformation indirectly, by seeking for the starting point and/or possible copying and altering operations along the history of the various streams. For instance, "TinEye Reverse Image Search"[9] and "Search by Image (by Google)"[10] allow users to monitor the origin of a picture and its past use, or even to find multiple matching versions, with possible higher resolution. While these approaches evaluate all the available information (i.e. content-features, keywords, semantic tags, etc.), there are also utilities that are explicitly relying on metadata processing. Specifically, "Send to Exif Viewer"[11] enhances the contextual framework by inspecting visual parts /entities in a metadata viewer (EXIF), which provides valuable information about the source of the photos (i.e. time, location, indication of processing by specific software, capturing parameters like shutter speed, exposure, F-number, etc.). Moving one step further, the "Image Tools"[12] is an extension that adds several context menu items (i.e. "Jeffrey's Exif Viewer"[13], "Metapicz online metadata Exif viewer"[14], "TinEye Reverse Image Search", "Google Search by Image" and others), which offer diverse metadata-driven image searching and retrieval mechanisms (e.g. "SauceNAO Image Search"[15], "Multi-service image search"[16] etc.). Going closer to the core of the problem, "Snopes Searcher"[17] allows users to highlight text and search for potential matches with popular /listed rumors (debunked Snopes). Likewise, "Instant Snopes Checker (Unofficial)"[18] checks the title and the keywords of a page within the records of the official "Snopes.com' site, thus making a simple and easy to operate browser addon. Specialized web interfaces are also available through online/free platforms dealing with most of the image forgery problems and techniques. Notable examples are the Forensically[19], created by Jonas Wagner, the "Media Verification Assistant"[20], implemented in the framework of the REVEAL project[21], and other environments like Ghiro[22], Imageforensic.org[23], Fotoforensics[24], etc. Fewer efforts are related to the case of motion pictures, such as the InVID Project[25], which aims at detecting, checking and authenticating newsworthy video material, spread through social media, thus exporting credibility marks. Recently, InVID has released its "fake video news debunker"[26] browser extension, providing the code in open source, under MIT license. Table 1 summarizes the most popular /worth mentioning veracity assistance tools, including the above-described, grouping them by the content they examine, so that the perception of the whole picture in this matter could be better served.

Skipping the philosophical debate about the efficiency of each addressing method, researchers and media professionals seem to agree that the most effective way to debunk the fake stories is with the help of fact-checking sites (i.e. Snopes.com, Buzzfeed.com, Politifact.com, Factcheck.org, Truthfiction. com, etc.). However, these services, analyzed in the previous chapter (Verification by humans), are not applicable when it comes to breaking news, because of the needed time to select and investigate a topic. Therefore, automations provided by machine-driven solutions are still considered to form an essential part, which can be really helpful in the future, subjected to their further advancement and testing in practice. Since most of the available tools do offer different /complementary views and evaluation outcomes, relying on a single authentication method and/or source can be considered utterly inadequate. Though the combination of multiple algorithms and procedures can propel the accuracy of the composite forgery detection results, technical and operational difficulties concerning interoperability and unification of the individual modalities need to be resolved before the materialization of the envisioned integration (Katsaounidou & Dimoulas, 2018).

To better illustrate the current state of the art and the research efforts that are being made in this area, three popular machine-driven platforms will be more thoroughly presented, namely Forensically, "Media Verification Assistance" and InVID. The former two focuses on photo-forensics, with Forensically being one of the initial efforts for verifying images trustworthiness, probably the most notable one. InVID can be thought as a pioneering venture in the more demanding area of video integrity evaluation, where integration with REVEAL (Media Verification Assistance) is pursued. Forensically, is a web environment that contains a set of free services for digital image forensics, namely clone detection, error level analysis, metadata extraction, and more. The simplest utility is the Magnifier tool, which enlarges the pixels of an image, allowing the more thorough inspection of a selected area, so that hidden details, likely connected to forgery trails, could be revealed (Figure 2a). Another function is the Clone Detection that allows the discovery of possible duplicated areas within a picture, using superimposed color indications (Figure 2b). Error Level Analysis compares the original image (under inspection) with its decompressed version, targeting to display areas with different noising patterns that might suggest potential forgery (Figure 2c).

Another essential technique is applied by the "Noise Analysis" function, which operates flipside from the classical de-noising goal, i.e. instead of removing the image noise, it isolates the estimated noise. Hence, the specific algorithm reveals noise inconsistences, thus it can be useful for detecting manipulations such as aerographs and distortions (Figure 3a). The "Level Sweep" process investigates different parts of the illumination values, allowing the quick sweep through the image-histogram that exposes the contrast of certain brightness levels (Figure 3b). Moving one step further, "Luminance Gradient" is based on the assumption that similar color should be observed in the parts of a photo under similar illumination (i.e. when they face light sources at similar angles /distances). As depicted in Figure 3c, its purpose is to find anomalies while inspecting the formed edges. Considering that similar edges should have comparable spatial transitions, if the gradients at one edge are significantly sharper than the rest, this can be taken as a sign that parts of the image could have been copy-pasted.

Table 1. An overview of user-friendly services, platforms and tools, classified respectively to their investigated multimedia elements and dissemination channels

Channels	Elements	Platforms and Tools
WWW Facebook, Google+ Twitter Instagram, Pinterest, Tumblr	Text	Dbpedia[27] Hoaxy[28] Instant Snopes Checker (Unofficial- Google Chrome Plugin) Snopes Searcher (Google Chrome Plugin) Tweet Verification Assistant TweetCred[29] (Google Chrome Plugin) Twitter Trails[30]
WWW Facebook, Google+, Twitter	Audio	EdiTracker[31] (Google Chrome Plugin) FIAS - Forensic Image Analysis System[32]
WWW Facebook, Google+, Twitter Instagram, Pinterest, Tumblr Messenger, Viber, Snapchat, Whats App	Image	eyewitnessproject.org[33] Forensically fotoforensics.com Ghiro Google Reverse Image Search Image Verification Assistant Izitru.com[34] tineye.com
WWW Facebook, Google+, Twitter Instagram, Pinterest, Tumblr	Video	InVID Project (Google Chrome Plugin-Fake video debunker)
WWW E-Mail, Newsletter Facebook, Google+, Twitter Instagram, Pinterest, Tumblr Messenger, Viber, Snapchat, Whats App	Tags (all applicable metadata)	Image Tools (Google Chrome Plugin) Jeffrey's Image Metadata Viewer Metapicz online metadata Exif viewer Multi-service image search- iqdb.org SauceNAO Image Search
WWW E-Mail, Newsletter Facebook, Google+, Twitter Instagram, Pinterest, Tumblr Messenger, Viber, Snapchat, Whats App	Source / Account	B.S Detector (Google Chrome Plugin) Pipl.com[35] Webmii[36] Wolframalpha[37] WOT: Web of Trust[38] (Google Chrome Plugin)

Elements: Text, Audio, Image, Video, Tags (all applicable metadata), Source /Account

Channels: WWW, E-Mail /Newsletter, Facebook /Google+, Twitter, Instagram/ Pinterest /Tumblr, Messenger /Viber / Snapchat /Whats App

Figure 2. Forensically tools: a. magnifier, b. clone detection, c. error level analysis

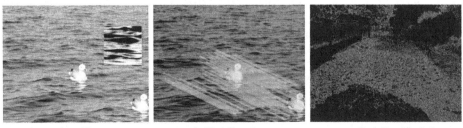

a. Magnifier   b. Clone Detection   c. Error Level Analysis

Figure 3. Forensically tools: a. Noise Analysis, b. Level Sweep, c. Luminance Gradient

a. Noise Analysis   b. Level Sweep   c. Luminance Gradient

"Principal Component Analysis" (Figure 4a) provides a different point of view, aiming at revealing specific manipulations through the more straightforward observation /indication of the projected details. Moreover, various metadata and geo-tag reading utilities (Figure 4b, 4c) can detect invisible in naked eye EXIF meta-information, which can be exploited in the detection of context- and location-aware inconsistencies (provided that these labels have been stored in the image files).

"Thumbnail Analysis" (Figure 5a) uncovers possible thumbnails /preview data that are hidden inside the original photo, which can reveal aspects about the original image and/or information related to the recording device. Moreover, relying on the fact that the most common /popular compression is the JPEG format, specialized "JPEG Analysis" can be applied for extracting EXIF metadata (even in the cases that such data were not saved in the first place), thus providing complementary evaluation insights (Figure 5b). Finally, "String Extraction" scans the image for binary content (i.e. looking

Figure 4. Forensically tools: a. Principal Component Analysis, b. Metadata inspector, c. Geotags (i.e. GPS-related information)

a. Principal Component Analysis   b. Metadata Inspector   . GPS-Related Information

Figure 5. Forensically tools: a. Thumbnail Analysis, b. JPEG Analysis, c. String Extraction

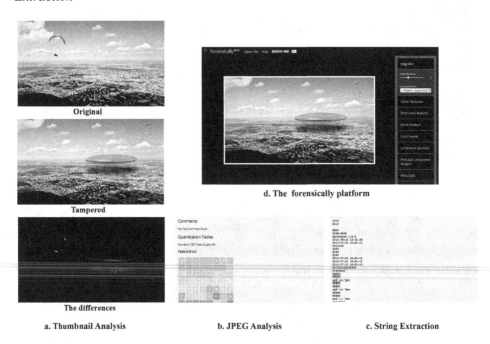

Original

Tampered

The differences

d. The forensically platform

a. Thumbnail Analysis   b. JPEG Analysis   c. String Extraction

for sequences of ASCII characters) which can be further exploited in the end-to-end contextual evaluation (Figure 5c).

As mentioned before, there are further initiatives following the efforts of the above platform. The most notable one is the "Media Verification Assistant", which is a set of free tools for digital image forensics, built by software engineers and researchers from CERTH-ITI[21] with the valuable cooperation of Deutsche Welle journalists. The platform features a multitude of image tampering detection techniques, including most of the already presented evaluation principles (i.e. noise, compression quantization /blocks, etc.), metadata analysis (GPS Geolocation, EXIF Thumbnail extraction, etc.), as well as integration with the Google reverse image search. Figure 6 provides an overview of the implemented services and their involvement in the different forgery operations. According to the shown diagram, some methods are best suited for detecting "object-wise" tampering operations and others for "image-wise" manipulations. For instance, the "Double JPEG quantization (DP)" evaluates the statistical inconsistencies at the compression level, as it is depicted in Figure 7, for a typical cloning /copy-move scenario. Particularly, the original JPEG document is initially compressed at a quality (A), and then an area is inserted into it (uncompressed, lower or higher quality). Following the applied processing, file saving triggers a recompression process, probably at a different quality (B). Hence, the image will have endured two compression levels, an issue that would probably leave some processing trails. Table 2 provides an overview of the tampering detection algorithms that are part of the "Media Verification Assistant"[20] platform (REVEAL project)[21], the web environment of which is presented in Figure 7, in a typical analysis example.

As already implied, video is considered as the most challenging forgery detection category, both due to the power, concerning mediated communication capabilities, and the involved difficulties. Hence, it worth mentioning the case of the InVID work, a pioneering effort in the demanding area of video

Figure 6. "Media Verification Assistant" algorithms and their use in the most common image manipulation operations

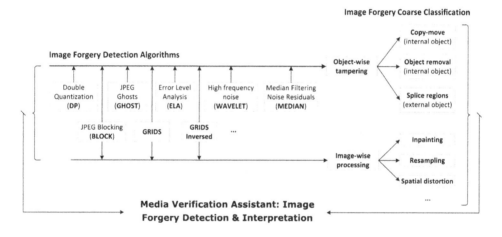

Figure 7. A typical scenario of clone forgery and the indications of the "Media Verification Assistant", while using "Double JPEG quantization (DP)"

121

Figure 8. The "Media Verification Assistant" environment (REVEAL project), presenting the analysis of an image tampering example by all the implemented algorithms

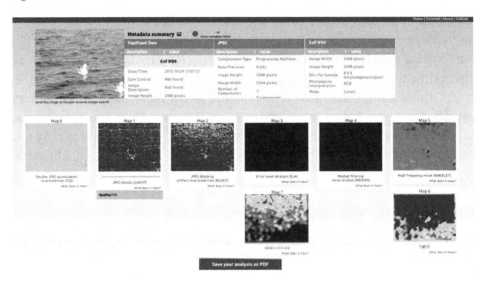

Table 2. Overview of the algorithms of the "Media Verification Assistant"[20] platform (REVEAL project)[21]

JPEG-Ghosts	This algorithm recompresses the JPEG image at all possible qualities (65-100%) and subtracts every produced image from the original, to generate a locally smaller difference.
Error Level Analysis	This algorithm removes the questionable recompressed version of JPEG image from the image itself. In contrary to "JPEG Ghosts", only a single version of the image is subtracted (quality 75%) to display areas with different noise patterns, which might pinpoint the potential falsification.
High Frequency Noise -Wavelets	This algorithm utilizes 2D Wavelet Transform to separate the image into multiple scales /levels. Then, it searches for significant /localized visual variances, based on the assumption that images with differentiated histories will feature dissimilar patterns of invisible high-frequency noise (i.e. due to different capturing devices, add-on image filters and other processing, compression, etc.).
Median Noise Residuals	This algorithm also relies on the expectation of altered high-frequency noise patterns, because of the tampering operations. Median filtering is applied as a mean for isolating noise and the filtered versions are subtracted from the original one. Thus, if areas of similar content exhibit different intensity residues, it is likely that the specific region has been originated from a different image source. As noise is generally an unreliable estimator of tampering, the specific algorithm should be considered valuable in confirming the output of other descriptors, rather than as an independent detector.
JPEG blocking	This algorithm investigates the appearance of artifacts related to JPEG block inconsistencies, seeking for traces that have been left during the procedures of splicing, copy-moving or inpainting.
GRIDS (and GRIDS-inversed)	The specific technique tries to locate grid alignment abnormalities in a JPEG compressed image, as an indicator of possible forgery. GRIDS-inversed is used in cases where tampering discontinuities appear as areas of averagely higher contribution, following an inverse mechanism, compared to GRIDS.

integrity evaluation. Funded by the European Union (Horizon 2020), the project has recently launched a plugin entitled "Fake video news debunker by InVID[39]". Upon its installation, users can be transferred to a web environment (by activating the corresponding button), where a set of services are online available, aiming at detecting, authenticating and checking the reliability and accuracy of spread newsworthy video content. InVID attempts to face the most popular cases of frame cropping and temporal processing (i.e. scenes removal, insertion, repetition, etc.), which are applied for concealing vital information (i.e. visual objects, subtitles and logos citing the footage sources, etc.). In this context, professional and citizen journalists may have valuable assistance when verifying videos and images, disseminated through SNSs, thus saving time and being more efficient in their fact-checking and debunking duties.

The interface contains a variety of tools (categorized at labels), which allows average users to get contextual information on Facebook and YouTube videos quickly. The plugin provides features that help to decompose videos (of various platforms) via key-frames extraction, so that a representational / sampled evaluation of all spatial, temporal and spatiotemporal manipulation operations can be conducted. The whole process is facilitated by various add-on functions /utilities, such as the magnifying lens for image inspection, reverse image search on related search engines, revealing visual metadata (i.e. associated with photos and motion pictures), performing Twitter queries concerning the appearance of linked multimedia content, and others. Table 3 provides an overview of the services (tabs) that are offered through the InVID environment (Figure 9), which is accessed after the activation of the corresponding plugin.

The presented tools form the current state of the art in the assisted / machine-driven multimedia veracity domain. Thus, they can be considered as automated solutions to the given problem of content and overall information authentication. As already explained and practically shown, an in-depth comprehension of the different methods and their algorithmic /operational attributes is rather necessary, in order to be familiar and confident with forensic investigation and validation processes. Therefore, proper instructions and training are urgently required, before professional journalists and average users could use these interesting services in their everyday practice. Moreover, integration and unification of the individual techniques are considered key-factors towards both the advancement and the real-world implementation of the acquired knowledge. Enhanced collaboration between researchers, journalists, professionals and various kinds of experts is truly necessary for

Table 3. Overview of the utilities (tabs) of the InVID[26] environment that are used for the purpose of video news debunking

Analysis tab	An enhanced metadata viewer for YouTube and Facebook videos that allows users to retrieve contextual information, location (if available /applicable), most interesting comments, as well as to apply reverse image search and check for tweets on the video (on YouTube).
Keyframes tab	A utility that allows user to copy a video URL (from YouTube, Twitter, Facebook, Daily Motion or Dropbox) or to upload a video file, in order to decompose it in key-frames, which can then be searched with a right click on Google, Yandex[40] and Chinese search engine Baidu[41]. The extracted key-frames are fed in the reverse image search tools, thus increasing the possibilities for finding related video.
Thumbnails tab	A service that allows users to quickly trigger a reverse image search on Google or Yandex Images with the four thumbnails, extracted from YouTube video.
Search tab	A function that allows users to perform an advanced search on Twitter for keywords or hashtags, using the "since" and "until" operators, either separately or together, to query within a time interval, up to one minute. It translates automatically the calendar date, hour and minutes into an unix timestamp to facilitate the query, e.g. of first eyewitness pictures or videos within a time range just after a breaking news event.
Magnifier tab	A tool that operates as a magnifying lens while displaying an image through its URL, thus helping to discover image-embedded information, such as written words, signs, banners, etc.
Metadata tab	A service that allows users to check the EXIF metadata of a JPEG picture, or the metadata of a video in mp4/m4v format, either through a link or through a local file upload process.
Forensic tab	An internal /i-frame opening of the "Media Verification Assistant" platform (Reveal project), which allows users to apply all the spatial /image-tampering inspection tools, mentioned before.

Figure 9. The InVID environment and its main features (tabs): a. Analysis, b. Keyframes, c. Thumbnails, d. Twitter Search, e. Magnifier, f. Metadata, g. Forensic ("Media Verification Assistant")

discovering difficulties and weaknesses, receiving useful feedback, planning system support, maintenance and updates, in favor of all the involved parties (Katsaounidou & Dimoulas, 2018). The above-listed directions can be considered as top-priority initiatives in the proposed solutions and recommendations.

CONCLUSION

The present chapter focuses on the algorithmic perspectives of media veracity and, especially, deals with machine-driven authentication solutions. Nowadays, algorithms have become a matter of public attention, having a more or less profound impact on various aspects of human life. Regarding their relation to the world of media and mass communications, these artificial systems have already entered the news-room, aiming at automating the journalistic reporting processes, in all the aspects of information covering, shaping and publishing (Singer, 2014; Belluck, 2015; Dourish, 2016). Robot journalism services have emerged, fueling fully- and semi-autonomous newsgathering (i.e. with little or no human interventions), while offering useful news alerting utilities to average users, citizen journalists and professional reporters. In this context, processing and editing of multimedia resources become easier and more efficient, even for the demanding audiovisual entities. The new computing capacities are ideal for serving modern needs of our ubiquitous society, such as the large-scale networking and exchanging of informatory data among various groups of specialists and individuals. A variety of tools and options is currently available for capturing, sharing and recreating events through digital content, in which the visual element is dominant. However, the new capabilities always bear the risk of misuse, such as in the case of intentional tampering and falsification of the news items. The above phenomenon did result in a corresponding rise in the dissemination of misleading articles and propaganda stories. While technology is partly the cause of the misinforming propagation and its unwanted consequences, computational models and algorithms can also offer the prosperous solutions for its decisive confrontation. In this framework, the field of digital forensics has been developed and is continuously elaborated ever since, aiming at exposing forgery attacks, thus helping the audience in the difficult fight against disinformation (Katsaounidou & Dimoulas, 2018).

Extending the preceding analysis, the dizzying speeds at which digital data and informing streams are spread, make it extremely difficult for traditional human-directed fact-checking processes to be fruitfully applied. Consequently, there is a turn to more sophisticated gatekeeping procedures, which could be assisted by the development of computerized automations. As already evidenced, there are several technologies for the detection of multimedia tampering based upon blind approaches (i.e. when the only accessible information is the digital item itself), a small number of which was thoroughly presented and reviewed. While every technique has its own advantages and disadvantages, it seems that different approaches are better suited in different cases. Hence, proper configuration of the planned authentication strategies, with respect to the encountered forgery operations and the available tools, is rather critical. Along with this, dedicated training and support in the use of the newfangled services seem to be equally essential. These prerequisites will facilitate easier integration and unification of all the offered cross-modal validation solutions, which could manage a decisive strike to the problem of misinformation. In conclusion, although the challenges of real-time verification intensify with the advance of social media platforms and the amount of the contributed volumes of content (i.e. UGC), marked improvements have already been achieved on individual parts of the whole process, thanks to social computing, incorporating intelligent information processing.

REFERENCES

Al-Sanjary, O. I., & Sulong, G. (2015). Detection of video forgery: A review of literature. *Journal of Theoretical & Applied Information Technology, 74*(2).

Alden, W. (2013). Separating the market-moving tweets from the chaff. *The New York Times,* p. 11.

Begault, D. R., Brustad, B. M., & Stanley, A. M. (2005, July). Tape analysis and authentication using multi-track recorders. In *Audio Engineering Society Conference: 26th International Conference: Audio Forensics in the Digital Age*. Audio Engineering Society.

Belluck, P. (2015). Chilly at work? Office formula was devised for men. *New York Times*. Available at: http://www.nytimes.com/2015/08/04/science/chilly-at-work-adecades-old-formula-may-be-to-blame.html

Bock, M. A. (2011). You really, truly, have to "be there": Video journalism as a social and material construction. *Journalism & Mass Communication Quarterly, 88*(4), 705–718. doi:10.1177/107769901108800402

Boididou, C., Middleton, S. E., Jin, Z., Papadopoulos, S., Dang-Nguyen, D. T., Boato, G., & Kompatsiaris, Y. (2017). Verifying information with multimedia content on twitter. *Multimedia Tools and Applications*, 1–27.

Boss, D. (2010, June). Visualization of magnetic features on analogue audiotapes is still an important task. In *Audio Engineering Society Conference: 39th International Conference: Audio Forensics: Practices and Challenges*. Audio Engineering Society.

Brandtzaeg, P. B., Lüders, M., Spangenberg, J., Rath-Wiggins, L., & Følstad, A. (2016). Emerging journalistic verification practices concerning social media. *Journalism Practice*, *10*(3), 323–342. doi:10.1080/17512786.2015.1020331

Buchholz, R., Kraetzer, C., & Dittmann, J. (2009). Microphone classification using Fourier coefficients. In Information hiding (pp. 235-246). Springer Berlin/Heidelberg. doi:10.1007/978-3-642-04431-1_17

Chao, J., Jiang, X., & Sun, T. (2013). A novel video inter-frame forgery model detection scheme based on optical flow consistency. In *The International Workshop on Digital Forensics and Watermarking 2012* (pp. 267-281). Springer. 10.1007/978-3-642-40099-5 22

Christian, A., & Sheth, R. (2016). Digital Video Forgery Detection and Authentication Technique-A Review. *IJSRST International Journal of Scientific Research in Science and Technology*, *2*(6), 138–143.

Cooper, A. J. (2008, June). The electric network frequency (ENF) as an aid to authenticating forensic digital audio recordings–an automated approach. In *Audio Engineering Society Conference: 33rd International Conference: Audio Forensics-Theory and Practice*. Audio Engineering Society.

Dayan, Z., & Cohen, Y. (2017). *Method for automatically transforming text into video*. U.S. Patent No. 9,607,611. Washington, DC: U.S. Patent and Trademark Office.

Diamantopoulos, T., Roth, M., Symeonidis, A., & Klein, E. (2017). Software requirements as an application domain for natural language processing. *Language Resources and Evaluation*, *51*(2), 495–524. doi:10.100710579-017-9381-z

Diplaris, S., Papadopoulos, S., Kompatsiaris, I., Goker, A., Macfarlane, A., Spangenberg, J., ... Klusch, M. (2012, April). Socialsensor: sensing user generated input for improved media discovery and experience. In *Proceedings of the 21st International Conference on World Wide Web* (pp. 243-246). ACM. 10.1145/2187980.2188020

Dourish, P. (2016). Algorithms and their others: Algorithmic culture in context. *Big Data & Society, 3*(2), 2053951716665128. doi:10.1177/2053951716665128

Fan, C. (2017). *Classifying Fake News*. Retrieved from http://www.conniefan. com/wp-content/uploads/2017/03/classifying-fake-news.pdf

Farid, H. (2009). Image forgery detection. *IEEE Signal Processing Magazine, 26*(2), 16–25. doi:10.1109/MSP.2008.931079

Garcia-Romero, D., & Espy-Wilson, C. Y. 2010, March. Automatic acquisition device identification from speech recordings. In *Acoustics Speech and Signal Processing (ICASSP), 2010 IEEE International Conference on* (pp. 1806-1809). IEEE. 10.1109/ICASSP.2010.5495407

Goodwin, J., & Chetty, G. (2011, December). Blind video tamper detection based on fusion of source features. In *Digital Image Computing Techniques and Applications (DICTA), 2011 International Conference on* (pp. 608-613). IEEE. 10.1109/DICTA.2011.108

Grigoras, C. (2007). Applications of ENF criterion in forensic audio, video, computer and telecommunication analysis. *Forensic Science International, 167*(2), 136–145. doi:10.1016/j.forsciint.2006.06.033 PMID:16884872

Gupta, S., Cho, S., & Kuo, C. C. J. (2012). Current developments and future trends in audio authentication. *IEEE MultiMedia, 19*(1), 50–59. doi:10.1109/MMUL.2011.74

Ho, A. T., & Li, S. (Eds.). (2015). *Handbook of digital forensics of multimedia data and devices*. John Wiley & Sons. doi:10.1002/9781118705773

Hsu, C. C., Hung, T. Y., Lin, C. W., & Hsu, C. T. (2008, October). Video forgery detection using correlation of noise residue. In *Multimedia Signal Processing, 2008 IEEE 10th Workshop on* (pp. 170-174). IEEE.

Kancherla, K., & Mukkamala, S. (2012, March). Novel blind video forgery detection using markov models on motion residue. In *Asian Conference on Intelligent Information and Database Systems* (pp. 308-315). Springer. 10.1007/978-3-642-28493-9_33

Katsaounidou, A., Vryzas, N., Kotsakis, R., & Dimoulas, C. 2016, October. Audio-Based Digital Content Authentication. *Proceedings of the 8th Greek National Conference "Acoustics 2016"*. (in Greek)

Katsaounidou, A. N., & Dimoulas, C. A. (2018). Integrating Content Authentication Support in Media Services. In Encyclopedia of Information Science and Technology, Fourth Edition (pp. 2908-2919). IGI Global. doi:10.4018/978-1-5225-2255-3.ch254

Kobayashi, M., Okabe, T., & Sato, Y. (2009). Detecting video forgeries based on noise characteristics. Advances in image and video technology, 306-317.

Kot, A. C., & Cao, H. (2013). Image and video source class identification. In *Digital Image Forensics* (pp. 157–178). Springer New York. doi:10.1007/978-1-4614-0757-7_5

Kraetzer, C., Oermann, A., Dittmann, J., & Lang, A. 2007, September. Digital audio forensics: a first practical evaluation on microphone and environment classification. In *Proceedings of the 9th workshop on Multimedia & security* (pp. 63-74). ACM. 10.1145/1288869.1288879

Kurniawan, F., Khalil, M. S., & Malik, H. (2015). Robust tampered detection method for digital audio using gabor filterbank. *Proc. ICIPCS*, 75-82.

Liu, M.H., & Xu, W.H. (2011). Detection of copy-move forgery image based on fractal and statistics. *Journal of Computer Applications, 8*, 61.

Mahdian, B., & Saic, S. (2007). Detection of copy–move forgery using a method based on blur moment invariants. *Forensic Science International, 171*(2), 180–189. doi:10.1016/j.forsciint.2006.11.002 PMID:17161569

Maher, R. (2010). *Overview of audio forensics.* Intelligent Multimedia Analysis for Security Applications.

Malik, H. (2013). Acoustic environment identification and its applications to audio forensics. *IEEE Transactions on Information Forensics and Security, 8*(11), 1827–1837. doi:10.1109/TIFS.2013.2280888

Malik, H. (2013). Acoustic environment identification and its applications to audio forensics. *IEEE Transactions on Information Forensics and Security, 8*(11), 1827–1837. doi:10.1109/TIFS.2013.2280888

Malik, H., & Farid, H. (2010, March). Audio forensics from acoustic reverberation. In *Acoustics Speech and Signal Processing (ICASSP), 2010 IEEE International Conference on* (pp. 1710-1713). IEEE. 10.1109/ICASSP.2010.5495479

Mendoza, M., Poblete, B., & Castillo, C. (2010, July). Twitter Under Crisis: Can we trust what we RT? In *Proceedings of the first workshop on social media analytics* (pp. 71-79). ACM. 10.1145/1964858.1964869

Menezes, A. J., Van Oorschot, P. C., & Vanstone, S. A. (1996). *Handbook of applied cryptography*. CRC press. doi:10.1201/9781439821916

Mizher, M. A., Ang, M. C., Mazhar, A. A., & Mizher, M. A. (2017). A review of video falsifying techniques and video forgery detection techniques. *International Journal of Electronic Security and Digital Forensics*, 9(3), 191–208. doi:10.1504/IJESDF.2017.085196

Mulla, M.U. & Bevinamarad, P.R. (2017). *Review of Techniques for the Detection of Passive Video Forgeries*. Academic Press.

Newman, N. (2016). *Journalism, media and technology predictions 2016*. Retrieved from https://ora.ox.ac.uk/objects/uuid:f15fac34-bafb-4883-898c-a53ade027e32

Owen, T. (1996). AES recommended practice for forensic purposes-managing recorded audio materials intended for examination. *Journal of the Audio Engineering Society*, 44(4), 275.

Popescu, A. C., & Farid, H. (2005). Exposing digital forgeries in color filter array interpolated images. *IEEE Transactions on Signal Processing*, 53(10), 3948–3959. doi:10.1109/TSP.2005.855406

Porter, S. V., Mirmehdi, M., & Thomas, B. T. (2000). Video cut detection using frequency domain correlation. In *Pattern Recognition, 2000. Proceedings. 15th International Conference on*(Vol. 3, pp. 409-412). IEEE. 10.1109/ICPR.2000.903571

Qureshi, M. A., & Deriche, M. (2015). A bibliography of pixel-based blind image forgery detection techniques. *Signal Processing Image Communication*, 39, 46–74. doi:10.1016/j.image.2015.08.008

Roth, M., Diamantopoulos, T., Klein, E., & Symeonidis, A. (2014, June). Software requirements: A new domain for semantic parsers. *Proceedings of the ACL 2014 Workshop on Semantic Parsing*, 50-54. 10.3115/v1/W14-2410

Saxena, S., Subramanyam, A. V., & Ravi, H. (2016, November). Video inpainting detection and localization using inconsistencies in optical flow. In Region 10 Conference (TENCON), 2016 IEEE (pp. 1361-1365). IEEE. doi:10.1109/TENCON.2016.7848236

Schwartz, R., Naaman, M., & Teodoro, R. (2015, April). Editorial Algorithms: Using Social Media to Discover and Report Local News. ICWSM, 407-415.

Silverman, C. (Ed.). (2013). *Verification handbook*. European Journalism Centre.

Singer, N. (2014). The scoreboards where you can't see your score. *New York Times*. Available at: http:// www.nytimes.com/2014/12/28/technology/the-scoreboards-where-you-cant-see-your-score.html

Stamm, M. C., Lin, W. S., & Liu, K. R. (2012). Temporal forensics and anti-forensics for motion compensated video. *IEEE Transactions on Information Forensics and Security*, *7*(4), 1315–1329. doi:10.1109/TIFS.2012.2205568

Su, L., Huang, T., & Yang, J. (2015). A video forgery detection algorithm based on compressive sensing. *Multimedia Tools and Applications*, *74*(17), 6641–6656. doi:10.100711042-014-1915-4

Su, Y., Zhang, J., & Liu, J. (2009, December). Exposing digital video forgery by detecting motion-compensated edge artifact. In *Computational Intelligence and Software Engineering, 2009. CiSE 2009. International Conference on* (pp. 1-4). IEEE. 10.1109/CISE.2009.5366884

Subramanyam, A. V., & Emmanuel, S. (2012, September). Video forgery detection using HOG features and compression properties. In *Multimedia Signal Processing (MMSP), 2012 IEEE 14th International Workshop on* (pp. 89-94). IEEE. 10.1109/MMSP.2012.6343421

Subramanyam, A. V., & Emmanuel, S. (2013, May). Pixel estimation based video forgery detection. In *Acoustics, Speech and Signal Processing (ICASSP), 2013 IEEE International Conference on* (pp. 3038-3042). IEEE. 10.1109/ICASSP.2013.6638216

Thajeel, S. A., & Sulong, G. B. (2013). State of the art of copy-move forgery detection techniques: A review. *International Journal of Computer Science Issues*, *10*(6), 174183.

Tralic, D., Grgic, S., & Zovko-Cihlar, B. (2014, October). Video frame copy-move forgery detection based on Cellular Automata and Local Binary Patterns. In *Telecommunications (BIHTEL), 2014 X International Symposium on* (pp. 1-4). IEEE. 10.1109/BIHTEL.2014.6987651

Upadhyay, S., & Singh, S. K. (2012). Video authentication: Issues and challenges. *International Journal of Computational Science*, *9*(1-3), 409–418.

Wang, W., & Farid, H. (2006, September). Exposing digital forgeries in video by detecting double MPEG compression. In *Proceedings of the 8th workshop on Multimedia and security* (pp. 37-47). ACM. 10.1145/1161366.1161375

Wang, W., & Farid, H. (2007). Exposing digital forgeries in interlaced and deinterlaced video. *IEEE Transactions on Information Forensics and Security*, 2(3), 438–449. doi:10.1109/TIFS.2007.902661

Woolley, S. C., & Howard, P. N. (2017). *Computational propaganda worldwide: Executive summary*. Working Paper 2017.11. Oxford Internet Institute.

Yang, J., Huang, T., & Su, L. (2016). Using similarity analysis to detect frame duplication forgery in videos. *Multimedia Tools and Applications*, 75(4), 1793–1811. doi:10.100711042-014-2374-7

Yin, P., & Hong, H. Y. (2001, November). Classification of video tampering methods and countermeasures using digital watermarking. In *ITCom 2001: International Symposium on the Convergence of IT and Communications* (pp. 239-246). International Society for Optics and Photonics. 10.1117/12.448208

Zubiaga, A., & Ji, H. (2014). Tweet, but verify: Epistemic study of information verification on twitter. *Social Network Analysis and Mining*, 4(1), 163. doi:10.100713278-014-0163-y

KEY TERMS AND DEFINITIONS

ASCII (American Standard Code for Information Interchange): A character encoding standard for electronic communication. ASCII codes represent text in computers, telecommunications equipment, and other devices.

Cellular Automation: A discrete model studied in computability theory, mathematics, physics, complexity science, theoretical biology, and microstructure modeling.

Deep Learning Approaches: Supervised, partially supervised or unsupervised deep structured learning or hierarchical learning is a part of a broader family of machine learning methods based on learning data representations, as opposed to task-specific algorithms.

Digital Image Forensics (DIF): This field emerged as a sub-field of digital image processing (DIP), aiming at providing tools for images tampering investigation.

Digital Signature: A digital signature is a mathematical technique used to validate the authenticity and integrity of a message, software or digital document.

Digital Watermark: A digital watermark is data embedded into digital intellectual property (IP) to identify its originator or owner.

Local Binary Patterns (LBP): A type of visual descriptor used for classification in computer vision.

Machine Learning: A scientific discipline that investigates algorithms and methods aiming at giving machines the ability to learn from experience (without being explicitly programed), in order to respond autonomously on specific tasks and automate various data-handling processes.

Markov Model: A stochastic model used to model randomly changing systems, where it is assumed that future states depend only on the current state, not on the events that occurred before it.

ENDNOTES

[1] See http://www.wibbitz.com/

[2] See https://www.samdesk.io/

[3] See https://www.dataminr.com/

[4] See http://www.socialsensor.eu/

[5] See https://github.com/selfagency/bs-detector

[6] See http://www.opensources.co/

[7] See https://github.com/BigMcLargeHuge/opensources

[8] See http://reveal-mklab.iti.gr/reveal/fake/

[9] See https://chrome.google.com/webstore/detail/tineye-reverse-image-sear/haebnnbpedcbhciplfhjjkbafijpncjl

[10] See https://chrome.google.com/webstore/detail/search-by-image-by-google/dajedkncpodkggklbegccjpmnglmnflm

[11] See https://chrome.google.com/webstore/detail/send-to-exif-viewer/gogiienhpamfmodmlnhdljokkjiapfck

[12] See https://chrome.google.com/webstore/detail/image-tools/jfhlbnfopnonplmphdkpphhakfplfjbp

[13] See http://exif.regex.info/exif.cgi

[14] See http://metapicz.com/#landing

[15] See https://saucenao.com/

[16] See https://www.iqdb.org/

[17] See https://chrome.google.com/webstore/detail/snopes-searcher/candgpmgkohdbipkdeoghbginhbbifam

[18] See https://chrome.google.com/webstore/detail/instant-snopes-checker-un/bbddjfjhfnafgfncmlbenehgionllfno

[19] See https://29a.ch/photo-forensics/#forensic-magnifier

[20] See http://reveal-mklab.iti.gr/reveal/

[21] See https://revealproject.eu/

[22] See http://www.getghiro.org/

[23] See http://www.imageforensic.org/

[24] See http://fotoforensics.com/

[25] See http://www.invid-project.eu/

[26] See https://chrome.google.com/webstore/detail/fake-video-news-debunker/mhccpoafgdgbhnjfhkcmgknndkeenfhe?hl=en

[27] See http://wiki.dbpedia.org/

[28] See https://hoaxy.iuni.iu.edu/

[29] See https://chrome.google.com/webstore/detail/tweetcred/fbokljinlogeihdnkikeeneiankdgikg

[30] See http://twittertrails.com/

[31] See http://speechpro-usa.com/product/forensic

[32] See http://www.forensicav.ro/software.htm

[33] See http://www.eyewitnessproject.org/

[34] See http://www.izitru.com/

[35] See https://pipl.com/

[36] See http://webmii.com/

[37] See https://www.wolframalpha.com/

[38] See https://chrome.google.com/webstore/detail/wot-web-of-trust-website/bhmmomiinigofkjcapegjjndpbikblnp

[39] chrome-extension://mhccpoafgdgbhnjfhkcmgknndkeenfhe/invid.html

[40] See https://www.yandex.com/

[41] See http://www.baidu.com/

Chapter 7
Cross–Media Publishing and Storytelling

ABSTRACT

Technological evolution on digital content processing and mediated communication has created multiple publication means, which can be employed for information channeling and dissemination. The present chapter analyzes in detail the important topic of cross-media publishing and storytelling that resulted in changes in the news reporting chain and created new ways of making journalism. It also involved fundamental changes in both ends of media production and consumption and consequently in the way that informing streams arrive to the end users. Taking into consideration that journalistic organizations utilize all the available propagation paths to spread their product, this section discusses the historic evolution of cross-media, defining multi-channel publishing procedures and presenting the various devices which can be utilized as receiving terminals. As a final point, the cross-modal attributes of the presented paradigms are studied for their potential usefulness in multimodal integrated authentication solutions.

DOI: 10.4018/978-1-5225-5592-6.ch007

INTRODUCTION

During the past thirty years, Information and Communication Technologies (ICTs) have transformed the media industry considerably. Digitization of media organizations and their procedures has facilitated changes in the main processes and practices of journalism (Erdal, 2007). A deriving consequence is that the complete control over news production and dissemination no longer belongs to the media companies, now that users can participate in every part of the process (Bruns, 2005; Ibrus & Scolari, 2012; Conrado, Neville, Woodworth, & O'Riordan, 2016; Mikos, 2017). Historically, newspapers, radio and TV mediums could publish news only on their designated channel. Specifically, newspapers were producing print editions, radio stations were transmitting radio programs and TV stations were broadcasting TV programs (Veglis, 2012). The convergence of ICTs created new opportunities and, for the first-time, media companies could utilize various channels in order to disseminate news.

In the heart of this development was the digitization of the production systems, enabling content to travel across-media boundaries, which were sealed in the previous decades. Television footage and radio soundbites could be published on the Web and television sound was frequently used on radio (Erdal, 2007; Veglis, 2012). This resulted in fundamental changes in the workflow of both media organizations and journalists (Sabelström, 2001; Papacharissi, 2017). The news is now produced once and deployed in various formats for different delivery channels. That allowed media companies to cover more audience needs, to deploy channels that complement each other, but also to attempt attracting younger users that tend not to consume news through traditional delivery channels (print, radio, TV). Trends in the worldwide media industry have clearly shown that, in order to guarantee long-term success with audience in the future, it is vital to change from a single product to a multimedia framework and a user-oriented approach (Dietmar, 2008). Thus, nowadays, media companies are changing and distribute news in a synchronized manner via different channels, guiding their readers from one medium to the other, in order to generate brand loyalty. According to Ibrus and Scolari (2012), the above practice is what we call cross-media storytelling (CS), in terms of popular knowledge, i.e. when news items are disseminated across multiple channels using a variety of media forms. The synchronous use of different transmission routes enables media outlets to make contact with their audience in a comprehensive and cross-modal way, using the involved channels as independent delivery paths. Thus, the same information is available via many different terminals and communication ways (Dena, 2004). Apart from CS, trans-media storytelling (TS) describes the narration of a single story across multiple platforms and formats, including modern interactive technologies that enable active user participation with possible content contributions (Jenkins, 2003; Ibrus & Scolari, 2012). The importance of cross-media publishing is due to many factors, namely the introduction of new technologies, changes in users consuming behavior, adoption of the new smart devices (smartphones and tablets) and new documentation capabilities (Rogobete, Peters, & Seruga, 2012; Heinrich, 2011; De Torres & Hermida, 2017). Along with the introduction of multiple media, co-production and cross-platform storytelling models, rethinking about copyright (Lessig, 2008; Bauman, 2013) and misinformation propagation (Katsaounidou & Dimoulas, 2018) emerge as side effects of the rapidly transforming media ecosystem.

CROSS-MEDIA FOUNDATION, EVOLUTION AND DEFINITIONS

Printing technology dominated the mass media industry until 1930's. Then radio was introduced and a couple of decades later television as well, so the field was completely reshaped. The last major evolution was the introduction of the Internet and its services during the last decade of the 20th century (Rogobete, Peters, & Seruga, 2012). During the first decade of the 21st century, media organizations witnessed another revolution with the introduction of the smart mobile devices (smartphones, tablets), that completely changed the way information is produced and consumed. The term cross-media was already used in the early days of electronic publishing during the 60's. In the print world, the term described database publishing (ACTeN, 2004). The first segment to automate cross-media was directory and reference publishing. When material was finally in a normalized database, creating new extract and transformation routines for CD-ROM and eventually Web production was not radically different from what publishers had been doing for the previous two decades of database print publishing. In the late 1980's, new cross-media publishing systems that were focused on "content-driven" publications emerged: manuals, books, treatises and other publications whose length is usually determined by the content, rather than trimmed to fit in a predefined space (Veglis, 2012; Walter, 1999). The print and publishing industries have incorporated cross-media for a long time. One driver was efficiency, but in newspaper and magazine publishing the technique is used for marketing and market penetration as well. In book printing and publishing, cross-media started out as media that were complementary to each other, such as a book and a CD-ROM. In magazine and newspaper publishing, cross-media are used more extensively to bridge the time between publications by providing information on the Internet and to create a community. In the most rudimentary form, newspapers and magazines had an electronic counterpart. They did not really add to the content of the magazine or the newspaper, but reproduced it (ACTeN, 2004; Veglis, 2012). This was the cross-media implementation in the early days of the internet.

Cross-media publishing can be defined as the production of any content (news, music, text images, etc.) for more than one media platform (for example print, Web and TV), within the same media organization (Erdal, 2011; Veglis, 2005, 2012). The content is posted once and it is available on many media distribution channels. Another term that is widely used is "Multiple media", which specifies the inter-platform or inter-device possibilities. The term "multiple media" indicates that the same content is delivered to end users in more than one medium, whereas a medium can be defined as means of communication or, more precisely, a system where transmission media are using more than one type of transmission path (e.g., optical fiber, radio and copper wire) to deliver information (Veglis, 2007; 2012). An alternative term for multiple media is multi-channel publishing. The same content is published on various channels or media. The term "multiple media" is broader than cross-media, as it expands the concept from devices to content (Antikainen, Kangas, & Vainikainen, 2004). Erdal (2011) proposes that cross-media is not synonymous with multi-platform. Other scholars perceive cross-media as an extension of multi-platform (Veglis, 2012). Multi-platform indicates the use of more than one media platform within the same 'communicative situation', but with no communicative relations or references between them.

Erdal (2011) believes that there must be a distinction between cross-media communication and production processes. If a news story is published on different mediums and involves cooperation between reporters for the different mediums' (i.e. television and web), either on the research stage or through content sharing, we have cross-media production process. The utilization of such publishing techniques in newspaper organizations has been investigated by some researchers (Sabelström, 2001; Sabelström, 2000; Veglis, 2007). However, the issue of cross-media publishing in broadcast media has drawn very little attention, although it is worth mentioning that there is a small number of important contributions (Cottle & Ashton, 1999; Duhe et al., 2004, Veglis, 2010).

CS is closely related to the cross-media term. Monique de Haas defined CS as the communication where the storyline is directing the user from one medium to the other (Hannele, Kangas, & Vainikainen, 2004). In this case, the user is navigated through different media, in order to obtain all the available information about a news story (Veglis, 2012). Cross-media publishing refers mainly to the utilization of multiple media and it focuses on the mean for conveying the message (news). On the other hand, CS is focused on the way the message is transmitted to the audience.

Another term that is related to CS is Trans-Media Storytelling (TS), where media providers are producing content across different channels and taking advantage of each channel's specific qualities and abilities (Bolin, 2007; Jenkins, 2003; Ibrus & Scolari, 2012). This technique attempts to engage audience members individually, validating their involvement and positively reinforcing personal participation in the narrative (Veglis, 2012). It involves the creation of a rich in-between space, an archive of shared meaning in-between different parts of the story. In different media, there are different "entry points" through which users can become immersed in the story. These entry-points have a unique and independent lifespan, but they play a definite role in the big narrative scheme. TS's field of application is mainly the entertainment industry. Although CS and TS have been around for quite some time, no specific theory has been introduced. In most cases scholars adapt existing media theories in order to study them.

MEDIA CONTENT AND CROSS-MEDIA DEVICES AND CHANNELS

Before discussing media channels, it is worth examining the available devices through which those channels are being accessed, namely PC/laptops, smartphones and tablets. PC/laptops, well known for their capabilities, are widely used since 1980's. Generally, they have sufficient processing power, above 12' screens with high resolution and internet access, usually through Wi-Fi or even cable connections. They are considered ideal for media consumption, but they lack portability (especially the PCs). Tablets are portable computer devices that include touch screens and wireless connections to the Internet. These devices offer relatively large high-resolution displays and an extensive storage capacity (in comparison with other mobile devices, for example smartphones, although high-end smartphones nowadays may offer extensive storage capacities) that allow publishers to provide readers with visually rich content in a fixed format that can retain each publication's established brand identity (Hassan & Alejandro, 2010; Wearden & Fidler, 2001; Veglis, 2012). Smartphones are devices that combine the functions of a personal digital assistant (PDA) and a mobile phone. They can serve as portable media players and camera phones with high-resolution touch screens, GPS navigation, Wi-Fi and mobile broadband access. They include browsers that enable users to access regular websites. However, these devices have small screens (in comparison with the PCs or even tablets) and thus web surfing is not an easy task. That is why many media companies are offering portals (with mobile themes) prepared for mobile devices that include all the necessary text and photographs for each article, but limited graphics (with basic navigation functions). This increases access speed and makes navigation more effortless for mobile readers (Veglis, 2012). Except the previously mentioned devices, there is one more category, the wearable devices, that is worth mentioning. Wearables are small electronic devices that are worn by users (usually on the wrist) (Mann, 2012). Some of them are standalone devices, but others work in conjunction with smartphones (smartwatches, wristbands, etc.) and support the display of smartphones' notifications. Although they are still at an early stage of adoption, and currently they can display only small notifications, it is worth mentioning them because, in the near future, they may play an important role in cross-media content consumption.

Channels for Publishing Content

Media companies have been employing various channels in order to relay news to their audience. These channels are being used in a cross-media scheme. It should be noted that they do not represent different categories of technology, but simply various methods for publishing news. They are the ways that the news is published by media organizations around the world. Next, the capabilities that each channel offers are briefly presented and discussed:

WWW

The main advantage of WWW is the transportation of information over great distances and the possibility of continuous updating (Negroponte,

1995). Surveys indicate that it is the first alternative publishing channel that newspapers adopted in the early years of WWW (Veglis, 2007). Newspapers publish the majority of their articles along with photos and, in some cases, they enrich articles with additional sources that cannot be included in the printed edition. On the other hand, WWW is also the main publication channel for every news organization. It is worth noting that it can be accessed from PCs laptops and from smart devices (smartphones and tablets). In the latter case, the websites must support mobile themes in order for the webpages to be more friendly to mobile users.

E-Mail

E-mail is employed by media companies in order to alert their readers about breaking news, relay them the headlines of the main stories (with links to the entire articles included in an online version), or send them the entire edition – in the case of a newspaper - in a PDF file (Schiff, 2003). E-mails can be accessed through all the devices being employed for the consumption of cross-media content.

Webcasting

Webcasting can be broadly defined as the delivery of media content on the Web (Veglis, 2007). Websites can be used for Webcasting of audio and video content. This content is available on demand and it is used in order to add value to the services offered by the WWW presence of the media company.

PDF

It is a file format. PDF files are portable, platform-independent and highly compressed. They are also searchable and can include features for interactive document use. That is why many newspapers have used this format to deliver exact copies of their printed edition (Schiff, 2003).

SMS

It is a service offered by network providers that allows customers to send text messages over their mobile phones. Many media companies employed SMS in order to send the main headlines to their readers or to alert them about breaking news (Gillmor, 2004). With the introduction of the smartphones along with the internet services they are able to support, the use of SMS as a publication channel has gradually decreased. Nevertheless, because this service is actively utilized by the majority of mobile phone users, it was included in the list of the available cross-media channels.

Blogs

A blog is a website where entries are written in chronological order and displayed in reverse chronological order. An important feature of blogs is the ability for readers to leave comments. That is the reason why media organizations have included blogs as a supplement to their web presence, thus giving their journalists the opportunity to comment onto current events and to their readers the ability to interact with them (Veglis, 2007).

Social Networks

They are web-based services that allow individuals to construct a public of semi-public profile within a bounded system, articulate a list of other users with whom they share a connection and view and traverse their list of connections and those made by others within the system (Ellison, 2007; Boyd & Ellison, 2010). The majority of media companies have established a presence in the most popular social networks (for example Facebook) in order to publish their news articles and attract other social network users to their web site. They have also integrated social media links in their web articles, so that users can link to them through their social network profiles. Moreover, their expansion outside the boundaries of their environments has institutionalize their function as an aggregator of news and other content (Wilson, Gosling, & Graham, 2012). A characteristic example is the like and share buttons of Facebook, which can be found outside the platform itself and allow people to share content from external sources (Gerlitz & Helmond, 2013; Mathieu & Pavlíčková, 2017). Users have also the ability to interact with the media companies by leaving comments (Veglis, 2012). A recently introduced type of social networking service that appears to have a growing popularity is Social or Content Curation (Kieu, Ichise, & Pham, 2015). It involves assembling, managing and presenting some types of collections of social content. It is considered to be a new type of journalism. Examples of such service are Storify, Pinterest, etc.

Twitter

Twitter is a social networking and micro-blogging service that enables its users to send and read other users' updates known as tweets. Twitter is often described as the "SMS of Internet", in that the site provides the back-end functionality to other desktop and web-based applications to send and receive short text messages, often obscuring the actual website itself. Tweets are text-based posts of up to 280 characters in length. Updates are displayed on the user's profile page and delivered to other users who have signed up to receive them. Users can send and receive updates via the Twitter website and through the Twitter application for mobile devices. Many media companies are using Twitter in order to alert their readers about breaking news. Although one may argue that Twitter belongs to the Social Network category, its distinct characteristics allow us to categorize it as a separate channel (Veglis, 2012).

Web Push Notifications

They are messages which are sent by a website through the user's web browser. They are considered to be a new publishing channel. The user has to accept once the initial request from the website to send notifications. The procedure is quite simple and it does not require any kind of registration. user receives notifications on his PC/laptop or other smart device even when the concerned web page is not open in his browser. The notification usually is comprised of the title of the news article, an image and a link to the news article.

RSS

It is a method of describing news or other Web content that is available for feeding from an online publisher to Web users. Today, many media companies are employing RSS in order to alert their readers about news headlines (Veglis, 2007). An RSS feed usually employs text and often photographs. RSS can also be utilized in smart devices, with the help of news readers apps. Typical examples are Google news, flipboard, freedly, etc. To some extent this solution is comparable with the smartphone apps (which are being discussed next), but it has the advantage that it can read feeds from many different media organizations.

Smartphone/Tablet Apps

They are special build apps for smartphones and tablets that display news and notifications from media organizations. They usually utilize the existing RSS feeds from the media organization's website and present the news in a format that retains the identity of the media organization. The problem is that the user must download and install the application for each media company. In some cases, media organizations offer different apps for smartphones and tablets, in order to exploit the larger screens employed by the tablets in a better way.

Social Broadcasting

Social Broadcasting can be defined as the broadcasting of video, text and pictures through social media channels (Yartey & Ha, 2015) such as Facebook, Twitter, Youtube and Instagram. This channel has been introduced recently (in spring of 2016) and it can be used for broadcasting live video of breaking news. The broadcasted content can also be available (in some social networks, Instagram does not support on demand viewing of social broadcasting) for on demand consumption, but in some cases for a limited time period (one week in Youtube). It is worth noting that this channel is available through the social media app, but in some cases (for example in the case of Twitter) it requires the installation of an additional application. Social broadcasting is aiming mainly for consumption through smart mobile devices, but is some cases is also available (for example Youtube) for access via PC/laptop devices.

SOLUTIONS AND RECOMMENDATIONS

News Dissemination and Storytelling Through Multiple Media

Based on the discussion presented in the previous section, it is evident that cross-media publishing is under constant evolution as far as its publishing channels are concerned. New channels appear every year that offer different characteristics and they are best suited for users with particular needs. Some of them are being accepted and used by the internet users, but others may be very short-lived. It is up to the media organization to choose and utilize the proper channel combination to best serve its target audience. Thus, in this section, the characteristics of each channel are discussed, offering certain usage guidelines for the media organization.

As various channels differ a lot, direct comparison is not an easy task. While, some of them are internet services (WWW, e-mail), others are specialized applications. However, we can make a general categorization based on the device through which a user can access them. Table 7-1 includes such a categorization. Most of the channels are accessible through PC/Laptop devices, but Smartphone/Tablet devices are able to utilize all the possible cross-media channels. It is worth noting that users cannot receive SMSs (which is considered to be an old channel not being utilized a lot in the last decade) through PC/laptop devices and they cannot install and use specialized apps, but one might argue that the later channel can be utilized in the PC/laptop devices by installing android emulators (i.e. bluestack, Duos, etc.) which support executing android apps. The latter is not an easy endeavor and it cannot be used on entry-level devices with limited processing power. Overall, there seems to be a redundancy in the devices a user can employ in order to access cross-media content. Nevertheless, the very slim advantage that smart devices exhibit over the traditional PC indicates that future cross-media publishing will focus on portable devices.

Table 1. Channels – devices

Channel	PC/Laptop	Smartphone/Tablet
www	✓	✓
E-mail	✓	✓
Webcasting	✓	✓
PDF	✓	✓
SMS		✓
Blogs	✓	✓
Social Networks	✓	✓
Twitter	✓	✓
Web push notifications	✓	✓
RSS	✓	✓
Apps		✓
Social broadcasting	✓ *	✓

*not all social networks support accessing social broadcasting through PC/laptop devices

The above classification suggests that some channels overlap. For example, RSS, apps and web push notifications usually include the exact same content. But we must also take into account that each channel may target different groups of users (Veglis, 2009) and users of different devices.

Different publishing channels can be classified as push or pull oriented, based on the way their content reaches internet users. Specifically, it is classified as push oriented when forced upon the end user without a specific request from him or her (typical examples are e-mail, RSS). On the other hand, it can be classified as pull oriented when the end user makes a deliberate action to access it (for example, WWW) (Veglis, 2012). Based on the above categories, Table 7-2 includes the channel classification as push and pull. It is worth noting that, in some cases, specific channels can be classified in both categories.

WWW is characterized as a pull channel. In the same category, Webcasting and blogs are also included, since their content is usually webpages. Of course, many blogs and web sites offer RSS feeds, but this is covered by the RSS channel. On the other hand, E-mail, RSS, Twitter, Web push notifications and SMS are considered to belong to the push category, since they deliver (push) information to readers (Veglis, 2012). In order to receive pushed information from a channel, the user has to actively choose it (for example, subscribe to an RSS feed, to a mailing list or follow a user on Twitter). Conversely, users usually do not know what they will receive when they access pull oriented information.

Finally, Table 2 includes a group of publishing channels (PDF, Social Networks, Apps and Social broadcasting) that can be classified to both push and pull categories. PDF files are mentioned as both push and pull channels, because they can be downloaded through a webpage and thus be considered as a pull channel, or they can be sent via an e-mail and thus be treated as a push channel. Social Networks can be characterized as pull when a user is accessing a profile, but also as a push channel in the case that a relationship is established between two users (or a user and a media organization) and content that is published by one user is sent to the other as notification. The same can be said in the case of apps. The user can use an app in order to access the news content from a media organization but at the same time he/she can receive notifications about new content (or breaking news) published by the organization. Finally, Social broadcasting can be classified in both categories since the live consumption can be viewed as a push channel for as much as a notification alerts the user to watch the broadcasting. However,

Table 2. Push – Pull orientation

Channel	Push	Pull
WWW		✓
E-mail	✓	
Webcasting		✓
PDF	✓	✓
SMS	✓	
Blogs		✓
Social Networks	✓	✓
Twitter	✓	
Web push notifications	✓	
RSS	✓	
Apps	✓	✓
Social broadcasting	✓	✓ *

*in the case of on-demand consumption

on-demand consumption can be considered as a pull channel since the user willingly accesses the recording.

All publishing channels consist of content elements which can be categorized into two categories, namely static and dynamic elements (Veglis, 2012). Text and images/graphics belong to the static content elements. They can be created and edited independently of each other and later compiled and logically connected in a news article. Static content elements can be created quite rapidly. In the second category, the dynamic elements, video and sound are included. Those elements are sequentially built up. It is quite obvious that the majority of publishing channels employ a combination of static and dynamic content elements, with the exception of some publishing channels that employ only video (Webcasting, Social broadcasting). As expected, preparing dynamic content is more time consuming than preparing static content. As a consequence, channels that are comprised of static content are always the fastest channels in disseminating breaking news. Content elements define the time required in order for the content to be produced. The first channels that relay the headlines of breaking news to the media audience are those based on text (RSS, Twitter, web push notifications). These channels are often characterized as info-alerts (Antikainen et al., 2004). and play an important role in cross-media communication (Veglis, 2012).

CONCLUSION

This chapter presents and discusses in detail the issues of cross-media publishing (CP) and storytelling (CS) in media organizations. The close related issue of transmedia (TS) is also examined. The available publishing channels have been presented, thoroughly analyzed and systematically categorized. Based on the characteristics of these channels, in conjunction with the needs of media companies, the specific cross-media strategy of a media organization can be planned. Initially, cross-media offered the opportunity to publish an article with the help of multiple channels. Thus, the produced content could be disseminated via CP. Gradually, the multichannel publishing trend focused on the exploitation of the alternative access points' features for enhancing users' engagement and interaction. That resulted in the introduction of more sophisticated digital narrations, namely CS and TS. Media industry is still focused on CS. Story narratives that were initially developed for newspapers and gradually transformed with the introduction of radio, TV and lastly the Internet, still have their roots in the early days of journalism. There were some attempts to introduce novel narratives in news organizations (Veglis, 2012), which included elements of TS. For example, Google's Living-Stories was a novel format for presenting and consuming online news, back in 2009 (Living-Stories, 2011). Although the format had the backing of Google and New York Times, the project was discontinued. Today, there are even more tools to tell a story and Internet users are more susceptible in embracing news narratives. There are tools that allow the flow of content across multiple channels. The kids who have grown up consuming content from various devices and services it is most likely that they are going to expect a similar experience when reading the news (Veglis, 2012). They have become information hunters and gatherers, taking pleasure in tracking information about things that interest them (Jenkins, 2003).

Another parameter that must be taken into account is that we are gradually moving away from PC/laptop devices and concentrating in media consumption with the help of smart mobile devices. This is evident from the number of cross-media channels that are accessed through mobile devices. In a past survey (Veglis, 2012) the situation was significantly different and the consumption through PC/laptops was the main target for cross-media projects. The appearance and rapid adoption of cross-media channels specifically created for consumption through mobile devices (for example Social broadcasting), is a clear indication of what to expect, in the near future. This shift to mobile devices is evident from the steady decrease in the sales of PC/laptops and the fast increase in the sales of smart mobile devices[1]. The utilized narratives must be adapted to the characteristics of the mobile devices and the consumers' habits. The future is mobile and it is already here.

Furthermore, CS and TS practices are significantly affected by the fake news phenomenon, which came in the spotlight during the last couple of years. Fortunately, the availability of multiple content versions and entities, adapted to the specific characteristics of each channel, require from potential news falsifiers to tamper the individual assets /resources across all instances of multiple media. Hence, the correlation of the various modalities, accompanying and describing the same event /news-article, could be useful in revealing possible informatory inconsistencies, therefore in detecting the associated forgery attacks. This evaluation approach forms the central principle and the motivation that lay beneath the envisioned cross-media authentication and verification model, which stand as the core topic of this book and it is thoroughly analyzed in the next chapter.

REFERENCES

ACTeN. (2004). *Cross-media E-Content Report 8*. Retrieved from http://www.sociologia.unimib.it/DATA/Insegnamenti/13_3299/materiale/04%20-%20jak%20boumans%20cross-media%20acten%20aug%202004.pdf

Antikainen, H., Kangas, S., & Vainikainen, S. (2004). *Three views on mobile cross-media entertainment*. VTT Information Technology, Research Report TTE4-2004-17, 22.3.

Bauman, Z. (2013). *Liquid modernity*. John Wiley & Sons.

Bolin, G. (2007). Media technologies, transmedia storytelling and commodification. *Ambivalence towards convergence: Digitalization and media change*, 237-248.

Boyd, D., & Ellison, N. (2010). Social network sites: Definition, history, and scholarship. *IEEE Engineering Management Review*, 3(38), 16–31. doi:10.1109/EMR.2010.5559139

Bruns, A. (2005). *Gatewatching: Collaborative online news production*. Peter Lang.

Conrado, S. P., Neville, K., Woodworth, S., & O'Riordan, S. (2016). Managing social media uncertainty to support the decision making process during emergencies. *Journal of Decision Systems, 25*(sup1), 171-181.

Cottle, S., & Ashton, M. (1999). From BBC Newsroom to BBC Newscentre: On Changing Technology and Journalist Practices. *Convergence (London), 5*(3), 22–43. doi:10.1177/135485659900500304

Dena, C. (2004). *Current State of Cross-media Storytelling: Preliminary observations for future design.* European Information Systems Technologies Event, The Hague, The Netherlands.

Dietmar, S. (2008). My view on cross-media communication for newspapers. *Nextnewsroom.* Retrieved from https://nextnewsroom.com/my-view-on-cross-media-communication-for-newspapers-d4ed76fdca5f

Dimoulas, C. A., & Symeonidis, A. L. (2015). Syncing shared multimedia through audiovisual bimodal segmentation. *IEEE MultiMedia, 22*(3), 26–42. doi:10.1109/MMUL.2015.33

Duhe, S. F., Mortimer, M., & Chow, S. S. (2004). Convergence in North American TV Newsrooms: A Nationwide Look. *Convergence (London), 10*(2), 81–104. doi:10.1177/135485650401000206

Ellison, N. B. (2007). Social network sites: Definition, history, and scholarship. *Journal of Computer-Mediated Communication, 13*(1), 210–230. doi:10.1111/j.1083-6101.2007.00393.x

Erdal, I. J. (2007). Researching Media Convergence and Cross-media News Production Mapping the Field. *Nordicom Review, 28*(2), 51–61. doi:10.1515/nor-2017-0209

Erdal, I. J. (2011). Coming to Terms with Convergence Journalism: Cross-Media as a Theoretical and Analytical Concept. *Convergence (London), 17*(2), 213–223. doi:10.1177/1354856510397109

García de Torres, E., & Hermida, A. (2017). The Social Reporter in Action: An analysis of the practice and discourse of Andy Carvin. *Journalism Practice, 11*(2-3), 177–194. doi:10.1080/17512786.2016.1245110

Gillmor, D. (2004). *We the Media - Grassroots Journalism by the People for the People.* O'Reilly.

Guerrini, F. (2013). *Newsroom Curators & Independent Storytellers: Content Curation as a new form of Journalism, Reuters Institute Fellowship Paper.* University of Oxford.

Hannele, A., Kangas, S., & Vainikainen, S. (2004). *GAIN Project: Three views on mobile cross-media entertainment.* VTT Information Technology. Retrieved from http://www.vtt.fi/inf/julkaisut/muut/2004 /cross-media_entertainment. pdf

Hassan, A., & Alejandro, J. (2010). *Tablets A Second Life for Newspapers and Magazines? A summary of proceedings at the Oxford Tablet Summit – May 19th.* Reuters Institute for the Study of Journalism, University of Oxford.

Heinrich, A. (2011). *Network journalism: Journalistic practice in interactive spheres* (Vol. 3). Routledge.

Ibrus, I., & Scolari, C. A. (2012). Cross-media innovations. *Texts, markets, institutions.* Peter Lang.

Jenkins, H. (2003). Transmedia Storytelling. *Technology Review.* Retrieved from http://www.technologyreview .com/articles/wo_jenkins011503.asp

Katsaounidou, A. N., & Dimoulas, C. A. (2018). Integrating Content Authentication Support in Media Services. In Encyclopedia of Information Science and Technology, Fourth Edition (pp. 2908-2919). IGI Global. doi:10.4018/978-1-5225-2255-3.ch254

Kieu, B. T., Ichise, R., & Pham, S. B. (2015). Predicting the Popularity of Social Curation. In V. H. Nguyen, A. C. Le, & V. N. Huynh (Eds.), *Knowledge and Systems Engineering. Advances in Intelligent Systems and Computing* (Vol. 326). Cham: Springer.

Living-Stories. (2011). *Living-Stories: A new format for online news.* Retrieved from http://code.google.com/p/living-stories/

Mann, S. (2012). Wearable Computing. In Encyclopedia of Human-Computer Interaction. Aarhus, Denmark: The Interaction-Design.org Foundation.

Mathieu, D., & Pavlíčková, T. (2017). Cross-media within the Facebook newsfeed: The role of the reader in cross-media uses. *Convergence.*

Mikos, L. (2017). Trans-media Storytelling and Mega-Narration: Audiovisual Production in Converged Media Environments. In *Media Convergence and Deconvergence* (pp. 159–175). Cham: Palgrave Macmillan. doi:10.1007/978-3-319-51289-1_8

Negroponte, N. (1995). *Being Digital*. Athens: Kastaniotis.

Papacharissi, Z. (2017). Commentary: Remaking Events, Storytelling, and the News. *Remaking the News: Essays on the Future of Journalism Scholarship in the Digital Age*, 147.

Rampazzo Gambarato, R., & Tárcia, L. P. T. (2017). Trans-media Strategies in Journalism: An analytical model for the news coverage of planned events. *Journalism Studies*, *18*(11), 1381–1399. doi:10.1080/146167 0X.2015.1127769

Rogobete, C., Peters, G., & Seruga, G. (2012). Cross-media and E-publishing. *International Journal of u- and e- Service. Science and Technology*, *5*(2), 17–31.

Sabelström, K. (2000). *The Multimedia News Reporter: Technology and Work Processes*. Presented at TAGA'S 52nd Annual Technical Conference, Colorado Springs, CO.

Sabelström, K. (2001). *Information Categories and Editorial Process in Multiple channel publishing* (PhD Thesis). Royal Institute of Technology, Department of NADA, Division of Media Technology and Graphics Arts, Stockholm, Sweden.

Schiff, F. (2003). Business models of news Web sites: A survey of empirical trends and expert opinion. *First Monday*, *8*(6). Retrieved from http://firstmonday.org/article/view/1061/981

Veglis, A. (2005). Implementation of a Computer Supported Collaborative Work System in a newspaper. *WSEAS Transactions on Information Science and Applications*, *2*(7), 891–902.

Veglis, A. (2007). Cross-media publishing by U.S. newspapers. *Journal of Electronic Publishing, 10*(2). Retrieved from https://quod.lib.umich.edu/j/jep/3336451.0010.211?view=text;rgn=main

Veglis, A. (2008, June). Comparison of alternative channels in cross-media publishing. Publishing Research Quarterly Journal, 111-123.

Veglis, A. (2010). Modeling Cross-media Publishing in Radio and TV Stations. *Proc of the Second International Conferences on Advances in Multimedia MMEDIA*, 196-201. 10.1109/MMEDIA.2010.16

Veglis, A. (2012). From Cross-media to Trans-media Reporting in Newspaper Articles. *Publishing Research Quarterly, 28*(4), 313–324. doi:10.100712109-012-9294-z

Veglis, A. (2012), Journalism and Cross-media Publishing: The case of Greece. In The Wiley-Blackwell Handbook of Online Journalism. Blackwell Publishing.

Veglis, A. A. (2009, September). *Cross-media Communication In Newspaper Organizations*. In 4th Mediterranean Conference on Information Systems, Athens, Greece.

Walter, M. (1999, October). Cross-Media Publishing Systems. *The Seybold Report on Internet Publishing*.

Wearden, S., & Fidler, R. (2001, Spring). Crain's Cleveland Business: Evaluating an e-Newspaper Concept for Tablet PCs. *Future of Print Media Journal*.

Wilson, R. E., Gosling, S. D., & Graham, L. T. (2012). A review of Facebook research in the social sciences. *Perspectives on Psychological Science, 7*(3), 203–220. doi:10.1177/1745691612442904 PMID:26168459

Yartey, F. N. A., & Ha, L. (2015). Smartphones and Self-Broadcasting among College Students in an Age of Social Media. In Human Behavior, Psychology, and Social Interaction in the Digital Era. IGI Global.

KEY TERMS AND DEFINITIONS

Pull Channel: A channel for which the end user makes a deliberate action to access.

Push Channel: A channel which is forced upon the end user without a specific request from him or her.

Web Push Notifications: Messages appearing in the browser's environment which are send by web sites alerting users about new content.

ENDNOTE

[1]   See https://www.statista.com/statistics/272595/global-shipments-forecast-for-tablets-laptops-and-desktop-pcs/

Chapter 8
Cross–Media Authentication and Verification

ABSTRACT

The present chapter outlines the potentials of cross-media authentication solutions by correlating all the available information streams involved in multiple media (i.e., content/channel-adapted modalities, linking mechanisms, users' feedback, metadata). The proposed model attempts to thoroughly analyze the existed (and detected) diversities, aiming at seeking for "consistent inconsistencies" (i.e., specific dissimilarities that are proportionately steady in most "comparison pairs"). Full range of forgery detection strategies are taken into consideration (i.e., best practices adopted by humans, algorithms, and intelligent systems implemented through machine learning, their dynamic combination, etc.). Thus, the current framework ventures to concatenate all the involved approaches, which are related to both multiple publishing channels and news verification. Hence, the "cross-media" term has a broader meaning, encapsulating the sub-cases of cross-/trans-media publishing and storytelling, with respect to cross-validation of information, along with the entire landscape of digital media.

DOI: 10.4018/978-1-5225-5592-6.ch008

INTRODUCTION

During the last decade, the tremendous progress in the Information and Communication Technologies (ICTs) has drastically altered mass communications into a social networking environment, revolutionizing the processes of news informing. Apparently, the new era has been dominated by the contemporary forms of Journalism, where multiple publishing means and digital storytelling have prevailed. Nowadays, most media organizations utilize more than one channel to disseminate their news articles, while active user engagement is also propelled, taking advantage of content contribution, commenting and sharing services, through the models of User Generated Content (UGC). No doubt, the advent of citizens' and participatory journalism further extended the plurality and diversity of the exchanged news information, yet with the counterbalance of the potential propagation of unverified content and, therefore, with the associated necessity for reconsidering validation codebooks. Indeed, the wide expansion in the use of mobile devices / computing systems (i.e. smartphones and tablets), and their inherent multimedia capturing and networking capabilities, made possible the massive production and distribution of multimodal digital content. Moreover, the availability of easy to use software and cloud computing services expedited the potentials of "shaping" and altering multimedia documents (not only text, but also images and audiovisual streams, as well). Considering that, in many cases, these media assets are used as proof evidence of the corresponding news events, the convenience of the digital processing broadened the possibilities for intentional content tampering and falsification, thus opening another backdoor of misinformation propagation (Dimoulas, Veglis, & Kalliris, 2014, 2015, 2018; Ho & Li, 2015; Katsaounidou & Dimoulas, 2018; Pantti & Sirén, 2015; Pasquini, Brunetta, Vinci, Conotter, & Boato, 2015; Silverman, 2013; Veglis, Dimoulas, & Kalliris, 2016).

While cross- and trans-media publishing systems have become the everyday practice of the average journalist in most professional organizations, this is not the case for the arising cross-validation demands. For this reason, the Forensics (or Digital Forensics -DF) field has emerged, purposing to face the majority of the forgery detection problems, so as to force news authentication. Although multimedia veracity techniques form a rapidly evolving research area with remarkable progress, simple, accurate and reliable tools to be used in real-world scenarios are still missing (Katsaounidou 2016; Katsaounidou & Dimoulas, 2018). This fact is further complicated by the plurality of the involved media entities and their possible content "shaping" mechanisms, resulting in a very broad, disperse and quite inhomogeneous taxonomy of potential verification systems. Clearly, distinguished scientific background and knowledge are required in each of the encountered types of information for the detection of possible manipulation or falsification (i.e. text /messages, images /photos, audio-video recordings etc.). Thus, much effort has been put into text analysis (i.e. Twitter messages) and photo evaluation. The former due to its urgent character, since it is used for fast posting up /info propagation, and the latter because of its documentation capabilities, when pictures are used as evidence records of the accompanying news events (Boididou et al., 2017; Farid, 2009; Katsaounidou, 2016; Mendoza, Poblete, & Castillo, 2010; Zubiaga & Ji, 2014). Less progress has been succeeded in the fields of audio and video, where research projects were relatively delayed and they were not, actually, launched until recently. This hysteresis is justified on the more demanding character of audiovisual information, which is reflected in the processing needs of both tampering and tampering detection tasks (Al-Sanjary & Sulong, 2015; Gupta, Cho, & Kuo, 2012; Maher, 2010; Mizher, Ang, Mazhar, & Mizher, 2017; Thakur, 2014). Apart from algorithms and machine-assisted approaches, the human factor is also engaged in authenticity assessment procedures, either in specific tasks, conducted solely by experts, or through their collaboration with individuals, by collecting the users' massive responses (i.e. through crowd computing services). As a result, the full framing /context of the surrounding information that lay beneath or under a news-story is thoroughly inspected, seeking for potential inconsistencies that would reveal possible tweaking operations (Ho & Li, 2015; Katsaounidou & Dimoulas, 2018; Silverman, 2013).

Following the above remarks, it becomes clearer that different competencies and knowhow are required in each one of the aforementioned verification approaches, which have been progressed as distinctive sub-fields in both research and practical applications. Thus, the implicated methods feature great differences, concerning the achieved progress and the corresponding gained experience /maturity, as already implied. Most importantly, there is missing an integration of all the currently available techniques towards unified and collaborative solutions (Ho & Li, 2015; Katsaounidou & Dimoulas, 2018). Hence, each method (and content type) is usually treated individually, at the moment that forgeries are expected to be located in the differences among the involved entities (all the original material of the news stories and the associated / linked veracity outcomes). The primary objective of this chapter is to introduce more sophisticated cross-media authentication procedures by applying multimodal (and multilevel) correlations across multiple channels, content versions, inspection tools, users, semantic tags and other metadata. Therefore, the "cross-media" term, here, extends the narrower meaning of multi-path transmission and interaction, although the motivation of its use remains the same. Particularly, while the former paradigms imply the utilization of many alternative publishing and storytelling ways, the reason of multichannel engagement is different in the new model. More specifically, cross-validation and certification mechanisms are deployed across the encountered modalities, thus aiming at confirming information integrity (or revealing potential falsification actions). In fact, this approach seems to be more beneficial with regard to contemporary digital storytelling examples, where plural sources and types of informing streams are normally involved, i.e. "Multimodal Media Assets" –MMA (Katsaounidou & Dimoulas, 2018; Veglis et al., 2016). Overall, the convergence of commonplace cross- and trans-media practices with upcoming multimodal authentication techniques is attempted towards a meaningful breakthrough on verification integration.

CROSS-MEDIA AUTHENTICATION AND VERIFICATION MODEL

Background: Cross-Media and Authentication Technologies

Looking back at the early days of cross-media, the availability of multiple communication channels gave the opportunity to publish an article by means of multiple paths and terminals. The content was produced once, in its prototype form /medium, and then it was pushed further on different networks, disseminating the same story via additional routes (Cross-media Publishing, CP). The most characteristic example that someone could refer to, is the release of electronic editions for printed newspapers and magazines, which actually flagged the beginning of the multiple media paradigms (Veglis 2012a, 2012b; Veglis et al., 2016). Following the trends of multichannel publishing, the interest moved on the exploitation of the alternative access points for enhancing users' engagement and interaction, implementing more sophisticated digital narrations. Thereafter, Cross-/Trans-media Storytelling (CS, TS) models emerged, aiming at creating more appealing presentations, directed through the nonlinear hyperlinking mechanisms and the associated networking services (i.e. channels, like Web, Streaming, Social networks, Twitter, Blogs, Smartphone, Tablet, etc.). In the former case (CS), the storyline is composed of multiple successive streams, each one containing different portion of information, so that users have to navigate to all the interfacing nodes for accessing the entire narrative. In the later scenario (TS), parts of the story are offered in parallel, having differentiated /channel-adapted content, thus "creating a rich in-between space, an archive of shared meaning" (Dimoulas et al., 2015). While the majority of the average users that are nowadays using CP, CS and TS services cannot, actually, point out the differences among them, all of the above forms have been put into practice for such long time, so that the gained experience has resulted in high maturity levels (at least, at the side of media professionals).

On the other hand, the ICT evolution brought forward new trends that pose certain similarities with CP, CS and TS models, hence blurring further the borders between the different disciplines. Specifically, Web documentaries (Web Docs), adaptive and semantically-enhanced hypermedia, are currently combined with Drone and Immersive Journalism products, crafting novel TS mechanisms. A variety of "second screen" applications has been developed to accompany most infotainment services (e.g. news, sports, lifestyle, documentaries, etc.), whereas Virtual and Augmented Reality technologies (VR, AR) are often used for propelling users' active participation (Dimoulas et al., 2015; 2108; Dimoulas, Kalliris, Chatzara, Tsipas, & Papanikolaou, 2014; Katsaounidou, Matsiola, & Dimoulas, 2016; Matsiola, Dimoulas, Kalliris, & Veglis, 2015; Ntalakas, Dimoulas, Kalliris, & Veglis, 2017; Seijo, 2017). For instance, AR-books, fold-out magazines /newspapers and animated maps shape some of the recent examples that utilize both electronic and paper-media, indicating a possible interesting turn in news consuming. Consequently, traditional news-readers have the choice to use their favored printed versions, where tablets and smart-phones can explore the surroundings that lay beneath the written stories, by offering on-demand access to enriched multimedia material. Also, the newfangled forms can encompass multimodal adaptation, learning and gamification components, which, along with context- and location-aware interactions, can literately alter the whole digital narration experience. Hence, the communicability, vividness and learning capabilities of those TS styles are further extended, favoring stronger and more entertaining engagement. These features are capable of efficiently supporting both news-informing and continuous digital literacy needs (Pavlik & Bridges, 2013; Shelton, Warren, & Archambault, 2016; Weedon, Miller, Franco, Moorhead, & Pearce, 2014; Zeman, 2017). In all cases, enriched TS services have become quite common in the media market, which is dominated by the co-existence of multiple content entities, (re)-sources, dissemination pipelines, access terminals, end-users' categories and roles. As a result, the reconsideration of the applied cross-validation principles seems to be urgent, pointing in the direction of integrated authentication solutions, through extended correlations of all the involved modalities.

As already implied, researchers responded to the arisen media verification challenges, so that tremendous progress has been achieved in every associated individual domain. Obviously, the wanted aggregation and unification (of all the approaches) is still missing; nevertheless, this is quite reasonable and has been already justified on the large heterogeneity of the involved entities, methods and technologies (Katsaounidou, 2016; Katsaounidou & Dimoulas, 2018). Recalling parts of the Introduction section, all three types of fully-/semi-automated and manual authentication systems have been implemented. In the former two cases, algorithms and Machine Learning (ML) systems have been developed, either for providing the final decision making (in the first sub-case), or for the assistance of the users /experts, by locating and indicating possible forgeries (second sub-case). The third category, which preceded the other two, relies on the subjective assessment of information, taking advantage of the human experience. For instance, potential inconsistencies can be revealed in the text-syntax and/or in the physical /undisrupted continuity of the audiovisual captures (i.e. photos, audio and video records). Thus, much effort has been put on the evaluation of short messaging services (i.e. Twitter), which are used for fast dissemination of emerging /breaking news (so, the control of potential untrue alerts could slowdown overall misinformation propagation). More specifically, the absence of textual meaning might imply that the messages have been post-processed or entirely composed by machines. Likewise, the frequent appearance (or absence) of some particular words and/or punctuation symbols (e.g. capitalized letters, exclamation points, etc.) might be related to specific "writers" (humans or machines). Thoughts and emotions that are extracted from an article can be further crisscrossed, concerning their match to the side-views of the accompanied events or situations (topic, time, location, semantics, context, etc.). To this end, useful conclusions can be drawn, grounded in the detection of unjustified contradictories (e.g. a sad story cannot be covered /reported with unfitting humorous mood). Commonly, both the original news-reports and the remarked altering trails are stored and documented in dedicated data repositories, allowing users and experts of various fields to exchange useful ideas on the matters, whereas time-passing works in favor of forgery discovery (Dimoulas et al., 2014a, 2014b, 2015, 2018; Ho & Li, 2015; Katsaounidou, 2016; Katsaounidou & Dimoulas, 2018; Mendoza et al., 2010; Silverman, 2013; Veglis et al., 2016; Zubiaga & Ji, 2014).

Extending the above, text-based authentication systems can be used, not only for short messages, but also for more elongated corpora that are part of an article or a multimedia story. Indeed, the adopted practices are being propagated and gradually progressed to other /composite content modalities, while they are tested as potential inputs to machine-driven solutions. Related verification artifacts can also be listed for the cases of photos and generally images, i.e. within the frame of motion picture sequences. Hence, abrupt changes in the values /colors of blocks, edges or pixels, as well as "missing or unexpected shadows and reflections" can be interpreted as manipulation side effects. Furthermore, areas with almost identical visual data imply possible cloning operations, where observations of inconsistencies about the scale, the relative placement or the geometry of some objects (with respect to the whole image view) expose potential splicing actions (Farid, 2009; Katsaounidou & Dimoulas, 2018; Silverman, 2013). Likewise, audio continuity interruptions associated with groundless changes in background noise, music or reverb indicate regions of "novelty detection" that might be connected to possible sound treatment or tampering. The same applies to the appearance of unjustified alterations in speech rate, pitch and intonation shapes (Dimoulas & Symeonidis, 2015; Gupta et al., 2012; Katsaounidou & Dimoulas, 2018; Katsaounidou, Vryzas, Kotsakis, & Dimoulas, 2016; Maher, 2010). As far as it concerns the case of video, favorably, the above image forgery detection principles can be extended from the solely spatial analysis to the additional evaluation of temporal and spatiotemporal correlations, aiming at revealing frame deletion, cloning or processing fingerprints (Al-Sanjary & Sulong, 2015; Katsaounidou & Dimoulas, 2018; Stamm, Lin, & Liu, 2012).

Algorithm-driven solutions, both semi- and fully-automated ones, can take full advantage of the offered high resolution and the increased power of the contemporary computing systems, thus more thorough inspections can be applied (i.e. at pixel /sample level and beyond, by projecting /predicting missing data). In particular, multi-observations and their connections can discover various hidden patterns, both in the text streams, i.e. through Natural Language Processing (NLP) searching mechanisms, and in the cases of audiovisual recordings, i.e. by locating possible artifacts and altering traces in the different representations or signal domains (e.g. in various time /space, frequency or scale views, multi-dimensional feature-spaces, etc.). Further elements, which are not easily accessible by humans, can also be added to the evaluation, such as the signatures of the capturing sensors or the recording media, concerning their noising patterns, their expected responses or even specific nonlinear behaviors that might feature (i.e. lenses and camera transducers, microphones and audiovisual recorders; analog or digital). Hence, the recognition of multiple "capturing" and/or "recording fingerprints" implies that multi-sourced audio or video segments have been combined. Likewise, encoding and compression patterns can be used as audiovisual source indicators, while other related metadata, hidden in the digitized sequences or easily extracted after some mandatory processing, favor similar root-tracking utilities. Furthermore, context-, time- and location-aware metadata, as well as content-based extraction of topic, semantic and emotion tags, offer additional inspection (and correlation) sights that can assist the overall veracity assessment process. Among others, ML and Deep Learning (DL) architectures are implemented for detecting possible universal manipulations or even the order of each tampering operation in the entire processing chain (Bayar & Stamm, 2016; Chen, Zhao, & Ni, 2017). As it has already been stated, the genres of text and (especially) photo authentication have received significant attention from multitudinous and pioneering scientific groups (i.e. image processing societies), so remarkable research progress has been conducted in these fields. The cases of audio and video present some hysteresis, due to their more demanding character, but also because of the corresponding delay in achieving the wanted audiovisual processing and authoring capabilities (Al-Sanjary & Sulong, 2015; Gupta et al., 2012; Katsaounidou et al., 2016a, 2016b; Mahdian & Saic, 2010; Mendoza et al., 2010; Mizher et al., 2017; Qureshi & Deriche, 2015; Stamm et al., 2012; Zubiaga & Ji, 2014). Once again, today's posts and shares are dominated by multimodal information (MMA), which combine time-based (audio, video, animations, etc.) and page-based media (text, images, pages, etc.), along with their linked metadata (Dimoulas et al., 2014a, 2014b; Katsaounidou & Dimoulas, 2018). Therefore, the absence of a holistic framework, which could jointly evaluate (and cross-authenticate) all the encountered multimodal entities, deteriorate the real potentials of the currently available verification solutions.

Multiple Media and Authentication Needs: Issues, Controversies, Problems

Nowadays, we are experiencing a whole new world of digital communications, dominated by the Social Networking Sites (SNS), the plurality of cross-media publishing and storytelling models, as well as the liquefied journalism landscape, where related present-day tools continuously appear and rapidly evolve (e.g. Drone, Robot, Data Journalism, etc.). Social Media have become the most popular place for news organizations to broaden and impress their audience. Facebook, Twitter, YouTube and other web services are used by their members to spread "knowledge" and to seed topics for the news reporters. The race to publish and the desire to have "a fancy story be true" can blind journalists to their judgment about the facts, showing a preference to events that appeal to emotion and personal belief, which give people the opportunity to criticize rather than to applaud. For instance, information about the economy, politics, conspiracy ideations, paranormal beliefs, alternative medicine, etc., which address to excessively "open-minded" individuals, is a cause for serious concerns. Ideology, money, status and desire for attention are included among the reasons that motivate actors to create and spread disinformation, propaganda or fake news. Due to their popular nature and the lack of effective and reliable censorship safeguards, SNSs have turned to be the central space for spreading misinformation online (Marwick & Lewis, 2017). In all cases, there is an urgent need for re-inventing cross-validation and authentication codes (and ethics) in the era of multiple media and Digital Journalism, where misinforming propagation is entirely uncontrollable.

The above matters are further deteriorated by the plurality of the newly surfaced Digital Journalism forms, starting with the machine-generated and distributed content, and the overall involvement of algorithms in the news production and publishing automations (i.e. Robot, Automated or Algorithmic Journalism). Specifically, many posts and shares within social networks offer "related stories" through auto-generated links, retrieved and recommended by topic detection algorithms that attempt to match the subject or theme of the source article. These decision-making systems are regularly opaque in the criteria that use to select and classify information. In most cases, they are encompassing predictions of relevance based on past behaviors, content types, interactions and, of course, commercial goals, while not paying much attention to the accuracy of the reports (Bode & Vraga, 2015; Boididou et al., 2017; Gillespie, 2014; Messing & Westwood, 2014; Pariser, 2012). The fast advancement of those procedures, along with the absence of clarity and proper documentation, results in understanding difficulties, further hardening the comprehension of their operational attributes and usefulness. Therefore, lack of confidence might be induced in the involved actors (both journalists and their audience), who are unable to fully exploit the offered tools and facilities in their everyday practice. As a side effect, most people are becoming more vulnerable to potential forgery attacks through the newly surfaced and usually incomprehensive means (Katsaounidou, 2016, Katsaounidou & Dimoulas, 2016; Ntalakas et al., 2017). Similar deficiencies or disadvantages can be found in the rest trendy genres of Digital Journalism, such as Data, Multimedia, Immersive and Drone Journalism. Inadequacy of related knowledge, practical experience and knowhow tend to form a defending attitude, to all media professionals, actively-engaged /contributing users and news consumers. Likewise, technical and usability complications arise regarding the proper configuration and functioning of the new services, including the setup and use of the add-on software or hardware. Apart from that, legal, regulatory and ethical matters are faced in most of the above disciplines and especially in Drone Journalism. The emerging issues seem to have a negative impact on both production and consumption ends, affecting the end-to-end chain of news reporting. Consequently, small groups of users and journalists utilize these recently launched paradigms in practice, a fact that further deteriorates their possible misuse, including likely disinformation actions (Coddington, 2015; Dörr, 2015; Dörr & Hollnbuchner, 2017; Gynnild, 2016; Haim & Graefe, 2017; Linden, 2016, 2017; Montal & Reich, 2016; Ntalakas et al., 2017; Seijo, 2017; Van Dalen, 2012; Veglis & Bratsas, 2017a, 2017b).

Additional controversies emerge because of the turn to multimodal news storytelling (TS) and immersive services. For instance, there are some contradictory argumentations regarding the truthful or engaging character of news informing. Web-docs, hypermedia, AR-books, transmedia games, fold-out magazines /newspapers and animated maps are some of the augmentation elements that are used for expanding the story narration across multiple modalities. Similarly, VR technologies, aerial footage, multi-view /360° coverage, photorealistic 3D graphics and dedicated Human Machine Interaction (HMI) terminals are also "hired" for immersing the audience into the recreated news-world. In this manner, stronger engagement is encouraged via multisite interaction nodes or "places", which can have both physical and virtual nature. The cross-modal character of those novel models empowers audience participation, interconnecting all the involved actors with different content modalities and "words", in meaningful ways (Dimoulas et al., 2015,

2018; Sánchez-Mesa, Aarseth, & Pratten, 2016; Weedon et al., 2014). On-demand access to linked stories can be exploited to "x-ray" the surroundings behind the events, thus favoring diverse and multi-angled informing with rich media experience. End-users are expected to join equally pull and push activities, facilitating crowdsourcing and collaborative processing for the tasks of multimedia authoring and publishing, while enhancing the global character of the corresponding transmedia news coverage. Overall, multiple journalism styles can be embraced with the combination of reports and documents, opinion articles, comments, etc., either from the part of the news organizations or from the sides of users and citizen journalists. On the other hand, there is a different argumentation supporting that, instead of engaging the audience through appealing storytelling, the number one priority of news-report should be to defend the truth and to inform the people. Hence, investigative practices and facts are considered as more important than stories (and aesthetics), which could turn journalism into a myth-making job (Groot Kormelink & Costera Meijer, 2015; Rampazzo Gambarato & Tárcia, 2016; Sánchez-Mesa et al., 2016; Weedon et al., 2014). While this dilemma has just surfaced and will probably stay for the following few years, it is clear that the availability of multiple genres and tools tend to confuse and disorient all kinds of users (at least in the beginning). This weakness could also offer a fertile ground for media forgery and misinformation to grow. On the contrary, it can be supported that the proper and well-balanced use of the up-to-date digital communication services could be the only prosperous solution to deal with the root of all these problems.

There are many advantages that the new journalism styles can offer, concerning timely, accurate and unbiased informing, where built-in validation filters can automatically engage. For instance, Data and Robot Journalism can offer the wanted transparency by properly documenting the associated data repositories and algorithms and, mostly, by releasing these assets under open /public licenses and use rights. The same applies to the cases of Multimedia and Immersive Journalism, provided that the source authoring material (and its thorough description) is similarly made accessible to the public. In addition, putting aside current regulation deficiencies, drones can truly offer an undisputed eye witness from above, which can be used as proof evidence of the associated events (especially if the aerial photos or footage are accompanied with time- and location-aware sensing data, thus making available the overall context of the captured /transmitted stories) (Ntalakas et al., 2017). The immediate and geographically unconstrained coverage attributes of this perspective can be further extended, by putting

UGC models into equation (i.e. engaging drone enthusiast and amateurs into citizens' journalism duties). Likewise, dedicated surveillance networks and/ or robotic systems (i.e. security cameras, traffic monitoring grids, Unmanned Aerial /Ground Vehicles, UAV /UGV, etc.) can be part of cooperative media production and management. Hence, Mobile Journalism and UGC-interactions can further extend the diversity and complementarity of events that are captured, processed, stored and shared through multiple publishing channels and SNSs. Although large-scale heterogeneity and improper /inconsistent annotation of the "streams to be matched" deteriorate the possibilities for their successful collaborative exploitation, undoubtedly, much progress has been achieved for the detection and registration of multimodal assets belonging to the same event or story (Álvarez, 2017; Dimoulas et al., 2014a, 2015, 2018; Dimoulas et al., 2014b; Dimoulas & Symeonidis, 2015; Gynnild, 2014; 2016; Kim, Evans, Blat, & Hilton, 2016; Ntalakas et al., 2017; Papadopoulos, Cesar, Shamma, & Kelliher, 2015; Rodríguez & Freire, 2017). Subsequently, besides the obvious enhancements in the used data repositories and the offered storytelling experience, among others, multichannel synching can serve cross-validation and authentication aims.

The availability of different audiovisual captures (and overall data), describing an explicit story, works in favor of the authentication. Specifically, single-file content evaluations and cross-correlations between the different instances can be conducted by both human and machines, aiming at locating possible forgery attacks. Indisputably, a lot of effort has been put for the implementation of methods, capable of revealing potential manipulation of information, including their algorithmic automation. Human-driven approaches have been thoroughly studied by related groups of experts, leading to the adoption of some primary best practices (Ho & Li, 2015; Katsaounidou & Dimoulas, 2018; Silverman, 2013). However, we are still far away from the moment that an apt factchecking codebook will be available, empowering end-users with the necessary knowledge, flexibility and adaptation to deal with the tampering revealing challenges, encountered in their every-day practice. Outstanding research progress has also been achieved for the development of fully- and semi-automated machine-driven verification solutions. Unpleasantly, these decision-making systems feature broad heterogeneity and complexity, so that, even the interpretation of the extracted validation outcomes (i.e. color heat-maps in photo forgery evaluation) requires some basic knowledge of the underlying algorithmic principles. It has been observed that, in most cases, the higher the sophistication of the implemented technique, the more the requirements for in-depth understanding of its operational attributes. While quite a few useful tools have been released, they regularly focus on a single content entity and on the treatment of a specific manipulation operation. Apparently, this is considered as fairly inadequate, at the moment that most of the exchanged information has nowadays the form of linked multimodal assets. Hence, despite the availability of some solitary services, most users prefer traditional validation approaches, since there is a lack of an integrated system (both in term of content modalities and methods) to support media authentication from all of its aspects in real-world scenarios (Katsaounidou et al., 2016a, 2016b; Katsaounidou & Dimoulas, 2018; Silverman, 2013).

The challenge of addressing the misinformation phenomenon is heavily technical, not only semantic, so that it needs to be supported at multiple levels. The main question remains the discovery of the possible features that are common in fake content, which need to be further supplemented and validated through related journalistic factchecking rules. Cross-modal processing has become the commonplace for many contemporary and highly demanding media tasks, such as topic detection and tracking, content-based searching and retrieval, multimedia document understanding and others (Boididou et al., 2017; Dimoulas & Symeonidis, 2015; Diou et al., 2010; Katsaounidou & Dimoulas, 2018; Li, Joo, Qi, & Zhu, 2017; Lu, Jin, Su, Shivakumara, & Tan, 2015; Peng, Huang, & Zhao, 2017; Vryzas, Kotsakis, Dimoulas, & Kalliris, 2016). While most of these systems have not reached an adequate maturity level yet, it can be predicted that, given the rapid technology and research evolution in the implicated domains so far, a lot of the encountered difficulties will be decisively faced in the near future. Such kinds of solutions seem to perfectly match to the inherent multimodal character /nature of the media veracity problem. Synergies and integration with the aforementioned fields are anticipated towards a prosperous cross-media authentication solution, taking advantage of all of the involved modalities (i.e. tools, methods, content entities, channels, etc.). Figure 1 graphically presents the above listed issues and controversies that associate multichannel publishing and storytelling models with the information validation needs. As already argued, both problems and challenges arise, which are strongly connected to the progress of the new digital journalism styles and the consequent ideological, legal and moral questions concerning the future of news reporting. Among others, motives, opportunities and anticipated benefits, pointing in the direction of the proposed cross-modal integration, are brought forward.

Figure 1. Multiple media and authentication needs: Issues, controversies, problems

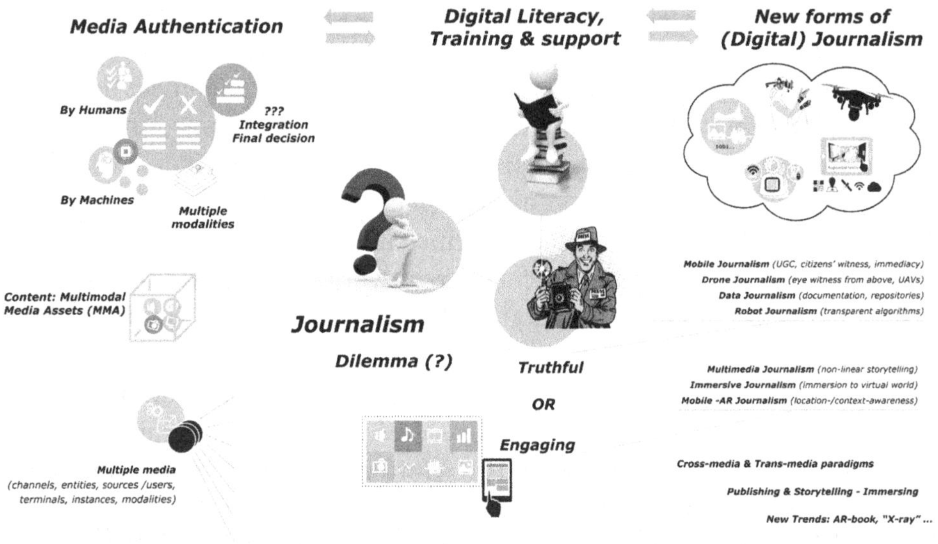

SOLUTIONS AND RECOMMENDATIONS

Integrating Cross-Media Authentication Models

Following the preceding analysis, cross-media authentication could be defined as an integrated veracity model, aiming at evaluating all the involved modalities across multiple channels (i.e. content entities /types, versions and forensic inspection outcomes), so that their unexpected contradictions could indicate possible tampering actions. In this approach, the different entities refer to the various types of information (i.e. text /messages, images /photos, audio, video, nonlinear multimedia, etc.), including the original multimodal assets and their accompanying metadata. The modified versions are related to the use of complementary publishing and storytelling ways, where slight variations are expected within the implicated terminals and news-products. The extraction of alternative validation instances is justified on the plurality of the above media forms and editions, as well as on the availability of several analysis methods, even within the exact same content type. For instance, photo manipulation can be checked by innumerous ways, such as through the estimation of inconsistent local noise patterns (implying different capturing locations, lighting conditions, sensing equipment, etc.), varying compression levels (indicating successive encoding /saving operations, therefore potential post-processing actions), and others (Bayar & Stamm, 2016; Chen et al., 2017; Farid, 2009; Katsaounidou & Dimoulas, 2018; Schetinger, Oliveira, da Silva, & Carvalho, 2015; Al-Sanjary & Sulong, 2015; Mizher et al., 2017). In the specific case of photo-forensics, it has been noticed that, though most forgery categories are generally detected by at least one method, the overall recognition accuracy remains at relatively low levels when algorithms are solely used. This also deteriorates the precision, hence the reliability of the provided results, which could erroneously lead to the registration of false positive marks (i.e. authentic /genuine images might be classified as fake / tampered). Reasonably, along with the technological and research progress, new algorithmic perspectives appear, practically offering unlimited implementation extensions that can be deployed for each one of the principle assessment ideas. In addition, the intervention of the human factor can be catalytic, whereas the adoption and appliance of best-practices, conducted by various investigators and expert groups, and their dynamic combination with the machine-drivel solutions, can further extend the potentials of the suggested integration. While such kind of modeling has been already proposed (Katsaounidou & Dimoulas, 2018), the novel part, here, lays in the targeted unification with the associated cross-media publishing and storytelling needs, taking into consideration the newly surfaced digital journalism models.

The motivation behind this cross-media veracity idea is quite obvious, if not self-evident, and it can be rationalized on the intensive multimodal character of today's information dissemination, as well as on the turning up of related cross-modal processing initiatives (Boididou et al., 2017; Dimoulas & Symeonidis, 2015; Li et al., 2017; Lu et al., 2015; Peng et al., 2017; Vryzas et al., 2016). Consequently, useful knowledge, concerning authenticity validation and disinformation prevention, could be mined by correlating all the engaged modalities (not only in terms of media assets, channels and storytelling means, but also with respect to different actors, i.e. professional and citizen journalists, informing and interacting audience, etc.). Indeed, such kinds of cross-modal processes have been already deployed for the urgent requirement of efficient content management, which came into view with the advent of Web 2.0 (UGC) and the domination of the participatory journalism models. The critical prerequisites for proper documentation and archiving of the massively exchanged multimedia streams resulted in the development of more sophisticated techniques and services, such as news alerting and recommendation systems, topic classification, searching and retrieval algorithms, semantic extraction and conceptualization forms, etc. (Dimoulas et al. 2014b; Dimoulas & Symeonidis, 2015; Diou et al., 2010; Katsaounidou

& Dimoulas, 2018; Li et al., 2017; Lu et al., 2015; Peng et al., 2017; Vryzas et al., 2016). Most of these approaches suffer from many difficulties at the moment, so that are mainly deployed at the research level. Nonetheless, it is more than certain that related practical applications will exponentially increase in the near future, aiming at dealing with the contemporary necessities in the journalism and mass communications business. Therefore, the convergence of the above trends towards collaborative cross-media authentication could bring forward some mutual benefits for all the involved parties, thus conjointly serving the arisen duties (i.e. semantic recognition and processing, multichannel publishing/storytelling, aggregated factchecking and verification integration). Subsequently, the broader meaning of the "cross-media" term incorporates the root concepts of the cross- and trans-media paradigms (CP, CS, TS), as well as the meta-processes of multimodal correlation and validation, across multiple users, networks and tools.

Considering the current state of the art (and research) of digital media technologies, presented in the previous paragraphs, and combining them with the accompanied argumentation that followed, a SWOT analysis was conducted for estimating Strengths, Weaknesses, Opportunities and Threats of the proposed model (Table 8-1). First of all, multimedia information (MMA) and cross-modal processes are already present, dominating the new networking landscape, an undisputed fact that can be listed in the strengths of the current project. Looking back at the proliferation of mobile computing and SNSs (including the paradigms of Web and Mobile Journalism), UGC production resulted in massive content exchange, on a daily basis. In the same way that this necessity brought forward smart Media Assets Management (MAM) systems and semantic services, it is similarly unavoidable that multimodal processing will prevail, both in the news informing and misinformation prevention practices. Likewise, the so-far progress of the involved technologies is considered among the strong points of the whole undertaking. Thus, new automation algorithms and artificial intelligence methods firmly appear and evolve (i.e. ML, DL), taking advantage of the continually increasing computational power, along with the associated progress in technical sophistication and elegance of the implemented solutions (Bayar & Stamm, 2016; Liu et al., 2017; Ota, Dao, Mezaris, & De Natale, 2017). In addition, the integration of all the encountered layers /instances of the news data and their verification outcomes could combine and jointly automate the individual base components, i.e. the models of multiple media (CP, CS, TS) and the processes of cross-validation. Overall, the advent of the contemporary digital communication ways and the increasing forgery attacks, therefore the intensification of the authentication needs, point in the direction of collaborative evaluation and interpretation of the authenticity remarks, which can be supported within the introduced framework. In this context, unique changes are offered for launching and continuously adapting digital literacy services, while, at the same time, supporting the engagement of the newfangled Digital Journalism genres. It is worth mentioning especially the cases that favor transparent informing /news-reporting that are related to some features of Drone, Robot, Mobile and broadly Computational Journalism, of course, with the prerequisites of proper documentation and availability of the used data and algorithms. Following the above arguments, it is expected that the anticipated progress will have an overall positive impact to the currently pursued far-reaching aims, such as the revolutionary notions of Semantic / Intelligent Web (Web 3.0/4.0) and the upcoming Internet of Things.

Besides the previously stated positive attributes (pros), certain difficulties or disadvantages can also be pinpointed and listed as weaknesses or threats (cons). In specific, a major drawback can be found in the need for central coordination of both the project deployment and its networking architecture. It is well known that the nature of social media and SNSs lacks such a centralized control mechanism, so that it would be difficult to be invented and applied hereafter. In spite of this, dedicated organizations or experts could start to coordinate the whole effort, with the expectation that additional news corporations would voluntarily join the venture, once the first practical benefits are visible. Therefore, the introduction of extra processing /analysis layers and entirely new aggregation mechanisms would allow to unify, better interpret and interoperate all the offered solutions, with the prerequisite cooperation agreements among the involved actors, for ensuring peer access to the repositories and execution codes. Closely linked with the above is the large-scale heterogeneity that is encountered across the entire news informing chain (i.e. content, users, terminals, dissemination and interaction ways, etc.). For instance, the training of artificial /smart systems relies on the availability of large datasets with consistent labeling /tagging that, even under the presence of a chief /supervising administration, is quite difficult to achieve (especially in the cases of DL). Nevertheless, semi-automated annotation procedures are, nowadays, emerging, either by interpreting the authoring and browsing history /analytics that "escort" the associated content, or by propagating related metadata across matched streams (Dimoulas et al., 2014a, 2014b, 2015, 2018; Dimoulas & Symeonidis, 2015; Diou et al., 2010; Ota et al., 2017; Tosi & Morasca, 2015; Sansone et al., 2017). Another strong weakness may be found in the fact that experienced reporters /investigators do face difficulties in

Table 1. SWOT Analysis: Strengths, Weaknesses, Opportunities and Threats of the proposed Cross-media Authentication Model

Strengths	Weaknesses
• Multimodal character of today's information exchange (multiple content entities, channels, storytelling means, users, etc.) • Cross-modal processes have been already deployed (i.e. topic detection and tracking, content-based searching and retrieval, semantic conceptualization, multimedia document understanding and others) • Rapid evolution of related technologies: new potentials • Urgent need for integrated authentication solutions • Urgent need for supporting new trends and, in general, digital literacy	• Need for central coordination • Contradictions to the "free" /non-controlled nature of social media and SNSs • Large-scale heterogeneity across the entire news-reporting chain (i.e. content, users, terminals, dissemination and interaction ways, etc.) • Need for proper /consistently annotated datasets • Experienced reporters /investigators cannot get with the pace of the new trends, while they could induct valuable knowledge and expertise: digital literacy is a critical prerequisite
Opportunities	**Threats**
• Combining and jointly automating the individual disciplines (i.e. multiple media publishing and storytelling, cross-validation, integrated information authentication) • Collaborative solutions: checking, interpreting and validating authenticity remarks • Propelling the employment and practice of the recent digital media genres, in the direction of enhancing transparent journalism (Drone, Robot, Mobile, Computational Journalism etc.) • Propelling active cooperation of all the involved actors through properly structured collaborative networks and services • Launching and continuously adapting digital literacy support services • Contribution to the overall progress of related far-reaching targets (i.e. Semantic /Intelligent Web –Web 3.0/4.0, Internet of Things)	• Misinforming propagation is most cases caused due to intentional disinformation actions • Major stakeholders do not actually desire fight against misinformation (i.e. political and media companies, professionals of various kinds, free-agents, opinion-makers, specific individuals, etc.) • Inconsistent progress along the involved domains (i.e. cross-media and authentication) could be further uncontrollably extended • Imbalance between complexity and sophistication of the implemented methods could deteriorate their usability • Powerful modern technologies could be held in the exclusive use of elite groups, actually acting in favor of subjective and falsified informing • Extracted knowledge could be used in opposite directions by misinformation players (i.e. counter- or anti-forensics)

getting along with the pace of the new trends. Consequently, digital literacy is again considered very important for avoiding the exclusion of this category of experts, who could induct valuable knowledge and expertise.

Last but not least, threats are always present, when such major breakthroughs are attempted. Principally, in most cases, misinforming propagation is caused due to intentional disinformation actions, so decisive confrontation of this negative phenomenon might not be really desired by some major stakeholders (i.e. political and media companies, professionals of various kinds, free-agents, opinion-makers, influencing individuals, etc.). Possible risk can also be justified on technical reasons, such as the inconsistent progress that has been conducted so far along the involved domains of cross-media and authentication. In specific, while some areas enclose remarkable progress and practical success, other developments feature a pure research character, thus failing to initiate the mass deployment of practical /real-world applications.

Likewise, the appearance of incomprehensible complexity or technical sophistication of the implemented solutions worsens the probabilities for their optimum exploitation (i.e. average users cannot easily operate complicated systems, regardless of their effectiveness). This fact might cause some additional obstacles in the required wide collaboration among multiple actors with ultra-diverse skills and interests (i.e. interdisciplinary research groups and academics, experienced reporters, journalism and governmental organizations, hobbyists of various emerging trends, end-users, etc.). In this context, there is another danger for the powerful modern technologies to be held in the exclusive control of elite groups, so that they can be used to propel, rather than to fight, subjective and falsified informing. Finally, a significant threat, also deriving from the rapid advancement of contemporary media tools, deteriorates the weaknesses of the inadequate digital-literacy-support to the heavier-impact risk of exploiting methods and knowhow in the reverse order, i.e. for serving information manipulation. Particularly, with the evolution of the veracity solutions the domain of counter- or anti-forensics has emerged, purposing to conceal content tampering operations, thus preventing or hardening proper forensic investigation (Katsaounidou & Dimoulas, 2018; Stamm et al., 2012). Hence, there is always an opening for competent "misinformation players" to infiltrate into the "verification world", exploiting mined knowledge in the exact opposite direction. Unfortunately, the skillful profiles of these actors, combined with the previously stated deficiencies (i.e. unstable media environment, lack of confidence in the new trends, urgent need for on-demand training and support, etc.), continue to act in favor of disinformation rather than its decisive confrontation (at least, in most practical situations).

Figure 2 presents the basic architecture and the data flow of the proposed integrated authentication model. Looking the diagram from the media production and dissemination sides, professional agencies have the opportunity of jointly serving the tasks of cross- /trans-media publishing and storytelling, along with the compulsory cross-validation and verification demands. Various automations can be applied in this direction (Veglis et al., 2016), aiming at autonomously producing all the required multimodal assets in the best possible quality (matched to the technical attributes of the different channels, terminals and storyline interaction nodes). Again, proper documentation and release of the implemented algorithms can guarantee the desired transparency, ensuring that the applied modifications were only made for serving multimedia authoring or adaptation needs, i.e. for confronting possible format compliance. In this context, processing logs and coding

Figure 2. The proposed cross-media authentication model

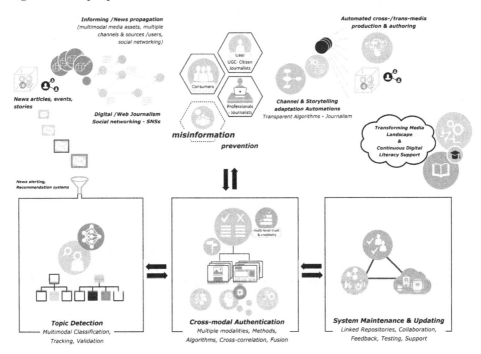

certifications eliminate the doubts for potential side-operations (i.e. linked to information manipulation), so that news organizations can claim their proper /unbiased newsgathering and reporting across the multiple modalities. Furthermore, newfangled journalism models can be employed, either for augmenting users' experience (i.e. Multimedia and Immersive Journalism) or for enhancing the authentication credibility, through supplementary views of timely and multi-angled footage or other data (i.e. Drone, Mobile and Data Journalism). As already discussed, surveillance grids, robotic systems and mobile UGC streams can be ingested in the informing streams, thus offering the possibility to further extend the diversity and objectivity of the captured events, while simultaneously promoting the more active audience engagement by means of nonlinear /HMI-augmented narrations (Álvarez, 2017; Dimoulas et al., 2014b, 2015, 2018; Dimoulas & Symeonidis, 2015; Gynnild, 2014, 2016; Kim et al., 2016; Ntalakas et al., 2017). Subsequently, both targets of engaging and truthful journalism can be served, depending on the nature of the stories and the associated preferences in the production and consumption ends. In addition, new trends can be used for delivering the extracted forgery detection outcomes (described next) in more entertained, comprehensive and vivid ways. For instance, the AR-book paradigm can be extended to AR-newspapers and magazines, allowing to X-ray, not only the surrounding info that accompanies a news-article, but mostly, the possible tampering indications. Likewise, digital literacy and technical support actions can be delivered through similar user-friendly mechanisms.

Apparently, professional and citizen journalists (in the broader meaning of contributing users) can equally be involved in the above production, publishing and authoring tasks, although they feature some different capabilities with respect to their specialty /training, the gained experience and the used infrastructures. Additional informing procedures (i.e. news alerts, recommendations, info-propagation monitoring, etc.) are even more important nowadays, both at the production and consumption ends. Particularly, journalists can exploit the warning services for catching up to timely coverage and breaking news reports, while end-users can utilize these feeds for staying tuned /informed. Algorithms of topic detection, classification and tracking are usually "hidden" in the back-ends of the corresponding systems, attempting to adapt to users' infotainment preferences, based on the selected configurations, their browsing history and interaction experience, etc. Nowadays, such automations play a key-role in the proposed cross-media authentication, purposing to locate all the alternative "versions" of the same story, which are disseminated along SNSs, through numerous channels, users and terminals (Dimoulas et al., 2014a, 2018; Diou et al., 2010; Lu et al., 2015; Matsiola et al., 2015; Ntalakas et al., 2017). Once new streams are located, matched and validated under a specific topic /article, multimodal assessment takes on, inspecting the associated modalities with regard to forgery detection: i.e. multimedia assets (text, image, audio, video, etc.), channel- and medium-adapted content versions, source profiles, human- and machine-driven authentication outcomes. Given that multiple approaches are used for detecting potential tampering attacks, the incorporation of all possible /applicable combinations allows for multilayered knowledge to be cross-correlated and verified. Therefore, performance accuracy of each method can be monitored and correlated with the associated altering operations, thus offering useful feedback that can propel the construction of dedicated ground-truth knowledge bases. Considering the large-scale inhomogeneity of the used resources /instances (and of the whole problem), unification of the provided results is considered very important, whereas continuous training and support actions are equally significant for informing users on how to exploit the implemented services. Although such kind of integration has already been presented (Katsaounidou & Dimoulas, 2018), cross-modal processes are further involved here, extending the used evaluation corpus, while also serving multiple contemporary needs (i.e. topic detection and tracking, news alerting /recommendation, stream alignment /registration, transmedia authoring /storytelling, and others).

In order the depicted dataflow to be better comprehended, it would be useful to examine a typical news-story example. Let us suppose that a fresh story /article has appeared and it is questioned about its validity. Firstly, topic detection and cross-modal inspection processes will run, targeting the localization of all the possible alternative versions and instances, either from the same source (cross-/trans- media paradigms) and/or from other producers (i.e. posts and shares propagated by journalists, professional organizations, actively-participating and regular users /news-consumers). After the validation and synchronization of the matched streams, forensic investigation will be executed for each of the individual content entities along all the applicable assessment methods. Hence, source, title and keywords of the article can be checked in human-directed hoax-fighting web sites, returning useful feedback about the credibility of the publisher and the potential controversies regarding similar subjects in the past. Text processing and meta-processing can be applied (i.e. through NLP) to estimate possible syntax inconsistencies (i.e. implying fake accounts, machine-composed messages, etc.) or divergences in the extracted semantics (i.e. subject /theme, opinion, emotions, etc.). Thereafter, the remaining media assets that accompany the corresponding event (usually having the role of proof-evident) will be analyzed along the entire evaluation toolset. Hence, photos will be examined by the applicable image forgery detection algorithms and the variant human-directed practices. The provided results can be crisscrossed, as long as unified data structures and visualization mechanisms are adopted (e.g. use of specific range color-maps, indicating the possibilities of altering operations across the entire image surface). After that, cross-inspection between all the extracted image tampering maps can be conducted, targeting to detect possible consistencies that are common /mutually presented in most of the matched instances (i.e. different channels, sources etc.). Next, similar rounds of investigations will be applied for the remaining content entities (audio, video, etc.), firstly along multiple evaluation methods and then across the registered versions / streams. Multimodal document understanding in terms of opinions, semantic and emotional conceptualization cues will supplement the existed metadata and tags (i.e. time-, location- and context-aware, user-inserted /selected, etc.), thus making it possible to conduct broader cross-modal correlations. It is essential for the entirety of the extracted remarks to be kept in publicly accessed linked repositories, featuring proper organization and structuring with dedicated documentation policies that need to be followed by all the engaged parties. Each time that a new story /informing stream appears, initiation of the applicable evaluation sessions is also triggered, allowing authored users to rank, classify, flag or archive the corresponding records. Furthermore, end-users' browsing history and interactions can be logged as "consuming annotations", while answers to specific questions and comments can similarly be crowd-sourced.

As already argued, a lot of technical and organization difficulties need to be faced, before the proposed model could become a viable solution. Continuous adaptation and system updates are needed each time that a new article /version, authentication method or technology appears, while large-scale heterogeneity always remains a big issue. Training on the latest tools and overall digital literacy support should also be solidly /on-demand provided, ordering to engage as many as possible users in the efficient operation of the offered services. Considering that crisp classification results are not very frequent in real-world examples, inconsistencies or controversies are very likely to be encountered among the evaluation outcomes of the various modalities. Consequently, networks of expert users and organizations must run and administrate the whole undertaking, where collaboration is more than essential for adopting best practices and overall policies, taking the right decisions when related questions arise. The above attributes form a typical, though highly demanding, big-data problem, requiring careful interdisciplinary analysis, planning and execution. However, there are certain advantages in this direction, as well, such as the construction of generic-purpose large repositories, the progress in the implementation of sophisticated DL algorithms and architectures, the availability of powerful computing systems (having high-end hardware and software resources), etc. (Bayar & Stamm, 2016; Dimoulas et al., 2015, 2018; Dimoulas & Symeonidis, 2015; Diou et al., 2010; Liu, Ma, Qi, Zhao, & Chen, 2017; Ota et al., 2017; Sansone et al., 2017; Tosi & Morasca, 2015). Joint advancement and convergence of these techniques are considered very important towards the materialization of the Semantic and Intelligent Web envisions, forming the forthcoming media breakthroughs. Looking forward at the far-reaching aim of the Internet of Things, similar cross-modal procedures are currently emerging, featuring comparable technical requirements in terms of elegance, maturity and sophistication. Therefore, anticipated synergies between all these projects are expected to work in favor of the individual targets, also propelling the incarnation of the proposed cross-media authentication model.

CONCLUSION

The present chapter provides a detailed view of the proposed cross-media authentication model. Multiple channels and nonlinear narration means have become the commonplace in most contemporary informing services, which exploit many different publishing and dissemination pathways. In specific, cross-modal storytelling and enhanced transmedia products have already begun to dominate mass communications and overall the news world. In this race, time works in favor of the new Digital Journalism models, the practical application and testing of which will offer the desired experience for gradually leading to their flourishing. Multimodal solutions have also emerged for providing efficient management, archiving and documentation utilities, as an answer to the innumerous users and content instances, involved in today's information exchange. Hence, new robotic systems have become available, utilizing high-end hardware and software components that can be deployed for both event capturing automations and multi-angled story augmentations. For example, dedicated aerial, ground and underwater vehicles that are currently being constructed, can provide fascinating footage from different environments, which might not be accessible to human journalists (Ntalakas et al., 2017). In this context, professionals and media organizations can adapt to the modern needs for continuous and timely newsgathering. On the contrary, massive propagation of unverified content is listed among the side-effect risks, caused by the uncontrollable news dissemination character. As a result, there is an urgent necessity for reconsidering cross-validation principles and rules. Undeniably, technological advances are expected to have a strongly positive impact, not only to the specific verification problem, but also to the entirety of the involved disciplines (Ho & Li, 2015; Katsaounidou & Dimoulas, 2018). However, the extreme rhythms that digital media services continue to evolve preserve a rather fluidly /unstable environment that creates anxiety and lack of confidence to the audience. In principle, it is very crucial to re-focus the central interest to the users' point of view, to fight both social exclusion and digital illiteracy. Thus, continuous training, updating and support actions are necessary for keeping up with the new trends, persistently notifying people for the entrance of new algorithms, computing systems, processing and interaction capabilities, veracity methods and practices.

Extending the above remarks in the news consumption side, humanoid robots, featuring multilingual, user-friendly and more humane-like interaction mechanisms, can now be part of innovative infotainment and journalism services, facilitating the joint promotion of social inclusion and digital literacy support. Gamification components and immersive experiences (AR, VR) are being deployed for connecting the physical world with multilayered virtual places, aiming at engaging the audience in more intensive and entertaining ways (Ntalakas et al., 2017; Tsardoulias, Thallas, Symeonidis, & Mitkas, 2016; Tsardoulias et al., 2017; Zeman, 2017). Portable devices like smartphones and tablets have become the natural extension of the human senses, so they can offer means for exploring the surrounding landscapes through visual searching, context- and location-aware metadata and other "X-ray" ways (i.e. AR-book applications). Thus, lookup information of various kinds can be extracted and projected, i.e. retrieving the background of a story, indicating possible forgeries, supporting digital literacy needs, etc. (Kim et al., 2016; Liu et al., 2017; Sánchez-Mesa et al., 2016; Weedon et al., 2014). The personalized character of the mobile communications can be used for perceiving users' preferences and adapting to the situated environments, while it can expedite crowdsourcing of multimedia semantics, by massively harvesting labeled data-pairs through fully- or semi-automated annotation tasks. Given that most of today's decision-making systems take advantage of the contemporary learning algorithms and frameworks (i.e. DL), the construction of related training repositories is considered vital. These ground-truth knowledge bases can be useful, not only in the current verification problem, but also in more general semantic services and artificial intelligence automations (Dimoulas et al., 2014a, 2015, 2018; Liu et al., 2017; Vrysis, Tsipas, Dimoulas, & Papanikolaou, 2016). In addition, the progress in software engineering technology has further extended algorithmic capabilities (i.e. NLP, media understanding, semantics, etc.), offering new developing approaches, even for the non-programmers. For instance, average users, being in the role of software engineers, can just provide their front-end needs through graphically interacting interfaces, letting machines to assemble the code of the corresponding back-ends, by locating generic-purpose ready to use software components (Diamantopoulos, Roth, Symeonidis, & Klein, 2017; Roth, Diamantopoulos, Klein, & Symeonidis, 2014; Tosi & Morasca, 2015; Zolotas, Diamantopoulos, Chatzidimitriou, & Symeonidis, 2016). In this perspective, future journalists would have better chances and prospects for designing their preferred algorithmic techniques on information collection, authentication and publishing.

The above technological facilities can be utilized by all, informing users, professional and citizen journalists that are involved in the news business. However, while remarkable research progress has been conducted in the implementation of related inspection methods (both human-operated and machine-assisted), still, a simple, accurate and reliable environment to support all aspects of verification in real-world scenarios is missing. An integrated model is suggested for this holistic cross-modal validation, taking into consideration all the involved modalities across multiple media (i.e. channels, users, content versions /instances, etc.), where different evaluation practices can be jointly applied. Estimated strengths, weaknesses, opportunities and threats of the proposed solution are thoroughly analyzed, while future directions are anticipated. Given that the required automations are directly and heavily connected to highly-progressed multidisciplinary areas, close-collaboration between experts of various kinds is judged as fully irreplaceable. Proper documentation and dissemination of the achieved results would help in the above directions, allowing professionals, scientists and researchers from different fields to serve better the interdisciplinary character of the project. Among others, monitoring of the competitor domain of counter- or anti-forensics is also intensively demanded, ordering to protect the useful research findings and to appropriately inform the engaged authorities. Overall, a balanced developing and supporting plan is needed for the prosperous implementation of the entire undertaking, aiming at equally propelling all the implicated processes, without effortlessly grounding priorities to some tasks over others. Under these prerequisites, constructive and effective cooperation among the involved parties will be more easily reached, which is the key factor for ensuring the success of the entire framework, as already pointed out.

REFERENCES

Al-Sanjary, O. I., & Sulong, G. (2015). Detection of video forgery: A review of literature. *Journal of Theoretical & Applied Information Technology, 74*(2).

Álvarez, M. V. (2017). The Future of Video-Journalism: Mobiles. In *Media and Metamedia Management* (pp. 463–469). Springer International Publishing. doi:10.1007/978-3-319-46068-0_61

Bayar, B., & Stamm, M. C. (2016), June. A deep learning approach to universal image manipulation detection using a new convolutional layer. In *Proceedings of the 4th ACM Workshop on Information Hiding and Multimedia Security* (pp. 5-10). ACM.

Bode, L., & Vraga, E. K. (2015). In related news, that was wrong: The correction of misinformation through related stories functionality in social media. *Journal of Communication*, *65*(4), 619–638. doi:10.1111/jcom.12166

Boididou, C., Middleton, S. E., Jin, Z., Papadopoulos, S., Dang-Nguyen, D. T., Boato, G., & Kompatsiaris, Y. (2017). Verifying information with multimedia content on twitter. *Multimedia Tools and Applications*, 1–27.

Chen, Z., Zhao, Y., & Ni, R. (2017). Detection of operation chain: JPEG-Resampling-JPEG. *Signal Processing Image Communication*, *57*, 8–20. doi:10.1016/j.image.2017.04.008

Coddington, M. (2015). Clarifying journalism's quantitative turn: A typology for evaluating data journalism, computational journalism, and computer-assisted reporting. *Digital Journalism*, *3*(3), 331–348. doi:10.1080/216708 11.2014.976400

Diamantopoulos, T., Roth, M., Symeonidis, A., & Klein, E. (2017). Software requirements as an application domain for natural language processing. *Language Resources and Evaluation*, *51*(2), 495–524. doi:10.100710579-017-9381-z

Dimoulas, C., Veglis, A., & Kalliris, G. (2014). Application of Mobile Cloud-Based Technologies. In J. Rodrigues, K. Lin, & J. Lloret (Eds.), *Mobile Networks and Cloud Computing Convergence for Progressive Services and Applications* (pp. 320–343). Hershey, PA: Information Science Reference. doi:10.4018/978-1-4666-4781-7.ch017

Dimoulas, C., Veglis, A., & Kalliris, G. (2015). Audiovisual hypermedia in the semantic Web. In M. Khosrow-Pour (Ed.), *Encyclopedia of Information Science and Technology* (3rd ed.; pp. 7594–7604). Hershey, PA: Information Science Reference. doi:10.4018/978-1-4666-5888-2.ch748

Dimoulas, C. A., Kalliris, G. M., Chatzara, E. G., Tsipas, N. K., & Papanikolaou, G. V. (2014). Audiovisual production, restoration-archiving and content management methods to preserve local tradition and folkloric heritage. *Journal of Cultural Heritage*, *15*(3), 234–241. doi:10.1016/j.culher.2013.05.003

Dimoulas, C. A., & Symeonidis, A. L. (2015). Syncing shared multimedia through audiovisual bimodal segmentation. *IEEE MultiMedia*, *22*(3), 26–42. doi:10.1109/MMUL.2015.33

Dimoulas, C. A., Veglis, A. A., & Kalliris, G. (2018). Semantically Enhanced Authoring of Shared Media. In Encyclopedia of Information Science and Technology, Fourth Edition (pp. 6476-6487). IGI Global. doi:10.4018/978-1-5225-2255-3.ch562

Diou, C., Stephanopoulos, G., Panagiotopoulos, P., Papachristou, C., Dimitriou, N., & Delopoulos, A. (2010). Large-scale concept detection in multimedia data using small training sets and cross-domain concept fusion. *IEEE Transactions on Circuits and Systems for Video Technology, 20*(12), 1808–1821. doi:10.1109/TCSVT.2010.2087814

Dörr, K. N. (2015). Mapping the field of Algorithmic Journalism. *Digital Journalism, 4*(6), 700–722. doi:10.1080/21670811.2015.1096748

Dörr, K. N., & Hollnbuchner, K. (2017). Ethical Challenges of Algorithmic Journalism. *Digital Journalism, 5*(4), 404–419. doi:10.1080/21670811.2016.1167612

Farid, H. (2009). Image forgery detection. *IEEE Signal Processing Magazine, 26*(2), 16–25. doi:10.1109/MSP.2008.931079

Gillespie, T. (2014). The relevance of algorithms. In T. Gillespie, P. J. Boczkowski, & K. A. Foot (Eds.), *Media technologies: Essays on communication, materiality, and society, 167*. MIT Press Scholarship Online. doi:10.7551/mitpress/9780262525374.003.0009

Groot Kormelink, T., & Costera Meijer, I. (2015). Truthful or Engaging? Surpassing the dilemma of reality versus storytelling in journalism. *Digital Journalism, 3*(2), 158–174. doi:10.1080/21670811.2014.1002514

Gynnild, A. (2014). Surveillance videos and visual transparency in journalism. *Journalism Studies, 15*(4), 449–463. doi:10.1080/1461670X.2013.831230

Gynnild, A. (2016). The robot eye witness: extending visual journalism through drone surveillance. *Digital Journalism, 2*(3), 334-343.

Haim, M., & Graefe, A. (2017). *Automated News: Better than expected?* Digital Journalism.

Ho, A. T., & Li, S. (Eds.). (2015). *Handbook of Digital Forensics of Multimedia Data and Devices*. John Wiley & Sons. doi:10.1002/9781118705773

Katsaounidou, A. (2016). *Content authenticity issues: detection (and validation) techniques of untruthful news stories from humans and machines* (Unpublished Master Thesis). Post-Graduate Program of the School of Journalism and Mass Communications, Aristotle University of Thessaloniki. (in Greek)

Katsaounidou, A., Matsiola, M., & Dimoulas, C. (2016, December). Controversial content broadcasting and the role of television. *Proceedings of the International Conference on 50 Years Greek TV.* (in Greek)

Katsaounidou, A., Vryzas, N., Kotsakis, R., & Dimoulas, C. (2016, October). Audio-Based Digital Content Authentication. *Proceedings of the 8th Greek National Conference "Acoustics 2016".* (in Greek)

Katsaounidou, A. N., & Dimoulas, C. A. (2018). Integrating Content Authentication Support in Media Services. In Encyclopedia of Information Science and Technology, Fourth Edition (pp. 2908-2919). IGI Global. doi:10.4018/978-1-5225-2255-3.ch254

Kim, H., Evans, A., Blat, J., & Hilton, A. (2016). Multi-modal Visual Data Registration for Web-based Visualisation in Media Production. *IEEE Transactions on Circuits and Systems for Video Technology.*

Li, W., Joo, J., Qi, H., & Zhu, S. C. (2017). Joint Image-Text News Topic Detection and Tracking by Multimodal Topic And-Or Graph. *IEEE Transactions on Multimedia, 19*(2), 367–381. doi:10.1109/TMM.2016.2616279

Linden, C. G. (2016). Decades of Automation in the Newsroom: Why are there still so many jobs in journalism? *Digital Journalism, 5*(2), 123–140. doi:10.1080/21670811.2016.1160791

Linden, C. G. (2017). Algorithms for journalism: The future of news work. *The Journal of Media Innovations, 4*(1), 60–76. doi:10.5617/jmi.v4i1.2420

Liu, W., Ma, H., Qi, H., Zhao, D., & Chen, Z. (2017). Deep learning hashing for mobile visual search. *EURASIP Journal on Image and Video Processing, 2017*(1), 17. doi:10.118613640-017-0167-4

Lu, T., Jin, Y., Su, F., Shivakumara, P., & Tan, C. L. (2015). Content-oriented multimedia document understanding through cross-media correlation. *Multimedia Tools and Applications, 74*(18), 8105–8135. doi:10.100711042-014-2044-9

Mahdian, B., & Saic, S. (2010). A bibliography on blind methods for identifying image forgery. *Signal Processing Image Communication, 25*(6), 389–399. doi:10.1016/j.image.2010.05.003

Maher, R. (2010). *Overview of audio forensics.* Intelligent Multimedia Analysis for Security Applications.

Marwick, A., & Lewis, R. (2017). Media manipulation and disinformation online. *Data & Society.* Retrieved from https://datasociety.net/pubs/oh/DataAndSociety_MediaManipulationAndDisinformationOnline.pdf

Matsiola, M., Dimoulas, C. A., Kalliris, G., & Veglis, A. A. (2015). Augmenting user interaction experience through embedded multimodal media agents in social networks. In Social media and the transformation of interaction in society (pp. 188-209). IGI Global. doi:10.4018/978-1-4666-8556-7.ch010

Mendoza, M., Poblete, B., & Castillo, C. (2010, July). Twitter Under Crisis: Can we trust what we RT? In *Proceedings of the first workshop on social media analytics* (pp. 71-79). ACM. 10.1145/1964858.1964869

Messing, S., & Westwood, S. J. (2014). Selective exposure in the age of social media: Endorsements trump partisan source affiliation when selecting news online. *Communication Research, 41*(8), 1042–1063. doi:10.1177/0093650212466406

Mizher, M. A., Ang, M. C., Mazhar, A. A., & Mizher, M. A. (2017). A review of video falsifying techniques and video forgery detection techniques. *International Journal of Electronic Security and Digital Forensics, 9*(3), 191–208. doi:10.1504/IJESDF.2017.085196

Montal, T., & Reich, Z. (2016). *I, Robot. You, Journalist. Who is the Author? Authorship, bylines and full disclosure in automated journalism.* Digital Journalism.

Ntalakas, A., Dimoulas, C. A., Kalliris, G., & Veglis, A. (2017). Drone journalism: Generating immersive experiences. *Journal of Media Critiques, 3*(11), 187–199. doi:10.17349/jmc117317

Ota, K., Dao, M. S., Mezaris, V., & De Natale, F. G. (2017). Deep Learning for Mobile Multimedia: A Survey. *ACM Transactions on Multimedia Computing Communications and Applications, 13*(3s), 34.

Pantti, M., & Sirén, S. (2015). The fragility of photo-truth: Verification of amateur images in Finnish newsrooms. *Digital Journalism, 3*(4), 495-512.

Papadopoulos, S., Cesar, P., Shamma, D. A., & Kelliher, S. (Eds.). (2015). Special issue on Social Multimedia and Storytelling. MultiMedia IEEE, 22(3), 10-65.

Pariser, E. (2011). *The filter bubble: How the new personalized web is changing what we read and how we think*. Penguin.

Pasquini, C., Brunetta, C., Vinci, A. F., Conotter, V., & Boato, G. (2015, June). Towards the verification of image integrity in online news. In *Multimedia & Expo Workshops (ICMEW), 2015 IEEE International Conference on* (pp. 1-6). IEEE. 10.1109/ICMEW.2015.7169801

Pavlik, J. V., & Bridges, F. (2013). The emergence of augmented reality (AR) as a storytelling medium in journalism. *Journalism & Communication Monographs*, *15*(1), 4–59. doi:10.1177/1522637912470819

Peng, Y., Huang, X., & Zhao, Y. (2017). An Overview of Cross-media Retrieval: Concepts, Methodologies, Benchmarks and Challenges. *IEEE Transactions on Circuits and Systems for Video Technology*, 1. doi:10.1109/TCSVT.2017.2705068

Qureshi, M. A., & Deriche, M. (2015). A bibliography of pixel-based blind image forgery detection techniques. *Signal Processing Image Communication*, *39*, 46–74. doi:10.1016/j.image.2015.08.008

Rampazzo Gambarato, R., & Tárcia, L. P. T. (2016). Transmedia Strategies in Journalism: An analytical model for the news coverage of planned events. *Journalism Studies*, 1–19.

Rodríguez, A. S., & Freire, F. C. (2017). Reports in and from Smartphones: A New Way of Doing Journalism. In Media and Metamedia Management (pp. 479-490). Springer International Publishing.

Roth, M., Diamantopoulos, T., Klein, E., & Symeonidis, A. (2014, June). Software requirements: A new domain for semantic parsers. *Proceedings of the ACL 2014 Workshop on Semantic Parsing*, 50-54. 10.3115/v1/W14-2410

Sánchez-Mesa, D., Aarseth, E., & Pratten, R. (2016). Transmedia (Storytelling?): A polyphonic critical review. *Artnodes. Journal of Art. Science & Technology*, *18*, 8–19.

Sansone, E., Apostolidis, K., Conci, N., Boato, G., Mezaris, V., & De Natale, F. G. (2017). Automatic synchronization of multi-user photo galleries. *IEEE Transactions on Multimedia*, *19*(6), 1285–1298. doi:10.1109/TMM.2017.2655446

Schetinger, V., Oliveira, M. M., da Silva, R., & Carvalho, T. J. (2015). *Humans are easily fooled by digital images.* arXiv preprint arXiv:1509.05301

Seijo, S. P. (2017). Immersive Journalism: From Audience to First-Person Experience of News. In Media and Metamedia Management (pp. 113-119). Springer International Publishing.

Shelton, C. C., Warren, A. E., & Archambault, L. M. (2016). Exploring the use of interactive digital storytelling video: Promoting student engagement and learning in a university hybrid course. *TechTrends*, *60*(5), 465–474. doi:10.100711528-016-0082-z

Silverman, C. (Ed.). (2013). *Verification handbook*. European Journalism Centre.

Stamm, M. C., Lin, W. S., & Liu, K. R. (2012). Temporal forensics and anti-forensics for motion compensated video. *IEEE Transactions on Information Forensics and Security*, *7*(4), 1315–1329. doi:10.1109/TIFS.2012.2205568

Thakur, M. K. (2014). *Tampered videos: detection and quality assessment* (Unpublished Doctoral dissertation). Jaypee Institute of Information Technology, Department of Computer Science Engineering & Information Technology. Retrieved from http://shodhganga.inflibnet.ac.in/handle/10603/44603

Tosi, D., & Morasca, S. (2015). Supporting the semi-automatic semantic annotation of web services: A systematic literature review. *Information and Software Technology*, *61*, 16–32. doi:10.1016/j.infsof.2015.01.007

Tsardoulias, E., Thallas, A. G., Symeonidis, A. L., & Mitkas, P. A. (2016). Improving Multilingual Interaction for Consumer Robots through Signal Enhancement in Multichannel Speech. *Journal of the Audio Engineering Society*, *64*(7/8), 514–524. doi:10.17743/jaes.2016.0022

Tsardoulias, E. G., Kintsakis, A. M., Panayiotou, K., Thallas, A. G., Reppou, S. E., Karagiannis, G. G., ... Psomopoulos, F. E. (2017). Towards an integrated robotics architecture for social inclusion–The RAPP paradigm. *Cognitive Systems Research*, *43*, 157–173. doi:10.1016/j.cogsys.2016.08.004

Van Dalen, A. (2012). The algorithms behind the headlines: How machine-written news redefines the core skills of human journalists. *Journalism Practice*, *6*(5-6), 648–658. doi:10.1080/17512786.2012.667268

Veglis, A. (2012a). Journalism and Cross-Media Publishing: The Case of Greece. The handbook of global online journalism, pp.209-230.

Veglis, A. (2012b). From cross media to transmedia reporting in newspaper articles. *Publishing Research Quarterly, 28*(4), 313–324. doi:10.100712109-012-9294-z

Veglis, A., & Bratsas, C. (2017a). Reporters in the age of data journalism. *Journal of Applied Journalism & Media Studies, 6*(2), 225–244. doi:10.1386/ajms.6.2.225_1

Veglis, A., & Bratsas, C. (2017b). Towards a taxonomy of data journalism. *Journal of Media Critiques, 3*(11), 109–121. doi:10.17349/jmc117309

Veglis, A., Dimoulas, C., & Kalliris, G. (2016). Towards intelligent cross-media publishing: media practices and technology convergence perspectives. In A. Lugmayr & C. Dal Zotto (Eds.), *Media Convergence Handbook-Vol. 1* (pp. 131–150). Springer Berlin Heidelberg. doi:10.1007/978-3-642-54484-2_8

Vrysis, L., Tsipas, N., Dimoulas, C., & Papanikolaou, G. (2016). Crowdsourcing Audio Semantics by Means of Hybrid Bimodal Segmentation with Hierarchical Classification. *Journal of the Audio Engineering Society, 64*(12), 1042–1054. doi:10.17743/jaes.2016.0051

Vryzas, N., Kotsakis, R., Dimoulas, C. A., & Kalliris, G. (2016). October. Investigating Multimodal Audiovisual Event Detection and Localization. *Proceedings of the Audio Mostly, 2016*, 97–104.

Weedon, A., Miller, D., Franco, C. P., Moorhead, D., & Pearce, S. (2014). Crossing media boundaries: Adaptations and new media forms of the book. *Convergence, 20*(1), 108–124. doi:10.1177/1354856513515968

Zeman, N. B. (2017). *Storytelling for Interactive Digital Media and Video Games*. CRC Press.

Zolotas, C., Diamantopoulos, T., Chatzidimitriou, K. C., & Symeonidis, A. L. (2016). From requirements to source code: A Model-Driven Engineering approach for RESTful web services. *Automated Software Engineering*, 1–48.

Zubiaga, A., & Ji, H. (2014). Tweet, but verify: Epistemic study of information verification on twitter. *Social Network Analysis and Mining, 4*(1), 163. doi:10.100713278-014-0163-y

KEY TERMS AND DEFINITIONS

Cross-Media Authentication: An integrated media veracity model that evaluates all of the involved modalities across multiple media, so that inconsistencies between the different content entities, versions and forensic validation outcomes (from multiple methods and practices) could reveal possible tampering actions.

Related Readings

To continue IGI Global's long-standing tradition of advancing innovation through emerging research, please find below a compiled list of recommended IGI Global book chapters and journal articles in the areas of cross-media, digital storytelling, and transmedia. These related readings will provide additional information and guidance to further enrich your knowledge and assist you with your own research.

Abdusselam, M. S., & Guntepe, E. T. (2018). New Media and Learning: Innovative Learning Technologies. In M. Yildiz, S. Funk, & B. De Abreu (Eds.), *Promoting Global Competencies Through Media Literacy* (pp. 41–63). Hershey, PA: IGI Global. doi:10.4018/978-1-5225-3082-4.ch003

Adam, F. (2016). Mobile Content and Walking Documentary: Teaching and Learning Science Step-by-Step with Smartphones. In J. Aguado, C. Feijóo, & I. Martínez (Eds.), *Emerging Perspectives on the Mobile Content Evolution* (pp. 313–335). Hershey, PA: IGI Global. doi:10.4018/978-1-4666-8838-4.ch016

Aggarwal, S., & Nayak, A. (2016). Mobile Big Data: A New Frontier of Innovation. In J. Aguado, C. Feijóo, & I. Martínez (Eds.), *Emerging Perspectives on the Mobile Content Evolution* (pp. 138–158). Hershey, PA: IGI Global. doi:10.4018/978-1-4666-8838-4.ch008

Aguado, J. M., & Martinez, I. J. (2016). Driving Media Transformations: Mobile Content and Personal Information. In J. Aguado, C. Feijóo, & I. Martínez (Eds.), *Emerging Perspectives on the Mobile Content Evolution* (pp. 160–176). Hershey, PA: IGI Global. doi:10.4018/978-1-4666-8838-4.ch009

Ahmed, S. T. (2017). Managing Information, Communication and Technologies in Schools: Overload as Mismanagement and Miscommunication. In R. Marques & J. Batista (Eds.), *Information and Communication Overload in the Digital Age* (pp. 72–92). Hershey, PA: IGI Global. doi:10.4018/978-1-5225-2061-0.ch004

Alvermann, D. E., Beach, C. L., & Boggs, G. L. (2016). What Does Digital Media Allow Us to "Do" to One Another?: Economic Significance of Content and Connection. In B. Guzzetti & M. Lesley (Eds.), *Handbook of Research on the Societal Impact of Digital Media* (pp. 1–23). Hershey, PA: IGI Global. doi:10.4018/978-1-4666-8310-5.ch001

Alzamora, G. C. (2018). The Transmedia Dynamics of TV3: Newscast "Especial 9-N" on Connections of Online Social Media. In R. Gambarato & G. Alzamora (Eds.), *Exploring Transmedia Journalism in the Digital Age* (pp. 222–234). Hershey, PA: IGI Global. doi:10.4018/978-1-5225-3781-6.ch013

Amador, J., & Piña-Garcia, C. A. (2017). Political Participation in Mexico Offline and Through Twitter. In S. Gordon (Ed.), *Online Communities as Agents of Change and Social Movements* (pp. 138–164). Hershey, PA: IGI Global. doi:10.4018/978-1-5225-2495-3.ch006

Andrews, K., & Mickahail, B. (2015). Business and Social Media: Collaboration for the Sixth Discipline. In J. Sahlin (Ed.), *Social Media and the Transformation of Interaction in Society* (pp. 158–172). Hershey, PA: IGI Global. doi:10.4018/978-1-4666-8556-7.ch008

Angiani, G., Fornacciari, P., Mordonini, M., Tomaiuolo, M., & Iotti, E. (2017). Models of Participation in Social Networks. In M. Brown Sr., (Ed.), *Social Media Performance Evaluation and Success Measurements* (pp. 196–224). Hershey, PA: IGI Global. doi:10.4018/978-1-5225-1963-8.ch010

Bailey, L. W. (2017). Social Media: A Discussion of Considerations for Modern Organizations and Professionals. In M. Brown Sr., (Ed.), *Social Media Performance Evaluation and Success Measurements* (pp. 64–77). Hershey, PA: IGI Global. doi:10.4018/978-1-5225-1963-8.ch004

Baker, E. B., Alfayez, A., Dalton, C., McInnish, R. S., Schwerdtfeger, R., & Khajeloo, M. (2016). The Irrevocable Alteration of Communication: A Glimpse into the Societal Impact of Digital Media. In B. Guzzetti & M. Lesley (Eds.), *Handbook of Research on the Societal Impact of Digital Media* (pp. 94–126). Hershey, PA: IGI Global. doi:10.4018/978-1-4666-8310-5.ch005

Bar-Tal, S., & Seifert, T. (2018). The Shluvim Social-Professional Network: A Bridge for Educational Challenges and Trailblazers in Education. In M. Yildiz, S. Funk, & B. De Abreu (Eds.), *Promoting Global Competencies Through Media Literacy* (pp. 138–159). Hershey, PA: IGI Global. doi:10.4018/978-1-5225-3082-4.ch009

Batista, J. C., & Marques, R. P. (2017). An Overview on Information and Communication Overload. In R. Marques & J. Batista (Eds.), *Information and Communication Overload in the Digital Age* (pp. 1–19). Hershey, PA: IGI Global. doi:10.4018/978-1-5225-2061-0.ch001

Beach, R., & Castek, J. (2016). Use of Apps and Devices for Fostering Mobile Learning of Literacy Practices. In B. Guzzetti & M. Lesley (Eds.), *Handbook of Research on the Societal Impact of Digital Media* (pp. 343–370). Hershey, PA: IGI Global. doi:10.4018/978-1-4666-8310-5.ch014

Bean, T. W. (2016). Digital Media and Cosmopolitan Critical Literacy: Research and Practice. In B. Guzzetti & M. Lesley (Eds.), *Handbook of Research on the Societal Impact of Digital Media* (pp. 46–68). Hershey, PA: IGI Global. doi:10.4018/978-1-4666-8310-5.ch003

Bekafigo, M., & Pingley, A. C. (2017). Do Campaigns "Go Negative" on Twitter? In Y. Ibrahim (Ed.), *Politics, Protest, and Empowerment in Digital Spaces* (pp. 178–191). Hershey, PA: IGI Global. doi:10.4018/978-1-5225-1862-4.ch011

Berke, B., Akarsu, G., & Obay, G. (2017). The Impact of Information and Communication Technologies on Economic Growth and Electricity Consumption: Evidence from Selected Balkan and Eastern European Countries. In R. Marques & J. Batista (Eds.), *Information and Communication Overload in the Digital Age* (pp. 176–200). Hershey, PA: IGI Global. doi:10.4018/978-1-5225-2061-0.ch008

Bicalho, L. A. (2018). Potential Mediations of Hashtags Within Transmedia Journalism. In R. Gambarato & G. Alzamora (Eds.), *Exploring Transmedia Journalism in the Digital Age* (pp. 202–221). Hershey, PA: IGI Global. doi:10.4018/978-1-5225-3781-6.ch012

Bishop, J. (2017). Developing and Validating the "This Is Why We Can't Have Nice Things Scale": Optimising Political Online Communities for Internet Trolling. In Y. Ibrahim (Ed.), *Politics, Protest, and Empowerment in Digital Spaces* (pp. 153–177). Hershey, PA: IGI Global. doi:10.4018/978-1-5225-1862-4.ch010

Bishop, J., & Beech, M. (2017). Exploring the Counting of Ballot Papers Using "Delegated Transferable Vote": Implications for Local and National Elections in the United Kingdom. In Y. Ibrahim (Ed.), *Politics, Protest, and Empowerment in Digital Spaces* (pp. 227–243). Hershey, PA: IGI Global. doi:10.4018/978-1-5225-1862-4.ch014

Blaney, A. (2017). Food Photography, Pixelated Produce, and Cameraless Images: A Photographic Journey from Farmville to Kheti Badi. In Y. Ibrahim (Ed.), *Politics, Protest, and Empowerment in Digital Spaces* (pp. 276–288). Hershey, PA: IGI Global. doi:10.4018/978-1-5225-1862-4.ch017

Bochmer, M. C. (2018). Teaching Digital and Media Literacy as Cross-Cultural Communication. In M. Yildiz, S. Funk, & B. De Abreu (Eds.), *Promoting Global Competencies Through Media Literacy* (pp. 240–249). Hershey, PA: IGI Global. doi:10.4018/978-1-5225-3082-4.ch015

Boggs, G. L. (2016). Economic Impact of Digital Media: Growing Nuance, Critique, and Direction for Education Research. In B. Guzzetti & M. Lesley (Eds.), *Handbook of Research on the Societal Impact of Digital Media* (pp. 178–207). Hershey, PA: IGI Global. doi:10.4018/978-1-4666-8310-5.ch008

Brown, M. A. Sr. (2017). SNIP: A Survey Instrument. In M. Brown Sr., (Ed.), *Social Media Performance Evaluation and Success Measurements* (pp. 15–45). Hershey, PA: IGI Global. doi:10.4018/978-1-5225-1963-8.ch002

Brown, M. A. Sr. (2017). Social Networking and Social Media Comparisons. In M. Brown Sr., (Ed.), *Social Media Performance Evaluation and Success Measurements* (pp. 1–14). Hershey, PA: IGI Global. doi:10.4018/978-1-5225-1963-8.ch001

Brown, M. A. Sr. (2017). Understanding Social Communication. In M. Brown Sr., (Ed.), *Social Media Performance Evaluation and Success Measurements* (pp. 47–63). Hershey, PA: IGI Global. doi:10.4018/978-1-5225-1963-8.ch003

Brown, V. (2018). Technology Access Gap for Postsecondary Education: A Statewide Case Study. In M. Yildiz, S. Funk, & B. De Abreu (Eds.), *Promoting Global Competencies Through Media Literacy* (pp. 20–40). Hershey, PA: IGI Global. doi:10.4018/978-1-5225-3082-4.ch002

Bruner, M. S., Valine, K., & Ceja, B. (2017). Women Can't Win: Gender Irony and the E-Politics of The Biggest Loser. In Y. Ibrahim (Ed.), *Politics, Protest, and Empowerment in Digital Spaces* (pp. 244–262). Hershey, PA: IGI Global. doi:10.4018/978-1-5225-1862-4.ch015

Canavilhas, J. (2018). Journalism in the Twenty-First Century: To Be or Not to Be Transmedia? In R. Gambarato & G. Alzamora (Eds.), *Exploring Transmedia Journalism in the Digital Age* (pp. 1–14). Hershey, PA: IGI Global. doi:10.4018/978-1-5225-3781-6.ch001

Canavilhas, J., & Satuf, I. (2016). Who Brings the News?: Exploring the Aggregators Apps for Mobile Devices. In J. Aguado, C. Feijóo, & I. Martínez (Eds.), *Emerging Perspectives on the Mobile Content Evolution* (pp. 220–238). Hershey, PA: IGI Global. doi:10.4018/978-1-4666-8838-4.ch012

Castellet, A. (2016). A Reflection on Wearables and Innovation in the Mobile Ecosystem: Two Possible Scenarios. In J. Aguado, C. Feijóo, & I. Martínez (Eds.), *Emerging Perspectives on the Mobile Content Evolution* (pp. 58–86). Hershey, PA: IGI Global. doi:10.4018/978-1-4666-8838-4.ch004

Castellet, A., & Westlund, O. (2016). Examining Mobile Search Adoption: The Swedish Experience in the Uptake Phase. In J. Aguado, C. Feijóo, & I. Martínez (Eds.), *Emerging Perspectives on the Mobile Content Evolution* (pp. 105–123). Hershey, PA: IGI Global. doi:10.4018/978-1-4666-8838-4.ch006

Castelló-Mayo, E., Fernández, R. M., Gómez, A. M., González, J. F., & Sánchez-Vila, E. (2016). Research, Development and Creativity in Ubiquitous Technologies in University: CIDUS Contribution. In J. Aguado, C. Feijóo, & I. Martínez (Eds.), *Emerging Perspectives on the Mobile Content Evolution* (pp. 284–312). Hershey, PA: IGI Global. doi:10.4018/978-1-4666-8838-4.ch015

Ciancia, M., & Mattei, M. (2018). Tell Me a Story, but It Should Be Real!: Design Practice in Transmedia Journalism. In R. Gambarato & G. Alzamora (Eds.), *Exploring Transmedia Journalism in the Digital Age* (pp. 104–125). Hershey, PA: IGI Global. doi:10.4018/978-1-5225-3781-6.ch007

Corrêa, C. H. (2017). Social Media Support for the Occupation of Public Schools in São Paulo, Brazil. In S. Gordon (Ed.), *Online Communities as Agents of Change and Social Movements* (pp. 67–88). Hershey, PA: IGI Global. doi:10.4018/978-1-5225-2495-3.ch003

Cottrell, T. (2016). Digital Media Affecting Society: Instruction and Learning. In B. Guzzetti & M. Lesley (Eds.), *Handbook of Research on the Societal Impact of Digital Media* (pp. 208–236). Hershey, PA: IGI Global. doi:10.4018/978-1-4666-8310-5.ch009

Cuevas, A., & Kohle, F. (2015). Social Media: Changing the Way We Teach and Changing the Way We Learn. In J. Sahlin (Ed.), *Social Media and the Transformation of Interaction in Society* (pp. 15–23). Hershey, PA: IGI Global. doi:10.4018/978-1-4666-8556-7.ch002

Dalisay, F., Kushin, M. J., & Yamamoto, M. (2017). The Demobilizing Potential of Conflict for Web and Mobile Political Participation. In Y. Ibrahim (Ed.), *Politics, Protest, and Empowerment in Digital Spaces* (pp. 52–71). Hershey, PA: IGI Global. doi:10.4018/978-1-5225-1862-4.ch004

Damásio, M. J., Henriques, S., Teixeira-Botelho, I., & Dias, P. (2016). Mobile Media and Social Interaction: Mobile Services and Content as Drivers of Social Interaction. In J. Aguado, C. Feijóo, & I. Martínez (Eds.), *Emerging Perspectives on the Mobile Content Evolution* (pp. 357–379). Hershey, PA: IGI Global. doi:10.4018/978-1-4666-8838-4.ch018

Davis, A., & Foley, L. (2016). Digital Storytelling. In B. Guzzetti & M. Lesley (Eds.), *Handbook of Research on the Societal Impact of Digital Media* (pp. 317–342). Hershey, PA: IGI Global. doi:10.4018/978-1-4666-8310-5.ch013

de Prato, G., & Simon, J. P. (2016). Global Trends in Mobile: A New Global Landscape for Supply And Demand. In J. Aguado, C. Feijóo, & I. Martínez (Eds.), *Emerging Perspectives on the Mobile Content Evolution* (pp. 1–31). Hershey, PA: IGI Global. doi:10.4018/978-1-4666-8838-4.ch001

Delello, J. A., & McWhorter, R. R. (2016). New Visual Literacies and Competencies for Education and the Workplace. In B. Guzzetti & M. Lesley (Eds.), *Handbook of Research on the Societal Impact of Digital Media* (pp. 127–162). Hershey, PA: IGI Global. doi:10.4018/978-1-4666-8310-5.ch006

Denner, J., & Martinez, J. (2016). Children and Youth Making Digital Media for the Social Good. In B. Guzzetti & M. Lesley (Eds.), *Handbook of Research on the Societal Impact of Digital Media* (pp. 398–416). Hershey, PA: IGI Global. doi:10.4018/978-1-4666-8310-5.ch016

Deshmukh, G. K., & Joseph, S. (2015). Referencing in the Virtual World: A Study. *International Journal of Social and Organizational Dynamics in IT*, *4*(2), 12–29. doi:10.4018/IJSODIT.2015070102

Di Cesare, D. M., Harwood, D., & Rowsell, J. (2016). It Is Real Colouring?: Mapping Children's Im/Material Thinking in a Digital World. In B. Guzzetti & M. Lesley (Eds.), *Handbook of Research on the Societal Impact of Digital Media* (pp. 69–93). Hershey, PA: IGI Global. doi:10.4018/978-1-4666-8310-5.ch004

Dickenson, P., Hall, M. T., & Courduff, J. (2016). Moving beyond the Basics: The Evolution of Web 2.0 Tools from Preview to Participate. In B. Guzzetti & M. Lesley (Eds.), *Handbook of Research on the Societal Impact of Digital Media* (pp. 24–45). Hershey, PA: IGI Global. doi:10.4018/978-1-4666-8310-5.ch002

Dieck-Assad, F. A. (2018). Teaching Undergraduate Finance via a Digital Literacy Platform. In M. Yildiz, S. Funk, & B. De Abreu (Eds.), *Promoting Global Competencies Through Media Literacy* (pp. 193–215). Hershey, PA: IGI Global. doi:10.4018/978-1-5225-3082-4.ch013

Dogan, B., & Almus, K. (2018). Developing and Assessing Media Literacy Through Digital Storytelling. In M. Yildiz, S. Funk, & B. De Abreu (Eds.), *Promoting Global Competencies Through Media Literacy* (pp. 65–78). Hershey, PA: IGI Global. doi:10.4018/978-1-5225-3082-4.ch004

Dunkerly-Bean, J. M., & Crompton, H. (2016). The Role of Mobile Learning in Promoting Literacy and Human Rights for Women and Girls. In B. Guzzetti & M. Lesley (Eds.), *Handbook of Research on the Societal Impact of Digital Media* (pp. 581–608). Hershey, PA: IGI Global. doi:10.4018/978-1-4666-8310-5.ch023

Dunne, K. (2017). ICTs: Ancillary Tools for Indirect Democracy? In Y. Ibrahim (Ed.), *Politics, Protest, and Empowerment in Digital Spaces* (pp. 91–106). Hershey, PA: IGI Global. doi:10.4018/978-1-5225-1862-4.ch006

Eberwein, T. (2018). A Question of Trust: Functions and Effects of Transmedia Journalism. In R. Gambarato & G. Alzamora (Eds.), *Exploring Transmedia Journalism in the Digital Age* (pp. 15–30). Hershey, PA: IGI Global. doi:10.4018/978-1-5225-3781-6.ch002

Ecenbarger, C. (2016). Comic Books, Video Games, and Transmedia Storytelling: A Case Study of The Walking Dead. *International Journal of Gaming and Computer-Mediated Simulations*, 8(2), 34–42. doi:10.4018/ IJGCMS.2016040103

Ellwart, T., & Antoni, C. H. (2017). Shared and Distributed Team Cognition and Information Overload: Evidence and Approaches for Team Adaptation. In R. Marques & J. Batista (Eds.), *Information and Communication Overload in the Digital Age* (pp. 223–245). Hershey, PA: IGI Global. doi:10.4018/978-1-5225-2061-0.ch010

Eren-Erdoğmuş, İ., & Ergun, S. (2017). The Impact of Social Media on Social Movements: The Case of Anti-Consumption. In S. Gordon (Ed.), *Online Communities as Agents of Change and Social Movements* (pp. 224–252). Hershey, PA: IGI Global. doi:10.4018/978-1-5225-2495-3.ch009

Erragcha, N. (2017). Using Social Media Tools in Marketing: Opportunities and Challenges. In M. Brown Sr., (Ed.), *Social Media Performance Evaluation and Success Measurements* (pp. 106–129). Hershey, PA: IGI Global. doi:10.4018/978-1-5225-1963-8.ch006

Fechine, Y., & Rêgo, S. C. (2018). Transmedia Television Journalism in Brazil: Jornal da Record News as Reference. In R. Gambarato & G. Alzamora (Eds.), *Exploring Transmedia Journalism in the Digital Age* (pp. 253–265). Hershey, PA: IGI Global. doi:10.4018/978-1-5225-3781-6.ch015

Feijóo, C., Ramos, S., & Bleda, V. (2016). Mobile Music: An Overview. In J. Aguado, C. Feijóo, & I. Martínez (Eds.), *Emerging Perspectives on the Mobile Content Evolution* (pp. 87–104). Hershey, PA: IGI Global. doi:10.4018/978-1-4666-8838-4.ch005

Funk, S. S. (2018). A Trans*+ Media Literacy Framework for Navigating the Dynamically Shifting Terrain of Gender in Media: Considering Assessment of Key Competencies. In M. Yildiz, S. Funk, & B. De Abreu (Eds.), *Promoting Global Competencies Through Media Literacy* (pp. 216–239). Hershey, PA: IGI Global. doi:10.4018/978-1-5225-3082-4.ch014

Gambarato, R. R. (2018). Transmedia Journalism and the City: Participation, Information, and Storytelling Within the Urban Fabric. In R. Gambarato & G. Alzamora (Eds.), *Exploring Transmedia Journalism in the Digital Age* (pp. 147–161). Hershey, PA: IGI Global. doi:10.4018/978-1-5225-3781-6.ch009

Gambarato, R. R., Alzamora, G. C., & Tárcia, L. P. (2018). 2016 Rio Summer Olympics and the Transmedia Journalism of Planned Events. In R. Gambarato & G. Alzamora (Eds.), *Exploring Transmedia Journalism in the Digital Age* (pp. 126–146). Hershey, PA: IGI Global. doi:10.4018/978-1-5225-3781-6.ch008

Gambarato, R. R., & Medvedev, S. A. (2015). Fish Fight: Transmedia Storytelling Strategies for Food Policy Change. *International Journal of E-Politics*, *6*(3), 43–59. doi:10.4018/IJEP.2015070104

Gambarato, R. R., & Medvedev, S. A. (2017). Transmedia Storytelling Impact on Government Policy Change. In Y. Ibrahim (Ed.), *Politics, Protest, and Empowerment in Digital Spaces* (pp. 31–51). Hershey, PA: IGI Global. doi:10.4018/978-1-5225-1862-4.ch003

Ganguin, S., Gemkow, J., & Haubold, R. (2017). Information Overload as a Challenge and Changing Point for Educational Media Literacies. In R. Marques & J. Batista (Eds.), *Information and Communication Overload in the Digital Age* (pp. 302–328). Hershey, PA: IGI Global. doi:10.4018/978-1-5225-2061-0.ch013

Garcia-Murillo, M., Zaber, M., & Wohlers de Almeida, M. (2017). Information and Communication Technologies as Drivers of Social Unrest. In S. Gordon (Ed.), *Online Communities as Agents of Change and Social Movements* (pp. 89–115). Hershey, PA: IGI Global. doi:10.4018/978-1-5225-2495-3.ch004

Gee, E. R., & Tran, K. M. (2016). Video Game Making and Modding. In B. Guzzetti & M. Lesley (Eds.), *Handbook of Research on the Societal Impact of Digital Media* (pp. 238–267). Hershey, PA: IGI Global. doi:10.4018/978-1-4666-8310-5.ch010

Godulla, A., & Wolf, C. (2018). Future of Food: Transmedia Strategies of National Geographic. In R. Gambarato & G. Alzamora (Eds.), *Exploring Transmedia Journalism in the Digital Age* (pp. 162–182). Hershey, PA: IGI Global. doi:10.4018/978-1-5225-3781-6.ch010

Gómez, H. G., & Crespo, E. C. (2017). Photographers without Photographs: The Internet as Primary Resource. In R. Marques & J. Batista (Eds.), *Information and Communication Overload in the Digital Age* (pp. 44–70). Hershey, PA: IGI Global. doi:10.4018/978-1-5225-2061-0.ch003

Gómez-Barroso, J. L., & Ruiz, J. Á. (2016). Behavioural Targeting in the Mobile Ecosystem. In J. Aguado, C. Feijóo, & I. Martínez (Eds.), *Emerging Perspectives on the Mobile Content Evolution* (pp. 44–57). Hershey, PA: IGI Global. doi:10.4018/978-1-4666-8838-4.ch003

Hasan, H., & Linger, H. (2017). Connected Living for Positive Ageing. In S. Gordon (Ed.), *Online Communities as Agents of Change and Social Movements* (pp. 203–223). Hershey, PA: IGI Global. doi:10.4018/978-1-5225-2495-3.ch008

He, X., & Lu, H. (2016). Catch a Fad or Capture a Value?: Social Media Leverage in SMEs. *Journal of Organizational and End User Computing*, 28(3), 67–81. doi:10.4018/JOEUC.2016070105

Hersey, L. N. (2017). CHOICES: Measuring Return on Investment in a Nonprofit Organization. In M. Brown Sr., (Ed.), *Social Media Performance Evaluation and Success Measurements* (pp. 157–179). Hershey, PA: IGI Global. doi:10.4018/978-1-5225-1963-8.ch008

Holmberg, C. (2017). Using the Blogosphere to Promote Disputed Diets: The Swedish Low-Carb High-Fat Movement. In Y. Ibrahim (Ed.), *Politics, Protest, and Empowerment in Digital Spaces* (pp. 10–30). Hershey, PA: IGI Global. doi:10.4018/978-1-5225-1862-4.ch002

Honari, A. (2017). The Formation of Consensus in Iranian Online Communities. In S. Gordon (Ed.), *Online Communities as Agents of Change and Social Movements* (pp. 165–201). Hershey, PA: IGI Global. doi:10.4018/978-1-5225-2495-3.ch007

Howarth, A. (2017). Challenging the De-Politicization of Food Poverty: Austerity Food Blogs. In Y. Ibrahim (Ed.), *Politics, Protest, and Empowerment in Digital Spaces* (pp. 123–140). Hershey, PA: IGI Global. doi:10.4018/978-1-5225-1862-4.ch008

Hsu, H., & Wang, S. (2018). Gaming Literacies and Learning. In M. Yildiz, S. Funk, & B. De Abreu (Eds.), *Promoting Global Competencies Through Media Literacy* (pp. 79–95). Hershey, PA: IGI Global. doi:10.4018/978-1-5225-3082-4.ch005

Hundley, M. K., & Holbrook, T. (2016). New and Strange Sorts of Texts: The Shaping and Reshaping of Digital and Multimodal Books and Young Adult Novels. In B. Guzzetti & M. Lesley (Eds.), *Handbook of Research on the Societal Impact of Digital Media* (pp. 437–466). Hershey, PA: IGI Global. doi:10.4018/978-1-4666-8310-5.ch018

Ibrahim, Y. (2017). Self and the Relationship with the Screen: Interrogating the Fictive and Banal in Self Production. In Y. Ibrahim (Ed.), *Politics, Protest, and Empowerment in Digital Spaces* (pp. 1–9). Hershey, PA: IGI Global. doi:10.4018/978-1-5225-1862-4.ch001

Ibrahim, Y. (2017). Ubiquitous Food Imaging: Food Images as Digital Spectacle. In Y. Ibrahim (Ed.), *Politics, Protest, and Empowerment in Digital Spaces* (pp. 141–152). Hershey, PA: IGI Global. doi:10.4018/978-1-5225-1862-4.ch009

Iskandarova, S., & Griffin, O. T. (2018). Assessing Multilingual Multicultural Teachers' Communication Styles. In M. Yildiz, S. Funk, & B. De Abreu (Eds.), *Promoting Global Competencies Through Media Literacy* (pp. 111–123). Hershey, PA: IGI Global. doi:10.4018/978-1-5225-3082-4.ch007

Jabbarova, L. (2018). The Psychological Effects of Violence-Related Information From the Media. In M. Yildiz, S. Funk, & B. De Abreu (Eds.), *Promoting Global Competencies Through Media Literacy* (pp. 175–183). Hershey, PA: IGI Global. doi:10.4018/978-1-5225-3082-4.ch011

Jacobs, G. E. (2016). Instant Messaging and Texting. In B. Guzzetti & M. Lesley (Eds.), *Handbook of Research on the Societal Impact of Digital Media* (pp. 493–527). Hershey, PA: IGI Global. doi:10.4018/978-1-4666-8310-5.ch020

Johnston, K. M., & Phillips, T. (2016). A 'Step into the Abyss'?: Transmedia in the U.K. Games and Television Industries. *International Journal of Gaming and Computer-Mediated Simulations*, 8(2), 43–58. doi:10.4018/IJGCMS.2016040104

Jones, B. L. (2016). Deviously Deviant: The Strange Tapestry that is deviantART.com. In B. Guzzetti & M. Lesley (Eds.), *Handbook of Research on the Societal Impact of Digital Media* (pp. 371–397). Hershey, PA: IGI Global. doi:10.4018/978-1-4666-8310-5.ch015

Kaur, M., & Verma, R. (2016). Social Media: An Emerging Tool for Political Participation. *International Journal of Social and Organizational Dynamics in IT*, 5(2), 31–38. doi:10.4018/IJSODIT.2016070103

Kelly, D. M., & Arnold, C. (2016). Cyberbullying and Internet Safety. In B. Guzzetti & M. Lesley (Eds.), *Handbook of Research on the Societal Impact of Digital Media* (pp. 529–559). Hershey, PA: IGI Global. doi:10.4018/978-1-4666-8310-5.ch021

Kneidinger-Müller, B. (2017). Perpetual Mobile Availability as a Reason for Communication Overload: Experiences and Coping Strategies of Smartphone Users. In R. Marques & J. Batista (Eds.), *Information and Communication Overload in the Digital Age* (pp. 93–119). Hershey, PA: IGI Global. doi:10.4018/978-1-5225-2061-0.ch005

Kohle, F. H. (2015). The Social Media "Information Explosion" Spectacle: Perspectives for Documentary Producers. In J. Sahlin (Ed.), *Social Media and the Transformation of Interaction in Society* (pp. 173–187). Hershey, PA: IGI Global. doi:10.4018/978-1-4666-8556-7.ch009

Kulesza, J. (2017). Online Free Expression and Its Gatekeepers. In Y. Ibrahim (Ed.), *Politics, Protest, and Empowerment in Digital Spaces* (pp. 215–226). Hershey, PA: IGI Global. doi:10.4018/978-1-5225-1862-4.ch013

Kurambayev, B. (2017). Social Media Users Collectively Speak Up: Evidence From Central Asian Kyrgyz Republic. In S. Gordon (Ed.), *Online Communities as Agents of Change and Social Movements* (pp. 44–66). Hershey, PA: IGI Global. doi:10.4018/978-1-5225-2495-3.ch002

Lay, T. (2017). Protests, Social Movements and Media Legislation in Mexico 2012-2014. In S. Gordon (Ed.), *Online Communities as Agents of Change and Social Movements* (pp. 116–136). Hershey, PA: IGI Global. doi:10.4018/978-1-5225-2495-3.ch005

Lewerenz, M. E. (2018). Learning to Unlearn: Using Taoism and Critical Pedagogy in Language Education to Foster Global Unity. In M. Yildiz, S. Funk, & B. De Abreu (Eds.), *Promoting Global Competencies Through Media Literacy* (pp. 185–192). Hershey, PA: IGI Global. doi:10.4018/978-1-5225-3082-4.ch012

Lovato, A. (2018). The Transmedia Script for Nonfictional Narratives. In R. Gambarato & G. Alzamora (Eds.), *Exploring Transmedia Journalism in the Digital Age* (pp. 235–252). Hershey, PA: IGI Global. doi:10.4018/978-1-5225-3781-6.ch014

Lucas, M., & Moreira, A. A. (2017). Information and Communication Overload: Can DigComp Help? In R. Marques & J. Batista (Eds.), *Information and Communication Overload in the Digital Age* (pp. 157–175). Hershey, PA: IGI Global. doi:10.4018/978-1-5225-2061-0.ch007

Luchessi, L. (2018). Viral News Content, Instantaneity, and Newsworthiness Criteria. In R. Gambarato & G. Alzamora (Eds.), *Exploring Transmedia Journalism in the Digital Age* (pp. 31–48). Hershey, PA: IGI Global. doi:10.4018/978-1-5225-3781-6.ch003

Manzoor, A. (2016). Social Media for Promoting Grassroots Political Movements and Social Change. In B. Guzzetti & M. Lesley (Eds.), *Handbook of Research on the Societal Impact of Digital Media* (pp. 609–637). Hershey, PA: IGI Global. doi:10.4018/978-1-4666-8310-5.ch024

Maravilhas, S., & Martins, J. S. (2017). Information Management in Fab Labs: Avoiding Information and Communication Overload in Digital Manufacturing. In R. Marques & J. Batista (Eds.), *Information and Communication Overload in the Digital Age* (pp. 246–270). Hershey, PA: IGI Global. doi:10.4018/978-1-5225-2061-0.ch011

Marovitz, M. (2017). Social Networking Engagement and Crisis Communication Considerations. In M. Brown Sr., (Ed.), *Social Media Performance Evaluation and Success Measurements* (pp. 130–155). Hershey, PA: IGI Global. doi:10.4018/978-1-5225-1963-8.ch007

Martens, S. (2016). Struggle for the Universe: Maneuvering the Narrative World of Assassin's Creed. *International Journal of Gaming and Computer-Mediated Simulations*, 8(2), 20–33. doi:10.4018/IJGCMS.2016040102

Marzano, G. (2015). Cyberbullying Prevention: Some Preventing Tips. In J. Sahlin (Ed.), *Social Media and the Transformation of Interaction in Society* (pp. 133–157). Hershey, PA: IGI Global. doi:10.4018/978-1-4666-8556-7.ch007

Matsiola, M., Dimoulas, C. A., Kalliris, G., & Veglis, A. A. (2015). Augmenting User Interaction Experience through Embedded Multimodal Media Agents in Social Networks. In J. Sahlin (Ed.), *Social Media and the Transformation of Interaction in Society* (pp. 188–209). Hershey, PA: IGI Global. doi:10.4018/978-1-4666-8556-7.ch010

Maziad, M., Abokhodair, N., & Garrido, M. (2017). The Road to Egypt's Tahrir Square: Social Movements in Convergence, Coalitions and Networks. In S. Gordon (Ed.), *Online Communities as Agents of Change and Social Movements* (pp. 1–43). Hershey, PA: IGI Global. doi:10.4018/978-1-5225-2495-3.ch001

McNeal, R. S., & Schmeida, M. (2015). Digital Paranoia: Unfriendly Social Media Climate Affecting Social Networking Activities. In J. Sahlin (Ed.), *Social Media and the Transformation of Interaction in Society* (pp. 210–227). Hershey, PA: IGI Global. doi:10.4018/978-1-4666-8556-7.ch011

Merchant, G. (2016). Virtual Worlds and Online Videogames for Children and Young People: Promises and Challenges. In B. Guzzetti & M. Lesley (Eds.), *Handbook of Research on the Societal Impact of Digital Media* (pp. 291–316). Hershey, PA: IGI Global. doi:10.4018/978-1-4666-8310-5.ch012

Moloney, K. (2018). Designing Transmedia Journalism Projects. In R. Gambarato & G. Alzamora (Eds.), *Exploring Transmedia Journalism in the Digital Age* (pp. 83–103). Hershey, PA: IGI Global. doi:10.4018/978-1-5225-3781-6.ch006

Montiel, A. V. (2017). Critical Issues on Gender Equality and ICTs in Latin America. In Y. Ibrahim (Ed.), *Politics, Protest, and Empowerment in Digital Spaces* (pp. 263–275). Hershey, PA: IGI Global. doi:10.4018/978-1-5225-1862-4.ch016

Mystakidis, S., & Berki, E. (2018). The Case of Literacy Motivation: Playful 3D Immersive Learning Environments and Problem-Focused Education for Blended Digital Storytelling. *International Journal of Web-Based Learning and Teaching Technologies, 13*(1), 64–79. doi:10.4018/IJWLTT.2018010105

Naghiyeva, S. (2018). A Counterpoint on American Education and Media: One Fulbright Scholar's Quest to Prepare Students for Travel to America. In M. Yildiz, S. Funk, & B. De Abreu (Eds.), *Promoting Global Competencies Through Media Literacy* (pp. 250–255). Hershey, PA: IGI Global. doi:10.4018/978-1-5225-3082-4.ch016

O'Brien, D. G., & Van Deventer, M. M. (2016). The Appification of Literacy. In B. Guzzetti & M. Lesley (Eds.), *Handbook of Research on the Societal Impact of Digital Media* (pp. 417–436). Hershey, PA: IGI Global. doi:10.4018/978-1-4666-8310-5.ch017

Olin, J. R. (2016). Libraries and Digital Media. In B. Guzzetti & M. Lesley (Eds.), *Handbook of Research on the Societal Impact of Digital Media* (pp. 163–177). Hershey, PA: IGI Global. doi:10.4018/978-1-4666-8310-5.ch007

Oppegaard, B. (2016). Mobility Matters: Classifying Locative Mobile Apps through an Affordances Approach. In J. Aguado, C. Feijóo, & I. Martínez (Eds.), *Emerging Perspectives on the Mobile Content Evolution* (pp. 200–219). Hershey, PA: IGI Global. doi:10.4018/978-1-4666-8838-4.ch011

Palacios, M., Barbosa, S., Firmino da Silva, F., & da Cunha, R. (2016). Mobile Journalism and Innovation: A Study on Content Formats of Autochthonous News Apps for Tablets. In J. Aguado, C. Feijóo, & I. Martínez (Eds.), *Emerging Perspectives on the Mobile Content Evolution* (pp. 239–262). Hershey, PA: IGI Global. doi:10.4018/978-1-4666-8838-4.ch013

Pascoal, R. M., & Guerreiro, S. L. (2017). Information Overload in Augmented Reality: The Outdoor Sports Environments. In R. Marques & J. Batista (Eds.), *Information and Communication Overload in the Digital Age* (pp. 271–301). Hershey, PA: IGI Global. doi:10.4018/978-1-5225-2061-0.ch012

Pase, A. F., Goss, B. M., & Tietzmann, R. (2018). A Matter of Time: Transmedia Journalism Challenges. In R. Gambarato & G. Alzamora (Eds.), *Exploring Transmedia Journalism in the Digital Age* (pp. 49–66). Hershey, PA: IGI Global. doi:10.4018/978-1-5225-3781-6.ch004

Peppler, K. (2016). A Review of E-Textiles in Education and Society. In B. Guzzetti & M. Lesley (Eds.), *Handbook of Research on the Societal Impact of Digital Media* (pp. 268–290). Hershey, PA: IGI Global. doi:10.4018/978-1-4666-8310-5.ch011

Perales, V. (2016). The Message Is the Medium: Ecology, Mobility and Emergent Storytelling. In J. Aguado, C. Feijóo, & I. Martínez (Eds.), *Emerging Perspectives on the Mobile Content Evolution* (pp. 336–356). Hershey, PA: IGI Global. doi:10.4018/978-1-4666-8838-4.ch017

Pina, P. (2017). Free and Open Source Software Movements as Agents of an Alternative Use of Copyright Law. In S. Gordon (Ed.), *Online Communities as Agents of Change and Social Movements* (pp. 253–270). Hershey, PA: IGI Global. doi:10.4018/978-1-5225-2495-3.ch010

Porlezza, C., Benecchi, E., & Colapinto, C. (2018). The Transmedia Revitalization of Investigative Journalism: Opportunities and Challenges of the Serial Podcast. In R. Gambarato & G. Alzamora (Eds.), *Exploring Transmedia Journalism in the Digital Age* (pp. 183–201). Hershey, PA: IGI Global. doi:10.4018/978-1-5225-3781-6.ch011

Ramos, S., Armuña, C., Arenal, A., & Ferrandis, J. (2016). Mobile Communications and the Entrepreneurial Revolution. In J. Aguado, C. Feijóo, & I. Martínez (Eds.), *Emerging Perspectives on the Mobile Content Evolution* (pp. 32–43). Hershey, PA: IGI Global. doi:10.4018/978-1-4666-8838-4.ch002

Rodrigues, P., & Bidarra, J. (2016). Transmedia Storytelling as an Educational Strategy: A Prototype for Learning English as a Second Language. *International Journal of Creative Interfaces and Computer Graphics*, 7(2), 56–67. doi:10.4018/IJCICG.2016070105

Rodríguez, N. L. (2018). Immersive Journalism Design Within a Transmedia Space. In R. Gambarato & G. Alzamora (Eds.), *Exploring Transmedia Journalism in the Digital Age* (pp. 67–82). Hershey, PA: IGI Global. doi:10.4018/978-1-5225-3781-6.ch005

Romm-Livermore, C., Raisinghani, M. S., & Rippa, P. (2017). eLearning Political Strategies: A Four Act Play. In Y. Ibrahim (Ed.), Politics, Protest, and Empowerment in Digital Spaces (pp. 289-303). Hershey, PA: IGI Global. doi:10.4018/978-1-5225-1862-4.ch018

Romm-Livermore, C., Rippa, P., & Raisinghani, M. S. (2017). Towards a Political Theory of eLearning. In Y. Ibrahim (Ed.), *Politics, Protest, and Empowerment in Digital Spaces* (pp. 107–122). Hershey, PA: IGI Global. doi:10.4018/978-1-5225-1862-4.ch007

Rubinstein-Avila, E., & Sartori, A. (2016). Diversification and Nuanced Inequities in Digital Media Use in the United States. In B. Guzzetti & M. Lesley (Eds.), *Handbook of Research on the Societal Impact of Digital Media* (pp. 560–580). Hershey, PA: IGI Global. doi:10.4018/978-1-4666-8310-5.ch022

Sahlin, J. P. (2015). Social Bootstrapping: Microfunding Major Projects in the Arts and Nonprofit Organizations. In J. Sahlin (Ed.), *Social Media and the Transformation of Interaction in Society* (pp. 1–14). Hershey, PA: IGI Global. doi:10.4018/978-1-4666-8556-7.ch001

Sandoval-Almazan, R. (2017). Political Messaging in Digital Spaces: The Case of Twitter in Mexico's Presidential Campaign. In Y. Ibrahim (Ed.), *Politics, Protest, and Empowerment in Digital Spaces* (pp. 72–90). Hershey, PA: IGI Global. doi:10.4018/978-1-5225-1862-4.ch005

Sayan, A., Gorgulu, V., Erhart, I., & Aslanbay, Y. (2017). A Social Influence Perspective on Uses of Online Football Forums: The Case with Turkish Football Fans. In S. Gordon (Ed.), *Online Communities as Agents of Change and Social Movements* (pp. 271–292). Hershey, PA: IGI Global. doi:10.4018/978-1-5225-2495-3.ch011

Seifert, T. (2018). Digital Media and Social Network in the Training of Pre-Service Teachers. In M. Yildiz, S. Funk, & B. De Abreu (Eds.), *Promoting Global Competencies Through Media Literacy* (pp. 96–110). Hershey, PA: IGI Global. doi:10.4018/978-1-5225-3082-4.ch006

Serrano-Puche, J. (2017). Developing Healthy Habits in Media Consumption: A Proposal for Dealing with Information Overload. In R. Marques & J. Batista (Eds.), *Information and Communication Overload in the Digital Age* (pp. 202–222). Hershey, PA: IGI Global. doi:10.4018/978-1-5225-2061-0.ch009

Sharma, A. R. (2018). Promoting Global Competencies in India: Media and Information Literacy as Stepping Stone. In M. Yildiz, S. Funk, & B. De Abreu (Eds.), *Promoting Global Competencies Through Media Literacy* (pp. 160–174). Hershey, PA: IGI Global. doi:10.4018/978-1-5225-3082-4.ch010

Sillah, A. (2017). Nonprofit Organizations and Social Media Use: An Analysis of Nonprofit Organizations' Effective Use of Social Media Tools. In M. Brown Sr., (Ed.), *Social Media Performance Evaluation and Success Measurements* (pp. 180–195). Hershey, PA: IGI Global. doi:10.4018/978-1-5225-1963-8.ch009

Sonnenberg, C. (2016). Mobile Content Adaptation: An Analysis of Techniques and Frameworks. In J. Aguado, C. Feijóo, & I. Martínez (Eds.), *Emerging Perspectives on the Mobile Content Evolution* (pp. 177–199). Hershey, PA: IGI Global. doi:10.4018/978-1-4666-8838-4.ch010

Sosale, S. (2018). Learning Content Creation in the Field: Reflections on Multimedia Literacy in Global Context. In M. Yildiz, S. Funk, & B. De Abreu (Eds.), *Promoting Global Competencies Through Media Literacy* (pp. 125–137). Hershey, PA: IGI Global. doi:10.4018/978-1-5225-3082-4.ch008

Stiegler, C. (2017). The Politics of Immersive Storytelling: Virtual Reality and the Logics of Digital Ecosystems. *International Journal of E-Politics*, 8(3), 1–15. doi:10.4018/IJEP.2017070101

Tellería, A. S. (2016). The Role of the Profile and the Digital Identity on the Mobile Content. In J. Aguado, C. Feijóo, & I. Martínez (Eds.), *Emerging Perspectives on the Mobile Content Evolution* (pp. 263–282). Hershey, PA: IGI Global. doi:10.4018/978-1-4666-8838-4.ch014

ter Veen, J., Sarkani, S., & Mazzuchi, T. A. (2015). Seeking an Online Social Media Radar. In J. Sahlin (Ed.), *Social Media and the Transformation of Interaction in Society* (pp. 67–92). Hershey, PA: IGI Global. doi:10.4018/978-1-4666-8556-7.ch005

Terra, A. L. (2017). Email Overload: Framing the Concept and Solving the Problem – A Literature Review. In R. Marques & J. Batista (Eds.), *Information and Communication Overload in the Digital Age* (pp. 20–43). Hershey, PA: IGI Global. doi:10.4018/978-1-5225-2061-0.ch002

Tomé, V. (2018). Assessing Media Literacy in Teacher Education. In M. Yildiz, S. Funk, & B. De Abreu (Eds.), *Promoting Global Competencies Through Media Literacy* (pp. 1–19). Hershey, PA: IGI Global. doi:10.4018/978-1-5225-3082-4.ch001

Torsi, S. (2017). The Fishtank Paradigm of Experience: Merging Time, Space, Activities, Emotions, and People. In R. Marques & J. Batista (Eds.), *Information and Communication Overload in the Digital Age* (pp. 120–156). Hershey, PA: IGI Global. doi:10.4018/978-1-5225-2061-0.ch006

Veugen, C. (2016). Assassin's Creed and Transmedia Storytelling. *International Journal of Gaming and Computer-Mediated Simulations, 8*(2), 1–19. doi:10.4018/IJGCMS.2016040101

Villalba-Mora, E., Peinado, I., & Rodriguez-Mañas, L. (2016). From Personal to Mobile Healthcare: Challenges and Opportunities. In J. Aguado, C. Feijóo, & I. Martínez (Eds.), *Emerging Perspectives on the Mobile Content Evolution* (pp. 124–137). Hershey, PA: IGI Global. doi:10.4018/978-1-4666-8838-4.ch007

Virkar, S. (2015). Globalisation, the Internet, and the Nation-State: A Critical Analysis. In J. Sahlin (Ed.), *Social Media and the Transformation of Interaction in Society* (pp. 51–66). Hershey, PA: IGI Global. doi:10.4018/978-1-4666-8556-7.ch004

Wakabi, W. (2017). When Citizens in Authoritarian States Use Facebook for Social Ties but Not Political Participation. In Y. Ibrahim (Ed.), *Politics, Protest, and Empowerment in Digital Spaces* (pp. 192–214). Hershey, PA: IGI Global. doi:10.4018/978-1-5225-1862-4.ch012

Wang, Y. (2017). Framing and Mis-Framing in Micro-Blogging Sites in China: Online Propagation of an Animal Cruelty Campaign. In M. Brown Sr., (Ed.), *Social Media Performance Evaluation and Success Measurements* (pp. 78–105). Hershey, PA: IGI Global. doi:10.4018/978-1-5225-1963-8.ch005

Webb, L. M., & Temple, N. (2016). Social Media and Gender Issues. In B. Guzzetti & M. Lesley (Eds.), *Handbook of Research on the Societal Impact of Digital Media* (pp. 638–669). Hershey, PA: IGI Global. doi:10.4018/978-1-4666-8310-5.ch025

Wiggins, B. E. (2017). Navigating an Immersive Narratology: Factors to Explain the Reception of Fake News. *International Journal of E-Politics, 8*(3), 16–29. doi:10.4018/IJEP.2017070102

Yarchi, M., Wolfsfeld, G., Samuel-Azran, T., & Segev, E. (2017). Invest, Engage, and Win: Online Campaigns and Their Outcomes in an Israeli Election. In M. Brown Sr., (Ed.), *Social Media Performance Evaluation and Success Measurements* (pp. 225–248). Hershey, PA: IGI Global. doi:10.4018/978-1-5225-1963-8.ch011

Young-McLear, K., Mazzuchi, T. A., & Sarkani, S. (2015). Large-Scale Disaster Response Management: Social Media and Homeland Security. In J. Sahlin (Ed.), *Social Media and the Transformation of Interaction in Society* (pp. 93–131). Hershey, PA: IGI Global. doi:10.4018/978-1-4666-8556-7.ch006

Youssry, A., Winklehake, B., & Lobera, J. A. (2015). A Study of Two Microfinance Models and Their Suitability for Egypt. In J. Sahlin (Ed.), *Social Media and the Transformation of Interaction in Society* (pp. 24–49). Hershey, PA: IGI Global. doi:10.4018/978-1-4666-8556-7.ch003

Zammit, K. (2016). Collaborative Writing: Wikis and the Co-Construction of Meaning. In B. Guzzetti & M. Lesley (Eds.), *Handbook of Research on the Societal Impact of Digital Media* (pp. 467–492). Hershey, PA: IGI Global. doi:10.4018/978-1-4666-8310-5.ch019

About the Authors

Anastasia N. Katsaounidou is a PhD candidate in School of Journalism & Mass Communications researching *"Interactive and collaborative environments to support digital content authentication"* supported by the State Scholarships Foundation (IKY). She studied Political Sciences and received her Master's degree in Journalism and New Media from School of Journalism & Mass Media Communication, AUTH. Her Master Thesis deals with *'Content authenticity issues: detection of untruthful news stories from human and machines'*. Her interests include social media, user generated content and media authentication, Digital Forensics, non-linear storytelling, mediated learning, multimedia, user experience design and human-computer interaction.

Charalampos A. Dimoulas is an Assistant Professor of Electronic Media in the School of Journalism and Mass Communications, AUTH. He was the program chair of the AudioMostly 2015 conference on "Sound, semantics and social interaction," and co-editor of the associated ACM proceedings. He is also co-editor of the recently published JAES special issue(s) (2) on "Intelligent audio processing, Semantics, and interaction." His current scientific interests include media technologies, signal processing, machine learning, media authentication, audiovisual content description and management automation, cultural heritage, multimedia semantics, and more. Dr. Dimoulas is member of IEEE, EURASIP and AES.

Andreas Veglis is Professor, Head of the Media Informatics Lab at the School of Journalism & Mass Communications at the Aristotle University of Thessaloniki. He is member of the editorial board in nine peer review scientific journals in the area of journalism and mass communications. He is the author or co-author of 12 books, he has published 60 papers on scientific journals and he has presented 91 papers in international and national Conferences. His current research interests include media technology, cross media publishing, content authentication, Social content, User Generated Content, web 2.0/3.0 tools in media / new media, course support environments, data journalism, open data, social media content verification, Internet censorship and others.

Index

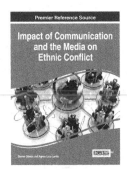

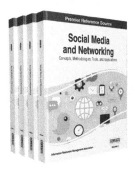
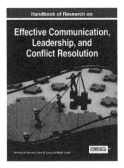

Stay Current on the Latest Emerging Research Developments

Become an IGI Global Reviewer for Authored Book Projects

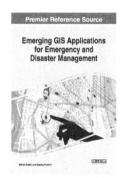

Premier Reference Source

Emerging GIS Applications for Emergency and Disaster Management

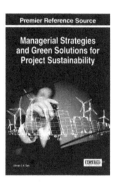

Premier Reference Source

Managerial Strategies and Green Solutions for Project Sustainability

Premier Reference Source

Comparative Approaches to Using R and Python for Statistical Data Analysis

Premier Reference Source

Solutions for High-Touch Communications in a High-Tech World

The overall success of an authored book project is dependent on quality and timely reviews.

In this competitive age of scholarly publishing, constructive and timely feedback significantly decreases the turnaround time of manuscripts from submission to acceptance, allowing the publication and discovery of progressive research at a much more expeditious rate. Several IGI Global authored book projects are currently seeking highly qualified experts in the field to fill vacancies on their respective editorial review boards:

Applications may be sent to:
development@igi-global.com

Applicants must have a doctorate (or an equivalent degree) as well as publishing and reviewing experience. Reviewers are asked to write reviews in a timely, collegial, and constructive manner. All reviewers will begin their role on an ad-hoc basis for a period of one year, and upon successful completion of this term can be considered for full editorial review board status, with the potential for a subsequent promotion to Associate Editor.

If you have a colleague that may be interested in this opportunity, we encourage you to share this information with them.

Printed in the United States
By Bookmasters